# World–
# Famous
# Acquittals

# World–
# Famous
# Acquittals

## Charles Franklin

Odhams Books

First published: 1970

Published for Odhams Books by
The Hamlyn Publishing Group Ltd,
Hamlyn House, 42 The Centre,
Feltham, Middlesex.

SBN 6007 2650 9

Printed by Cox & Wyman Ltd,
London, Fakenham and Reading

# Contents

# Illustrations

# Preface

To be acquitted in a court of law one does not of course have to be innocent. No country possesses an infallible legal process, though most would claim that the system they practise is superior to all others. A study of the great trials of history leads one inevitably to the conclusion that the pursuit of justice was not always the object of the legal tribunals of the past. Condemnation was more usual than acquittal until the eighteenth century when the legal conscience began to stir, particularly in England, and the principle of precedents was set up which made it difficult for the administration to interfere with justice.

In a book of trials I wrote a few years ago* there was not one acquittal in a series of historic cases ranging from Socrates to the Rosenbergs. Most of these trials were travesties of justice. Despite the sound judicial foundations laid down by the Romans, it is only in the last two and a half centuries that man has begun to take the idea of justice seriously, and even now there are many countries which believe themselves highly civilized, yet which judge individuals to be of less account than the supposed good of the state.

Anglo-Saxon justice, which is practised not only in the British Isles and America but in many places in the world where British influence has left its impress, lays down the important principle that the common law must not in any way be perverted in order that an obviously guilty person shall be condemned. All persons being equal before the law means that it doesn't matter what you have done in the past, or how bad your character may be, you will only be condemned upon evidence relating to the specific charge made against

* *World-Famous Trials* (Odhams 1966)

you. Thus many guilty persons have been acquitted. Of the fourteen cases of acquittal told in this book, it might be said that five of them were guilty and got away with it.

As for Queen Caroline, many think she was guilty of no more than well-nigh incredible indiscretion. The innocence of Adelaide Bartlett has always been in doubt – though not by me. Warren Hastings's trial was political; the true guilty party was that incredible institution, the East India Company. It was difficult to believe that Aimee Semple McPherson had committed a crime in the true sense of the word, but Thomas Picton did, and Henriette Caillaux blatantly got away with plain murder. Lizzie Borden's guilt was always obvious to the students of her case and now medical evidence establishes it as pretty conclusive, even if it does diminish her responsibility. The Montesi Scandal is perhaps one of the strangest legal stories of the century; and I make no apology for the inclusion of Oscar Wilde.

To my old friend and fellow-author, Hebe Elsna, I am indebted for suggesting a book of famous acquittals in the first place.

Most of the reference books which were consulted are listed separately. I am especially indebted to the following: H. Montgomery Hyde for granting me permission to reproduce copyright material from his book *The Trials of Oscar Wilde* (William Hodge, 1948); A. D. Peters and Co. for permission to make quotations from *The Montesi Scandal* by Wayland Young (Faber and Faber, 1957); Opera Mundi of Paris for permission to quote from Marie Besnard's remarkable book, *The Trial of Marie Besnard* (translated by Denise Folliot, William Heinemann Ltd, 1963); Roger Fulford for permission to make a quotation from *The Trial of Queen Caroline* (Batsford, 1967); and to James Hodge for permission to quote from various volumes of *Notable British Trials Series* (William Hodge, Edinburgh). Grateful acknowledgement is also made to Lately Thomas for his account of the trial of Aimee McPherson in his book *The Vanishing Evangelist* (William Heinemann, 1960).

Charles Franklin

# Chapter 1
# Queen Caroline

*God prosper, speed and save,*
*God raise from England's grave*
*Her murdered Queen.*
Percy Bysshe Shelley

Of all history's ill-used queens, few have aroused more turmoil and passion than Caroline, the consort of George IV. No one can pretend, however, that her cause was really worthwhile, that her behaviour or personality was in the least attractive. People championed her for the simple reason that they hated George IV so much.

Her trial was not a trial in the ordinary sense of the word. Stage-managed by the King's subservient ministers, it took the form of a Parliamentary Bill during the passage of which evidence was heard for and against her, with the House of Lords as judges and jury. It was a clumsy device the object of which was to deprive her of a proper legal trial; and it defeated its own ends by acquitting her, even though it produced what amounted to a verdict of guilty. It was a trial unparalleled in English history.

Caroline was the second daughter of the Duke of Brunswick who was married to the eldest sister of George III. Caroline, born in 1768, held the title of Princess, Brunswick being a famous ducal house related to the Romanoffs, the Hohenzollerns and the Habsburgs.

A contempt for the dynasties of continental Europe is one of the curiosities of the English mentality. It lay behind the public dislike of the Hanoverian monarchs – the four Georges, William IV, and even Victoria, who was only liked at the end of her long reign. The British royal family was of German origin and was looked down upon by the great aristocratic families of England. There had not been a true British monarch on the throne since Anne, the last of the Stuarts who were Scottish. Even the capable Tudors had been Welsh. Many English aristocrats considered that not since the Yorkist kings of the fifteenth century had a monarch of superior birth to them sat upon the throne of England. George III had enjoyed more popularity than his fellow Hanoverians, despite his acts of supreme unwisdom during his period of personal rule which ended in the loss of the American colonies; but his son, the Prince of Wales, was extremely disliked, undeservedly so in the opinion of modern historians.

Those who knew the Prince liked him well. But he was extremely unpopular with the public on account of his extravagance and because of his close connections with the Whig Party which was disliked by the middle classes. His reputation also suffered greatly from the fact that he had little political sense. He was rather a man of culture and taste, well read, and something of an intellectual. Unlike any other monarch of recent times, he could meet men of letters, artists and musicians on equal terms.

George IV's many detractors have portrayed him as a gross sensualist, a man without taste, feeling or sensitivity, a selfish coward and many other things besides. These opinions were strongly held by his contemporaries. Today only superficial students of history fail to recognize his real qualities.

In 1794 he was thirty-two (and already weighed seventeen

stone). The necessity to make a marriage appropriate to his position was strongly pressed upon him. His morganatic marriage to Mrs Fitzherbert was not legally binding and did not preclude him marrying Caroline of Brunswick, the only eligible princess in the eyes of George III and his ministers. The Prince had little choice. His father told him bluntly that that was the only way of getting his mountainous debts paid off.

Lord Malmesbury was sent to Brunswick to make the arrangements for the marriage. He was frankly dismayed when he met Princess Caroline. She was twenty-seven, and in some ways attractive, with a profusion of fair hair. What shocked Malmesbury was that she was dirty. She hardly ever washed and wore coarse underclothing and thick stockings. Worse, she had no tact or decorum. She spoke with the utmost recklessness and had a free and easy manner with her inferiors. She was in every way, except in the matter of birth, totally unsuitable to be Princess of Wales, let alone Queen of England.

But Malmesbury knew that George III had made up his mind about the marriage and it was more than he dare do to place any obstacles in the way. He could only lecture Caroline constantly upon the necessity of thinking before she spoke. But he was wasting his time. Caroline at twenty-seven was too set in her ways. Her indiscretions and eccentricities were to cause herself and her future husband endless trouble, and nearly bring the English monarchy crashing into the dust.

After an adventurous journey dodging the French Revolutionary armies, Caroline arrived in England in April, 1794. The first meeting between the intended bride and groom was an augury of what was to come. His Royal Highness called for brandy at the very sight of her, while she remarked with her usual tactlessness: 'I find him very fat and nothing like as handsome as his portrait.'

They were married in the Chapel Royal three days later. The Prince, according to an onlooker, had the appearance of 'death and confusion, as if he wished to hide himself from the looks of the whole world'. It was said that he was drunk, while she was in 'the highest of spirits'.

The honeymoon and their brief married life was spent at the Prince's London residence, Carlton House, at Windsor Castle and the Pavilion at Brighton.

As Caroline was none too cleanly in her habits and the Prince extremely fastidious in such matters, he found her physically repulsive. It was with great difficulty that he could bring himself to consummate the marriage. Caroline gave birth to Princess Charlotte on 7 January, 1796, and the child, it is believed on good authority, was conceived as the result of the one and only sexual act which took place between her parents.

The Prince was somewhat bitter about what he called his wife's 'personal nastiness', and after a while he felt that he could endure her no longer. At Brighton, some months before the birth of their child, they agreed to part and maintain separate establishments – a *mariage blanc* in fact, not unusual in dynastic unions. However, this marriage had been made in order to ensure the succession, and in the opinion of many the Prince was at fault for not performing his dynastic duties and attempting to produce a son, no matter how much the Princess might have offended his senses.

The public felt no such revulsion towards the Princess. On the contrary, they liked her from the start, and as soon as the Prince's feelings towards her became known, they took Caroline to their hearts, if merely out of spite towards the Prince. Caroline consoled herself by becoming London's sweetheart.

She presently left Carlton House and went to live, somewhat notoriously, near Greenwich where she made a series of rash and indiscreet friendships with certain naval officers who lived nearby. Her conduct caused such scandal that, in 1806, the Government were forced to set up a commission to investigate it. It was called the Delicate Investigation and so important was the matter considered, that its members included the Prime Minister, the Home Secretary, the Lord Chancellor and the Lord Chief Justice. Caroline was charged to have committed adultery with Sir Thomas Lawrence, Sir Sidney Smith, Captain Manby and others and – the gravest charge of all – that she had given birth to an illegitimate son.

Lady Douglas, wife of Sir John Douglas, told the Commission that the Princess of Wales herself had described her pregnancy with a wealth of physical detail. However, the Delicate Investigators discovered that what had happened was that in 1802 Caroline had taken into her establishment a baby, William Austin, belonging to a poor woman whose husband was out of work. Caroline had actually taken the child in out of the goodness of her heart, though she might have avoided a lot of trouble for herself if she had given its parents an allowance to save them from destitution.

The Delicate Commissioners did not believe Lady Douglas's story, though they had plenty of evidence of Caroline's reckless and unlicensed tongue, and the fact that she indulged in coarse and undignified prattle which ill became a Princess of Wales. For instance, on one occasion she had asserted: 'I have a bedfellow whenever I like. All men like a bedfellow, but Sir Sidney better than anyone else.'

Many found it difficult to resist the conclusion that the lady was overfond of sex and that she indulged herself whenever the opportunity occurred, and with a variety of men. Her Prince was doing the same thing with his own middle-aged *inamoratas*, but the double standard of morality held then as it does today, and according to an ancient act of Edward III, the Princess of Wales risked going to the scaffold every time she got into bed with a man who was not her husband.

In the end her conduct was reported on very unfavourably by the Delicate Investigators, though they discredited the worst of the scandal told them by members of her household. King George III, whom she always regarded as her friend and supporter, severely admonished her and refused to see her.

The whole business was something of a shock to Caroline who behaved herself for a while, and cultivated the society of men of learning and culture, though it must be admitted that she added more eccentricity than brilliance to these gatherings of intellectuals over which she presided. But at least she did try.

The end came when the King, regarded by her as her most powerful ally, lapsed into insanity from which there was no hope of recovery. In 1814 she left England, much against the advice and wishes of her political friends.

Why did she go? Perhaps she desired the freedom to choose her own friends, to have a lover, to be released from the boredom and frustration of her position, which would become even worse now that her husband was Prince Regent, a position which made him King in all but name. 'Since de English neither give me de great honour of being a Princesse de Galles, I will be Caroline, a happy, merry soul,' she rather ominously declared, and then embarked from Worthing for France on the frigate *Jason*, attended by a very respectable court of ladies and gentlemen who soon left her when it became obvious that 'Caroline, the happy, merry soul', was taking the ascendant over Caroline, Princess of Wales. And as she did not seem to have any plans for returning to England, they realized that to be in her service would mean exile, even banishment. So her 'court' became very small.

As she travelled through Switzerland to Italy, she was well aware that she was being spied upon, and that the Regent would get to hear everything that she did. All her friends and advisers urged upon her the importance of discretion, and behaviour befitting to her elevated station in life. However, she went out of her way to disgrace the English monarchy. She was in fact well aware of what she was doing. She once said to a friend: 'You say the Regent will hear of it. I hope he will. I love to mortify him.'

In Milan she met Bartolomeo Pergami, a splendid looking man of romantic latin appearance, but of doubtful origins, whom she appointed as her *cabinet courier*. With this handsome Italian as her personal bodyguard, Caroline then began seven years of exotic travel in hardly suitable circumstances which scandalized the whole of Europe. Her last English courtiers left her in alarm. She went to Naples surrounded by a rabble of foreign servants, then crossed the Mediterranean to Tunis where she took coffee with the Bey in his seraglio. She sailed for Athens, visited the Greek islands, Constantinople, Acre and Jerusalem which she entered on horseback in July, 1815. On return to Italy she bought a villa on Lake Como where she settled down. Between 1817 and 1819 she paid visits to Munich, Innsbruck and Vienna. She was wintering in Marseilles when she heard, early in 1820, that George III had died and that her husband was King of England.

Orders were given on the accession of George IV that the English Ambassadors should prevent the recognition of Princess Caroline as Queen at any foreign court, and her name was omitted from the Liturgy of the Church of England. George IV immediately wanted to divorce his wife on the grounds of adultery. There seemed ample evidence that she had been living with Pergami as her lover.

The King was advised that to take such proceedings would entail certain dangers for him, for Caroline would almost certainly defend herself with vigour and make counter-charges of adultery against him which would be difficult to disprove. After all, it was common knowledge that he had had a succession of mistresses. His Ministers feared that such action would bring damaging discredit upon the monarchy. The Hanoverian kings, by their indolence and stupidity, had brought the English monarchy pretty low anyway, and there were many who thought that national opinion was ripe for a republic. The French Revolution and the dismantling of the Bourbon monarchy had not been unpopular with certain sections of British public opinion.

It was not unnatural that Caroline should wish to return to England and take up her nominally rightful place as its Queen, although the King's desire that she should not do so is equally understandable.

Caroline claimed all the prerogatives of the fun-loving male. She once said of her husband: 'I should have been the man, he the woman.' It was evident that she envied the man's freedom to enjoy himself, and in being 'Caroline, the happy merry soul', she completely lost what royal dignity she possessed. Even Catherine of Russia, with her breath-taking immoralities – one of her ladies tested the sexual prowess of every man before he was permitted to the Empress's bed – managed to defy shocked public opinion without loss of royal dignity.

But Queen Caroline, as she now was, was quite outside the

pale. Those who supported the British monarchy did not want her on the throne. If George IV was a liability – and there was no love lost between him and his people – Caroline would have been even more so.

Yet Caroline, despite warnings that proceedings would be taken against her for adultery, set off for England. At St Omer, near Calais, she was met by emissaries of the King, as well as by her own sympathizers in England. Henry Brougham was empowered by the Government to offer her an annuity of £50,000, if she would not set foot on His Majesty's dominions again. There was some confusion about these negotiations which were bungled by both Brougham and the Cabinet. There is reason to believe that Caroline could have been bought off in this way if the negotiations had been more skilfully handled.

As it was she was antagonized from the start, particularly by the King's insistence that her name be omitted from the prayers for the Royal Family, which was as good as saying that so wicked a person could not be brought before the Throne of Grace – an outrageous thing to suggest in those days. And who was George IV to pass moral judgements anyway? Caroline decided to go to England and claim her rights. She was one of the fighting Brunswicks. Had not her brother fallen at Waterloo? Perhaps it was her great love of melodrama that triumphed over common sense.

There was certainly an almighty row at St Omer. Lord Hutchinson, one of the King's party, wrote: 'It is impossible for me to print the insolence, the violence and the precipitation of this woman's conduct; I never saw anything so outrageous, so undignified as a Queen, or so unamiable as a woman.'

If the King and his government could have foreseen what would be the effect on the populace of Caroline's return to England, they would probably have gone to much greater lengths to have kept her out of the country. If they had treated her with more tact at St Omer and generally with less contempt, they would probably have come to some agreement with her and avoided the most embarrassing royal trial in English history.

At Dover Caroline had an encouraging foretaste of the esteem in which she was held by her husband's subjects. She got a royal salute of guns from the garrison commander and was cheered by thousands as she disembarked. The crowd greeted her vociferously and demanded why she had not brought 'King Pergami' with her. After an address of welcome from the people of Dover, she drove to London in triumphant procession, escorted part of the way by a contingent of cavalry officers, but greeted or received nowhere by any representative of the King or his government.

King and government were busy elsewhere, cooking the Queen's goose for her, or so they thought.

The authorities were in possession of a collection of documents in which were set out statements by various people alleging that the Queen had been guilty of 'Conduct of the most licentious character' during her sojourn abroad. The documents were contained in a famous green bag, and the Parliamentary Committee which examined them stated that the charges 'affected the moral feeling and honour of the country'.

The Prime Minister, Lord Liverpool, introduced a Bill of Pains and Penalties. The Bill was designed to deprive Caroline of her rights and title of Queen of England and to dissolve the marriage between her and the King. It accused Caroline of a 'most unbecoming and disgusting intimacy' with Bartolomeo Pergami and alleged that she had behaved towards him, in various countries both in public and private, 'with indecent and offensive familiarity and freedom'. What is more, she was accused of having 'carried on a licentious, disgraceful and adulterous intercourse' with Pergami for a long period of time.

It was decided that the Bill was to be debated in the Lords only. This meant that all evidence would be heard there, that both sides would be represented by counsel, that witnesses could be questioned by any member of the House, who would finally vote on the Bill in the ordinary way.

The trial caused enormous excitement throughout England. There was countrywide backing for the Queen who received loyal addresses from supporters in Exeter,

Liverpool, Bath, Bristol, Halifax, Leeds, Nottingham and Sheffield.

The trial began with the second reading of the Bill on 17 August, 1820. The Lord Chancellor, Lord Eldon, was on the Woolsack. The Attorney-General, Sir Robert Gifford, opened the case for the Bill. The Queen was represented by Henry Brougham. The Whig leader, Lord Grey, immediately raised the legal point as to whether the Queen had not committed high treason by the fact that she had consented to violation of her marriage by someone not owing allegiance to the Crown. The judges, who were there throughout the trial to advise the House, considered the point and ruled that, even if proved, this fact would not amount to high treason.

In the opening speeches for and against, the supporters of the Bill alleged immoral sexual behaviour on the part of the Queen, while the Queen's partisans held that the evidence against her was false, as the witnesses brought from Europe were a 'perjured, abject pack of suborned wretches'. The Queen, declared her Solicitor-General, a handsome, golden-voiced man named Thomas Denham, was 'pure as unsunned snow' – a description which caused a certain amount of hilarity.

Those who had been sent to the Continent to inquire after the Queen's conduct with Pergami, pointed out that their bedrooms had been situated so close together that their life was to all appearance that of man and wife.

The Attorney-General explained that it was in Naples, in November, 1814, that Caroline's sleeping habits changed. William Austin, the child she had taken into her household at Greenwich, had then reached the age of puberty and no longer shared her bedroom. Pergami moved from the servants' quarters to a room adjoining the Queen's, and two people had been observed sleeping in Pergami's bed while the Queen's was empty. Pergami had also been watched helping the Queen to dress. While travelling in Syria he was seen going into her tent in a state of undress, and was often chosen to attend her while she was in the tent. The sleeping arrangements on board ship during Caroline's Mediterranean voyages were criticized similarly.

'No woman,' concluded the Attorney-General, 'would allow such a liberty to be taken with her unless by a man to whom she had granted the last favour.'

The first witness to be called was Theodore Majocchi. As soon as she saw him the Queen uttered a piercing exclamation: 'Theodore! Theodore! Oh, no!' Some people present thought she called him 'Traditore! Traditore!' It was considered likely they were right, though the newspapers of the day gave the other version, and that Caroline was horrified to see an old and trusted servant brought to give evidence against her. She hurriedly left the chamber looking, as one spectator described her, 'more like a fury than a woman'.

Majocchi gave his evidence through an interpreter. He declared he was a kind of servant to Pergami after that gentleman's promotion to the rank of *courier de cabinet*.

His evidence was confined mainly to the sleeping arrangements at various places of the Queen's travels. At Naples, he said, he slept on a sofa in the cabinet which was between the rooms occupied by Pergami and the Princess, for five or six nights. On two nights he saw the Princess come through after midnight and walk into Pergami's room, staying on each occasion about a quarter of an hour or twenty minutes.

He told of the domestic arrangements on board a sailing ship in which Caroline and her entourage travelled from Jaffa to Italy. Owing to the heat the Princess slept on deck. Two tents were pitched, one inside the other, and a sofa and travelling bed were placed in the inner tent. According to Majocchi the Princess slept in this tent every night, and Pergami slept with her. He said that he himself had slept in the deck immediately below, and had often heard a rhythmic creaking motion going on at night. Majocchi also maintained that on one occasion he had prepared hot water for the Princess, when Pergami had fetched it and remained in Caroline's cabin while she was bathing.

Majocchi also spoke of the Princess's travelling arrangements in European countries. It was his duty, as he mentioned, to prepare the carriage in which the Princess and Pergami travelled together. He described a dancing display given by Mahomet, the exhibitionist, which the Princess attended. It included a *guioco*: this was referred to as an indecent dance representing sexual intercourse, during which Mahomet had inserted a roll in his pantaloons to represent an erect penis, and then he had made backward and forward motions. The witness claimed that the Princess had enjoyed the exhibition of the *guioco* on more than one occasion. (As was established by later counter-evidence, Mahomet's dance was only a variation of the Spanish *bolero* and commonly performed all over southern Europe in the company of both ladies and gentlemen.)

Brougham, in his cross-examination of Majocchi, sought to establish that at Naples there was another passage from the Princess's room to that occupied by Pergami, and that there would have been no reason for her to have passed through the room he was occupying. Majocchi believed there was such a passage – an admission which rather damaged his evidence. To a whole series of Brougham's questions Majocchi made the single reply, *'Non mi ricordo'*. The precise translation of this was a matter of some discussion. Whether it meant 'I do not know', 'I do not remember', or 'I do not recollect', it was generally taken as meaning something which it was convenient to forget and the phrase passed into the early nineteenth-century English vernacular as such.

Much of Brougham's cross-examination was aimed at discrediting the witness and his motives for giving evidence, and putting him to ridicule. He did this with all the foreign witnesses, which did not create a good impression with their lordships who again and again called him to order for taking advantage of their simplicity and lack of education.

After counsel had finished with the witness, the members of the House questioned him. More details about the sleeping accommodation on board the Mediterranean ship were given by Gaetano Paturzo, the mate, who described familiarities he had seen both inside and outside the tent. He had observed the Princess sitting on Pergami's lap on a bench near the mainmast when they were cuddling each other. The master of the ship, Vincenzo Gargiulo, gave similar evidence. Various members of the Princess's staff stated they had seen

Pergami emerge from her bedroom in a state of undress. A member of the staff of an inn at Trieste, where the entourage had stayed overnight, alleged that on the next morning he found *two* chamberpots in the Princess's bedroom. 'There was a good deal in each,' he added.

Further familiarities between the Princess and Pergami were attested by Meidge Barbara Kress who before her marriage had been a maid at the Post Inn, Karlsruhe, where the Princess had spent one night. She said that when she entered Pergami's room she found him in bed, with the Princess sitting on it, and their arms had been around each other. The Princess had immediately jumped up when the maid came in. Meidge Kress also asserted that when she made Pergami's bed in the morning she found certain stains on the sheets.

Brougham, in his cross-examination, went to such lengths in his endeavours to discredit this witness and her motives that strong protests were made by the peers. Although she strongly denied that she had been given money to come to England, and had in fact begged to be excused giving evidence, Brougham got a lot of rather contemptible enjoyment out of putting her to ridicule. It remained for the peers to ask the rather more important questions about facts concerning her evidence, but her story could not be shaken.

One of the most damaging – and notorious – witnesses against Caroline was Louisa Demont who had been the Princess's *femme de chambre*. Creevey, the diarist, called her *la chienne Demont*. She told the now familiar story about the Princess and Pergami sleeping together, a fact which as before had only been adduced indirectly from the observation that of their two respective beds only one, to all appearances, had been slept in.

Further witnesses stated they had seen Pergami and the Princess kissing, walking arm-in-arm as though husband and wife, and one said he saw Pergami fondling her breasts.

Giuseppe Rastelli who had been superintendent of the Princess's stables took the story to even more outrageous lengths by saying that when the Princess and Pergami were out driving in her carriage, he saw the Princess's hand 'in the small clothes of Mr Pergami'. This had been in 1816. An Italian named Sacchi who had been the Princess's courier and equerry about that time was more explicit about this particular indecency. He claimed to have seen them on more than one occasion in their carriage, with their hands on each other's private parts. This outrageous evidence prompted the Queen's Counsel to make virulent personal attacks upon the witnesses who gave it. Little attempt seems to have been made by Brougham to shake their improbable story.

The atmosphere in which Queen Caroline's trial took place can be gauged by the fact that the witnesses who had come to England to give evidence against her had been so roughly handled by the Dover rabble, that others who had been summoned turned back at Calais, rather than face the terror of the pro-Caroline mobs, to say nothing of the character-assassination which awaited them in the House of Lords at the hands of her counsel.

The trial lasted for three months, and so intense was the interest and so detailed were the reports of the evidence of indecencies that all England, it was said, was discussing it in the most bawdy manner. Even the Archbishop of Canterbury was heard making risqué remarks about it in mixed company. Many parents forbade their daughters to read the newspapers during that period.

The case for the Bill was brought to a close by the Solicitor-General. He considered the circumstances were sufficient to establish Queen Caroline's adultery with Pergami.

The Lords then adjourned for three weeks to give the defence ample time to prepare their case. Brougham opened for the defence on 3 October with a brilliant speech which lasted two days. He made light of the evidence against the Queen in passages of splendid irony and sarcasm. He commented upon the unprecedented advantage enjoyed by Queen Caroline's prosecutors 'of having parties to proceed against who, from beginning to end, concealed no part of their conduct under the slightest or even most flimsy disguise. Throughout the whole of the proceedings knowing they were watched, they discarded all schemes of secrecy, showed an utter carelessness of the persons who were watching them, threw off all ordinary trammels, banished from their practice every suggestion of decorum and prudence, and in fact gave themselves up to the gratification and indulgence of their passion with that warmth which is only found in the hey-day of young blood.

'Thus it would be seen that they were sitting together in familiar proximity. The act is also seen with the addition of the lady's arm around the neck, or behind the back of her paramour. When it is necessary to trace their conduct a step higher in the scale of criminality, and exhibit the parties in such an attitude as to leave no room for explanation or equivocation, the act is done – not in a corner apart from any scrutinizing eye – but in a villa filled by servants. Especial pains are taken that the slander shall not be secret, but on the contrary that it shall be liable to the most widely-diffused publicity. Even the act of sitting on Pergami's knee upon the deck is adjusted to take place in the presence of crew and passengers. Care is taken that it shall be directly seen by at least eleven persons. The frequent and free saluting on the deck, which when committed in a particular manner, must leave little doubt of the subsisting intercourse between the parties – even that is done, not at night, nor in dark and privacy, but before everybody and in open daylight. But the case which their lordships were called upon to believe was not left there, for the parties were represented as having taken the indispensable precaution of granting even the last favours within the hearing of witnesses. They were described as habitually sleeping together in all their journeys by land and sea. She could not even retire to change her dress but Pergami must attend in the dressing-room – first of course the parties taking care to have a witness present to speak to the fact.

'No hidden places or recesses were selected or chosen by the parties for the free and safe indulgence of their passion from the prying eyes of those around them. They acted on the contrary before witnesses. They conducted themselves in open daylight, in the face of couriers, servants, and passengers. Was such folly ever known before in the history of human acts? Was ever folly so extravagant disclosed in the most unthinking acts of that youthful period when the blood boils in the veins? Was ever, even then, in that proverbial period of thoughtless levity, a being so recklessly insane as to have acted in this manner?' Brougham did not believe there was ever such an instance in the history of human passions.

In similar manner Brougham, who put up a strong defence for the Queen, covered the assertions of all the witnesses against her with biting sarcasm and scorn, alleging they had been bribed. (His attacks on George IV, in this connexion, were to bar him from taking silk for many years.)

The defence called evidence to show that Pergami and the Queen had always behaved with the greatest propriety. The most important witness for Caroline was Lieutenant J. R. Hownam, R.N. And yet it was he who did her case the most damage.

He had been in her service during her Mediterranean voyages when she was alleged to have slept with Pergami in the tent. He told the Lords that it had been extremely hot during that July, and the tent had been pitched on the deck on the Princess's instructions, because it was too oppressive to sleep below – particularly as the ship carried horses, the noise and smell of which she found intolerable in the cabins.

In cross-examination Hownam then conceded that in his view Pergami *did* sleep in the tent with the Princess – an admission which caused something of a sensation. And it certainly put a different light on Hownam's previous contention that it had been necessary for the Princess to have some responsible person near her while she was sleeping on deck, for her own safety. Many members of the Lords considered that Hownam's evidence was proof of Caroline's adultery. Charles Greville, the diarist, concluded in *The Greville Memoirs 1814–1860*: 'All unprejudiced men seem to think the adultery sufficiently proved.'

To top it all Thomas Denman, the Queen's Solicitor-General, perpetrated a memorable gaffe at the end of his speech in her defence which he concluded with the following reference to her: 'If no accuser can come forward to condemn thee, neither do I condemn thee. Go and sin no more.'

This was disastrous and was believed to be the thing which really ended the Queen's popularity. The lampooners soon got to work and the following verse was chanted in London's taverns:

> *Most gracious Queen, we thee implore*
> *To go away and sin no more.*
> *But if that effort be too great,*
> *To go away at any rate.*

Yet although a good majority of the Lords believed that the Queen's guilt had been established, many voted against the Bill.

The first reading of the Bill was passed by a majority of only 28. The Queen immediately presented a petition, declaring that 'before God she is wholly innocent of the crime laid to her charge'.

The Lords were plainly getting cold feet. The Bill was highly unpopular. It had involved the Crown in dire disgrace in the eyes of all sections of the community. And public opinion was rapidly turning against the Government. On 10 November the question was put that the Bill be read a third time. There was a majority of only nine and the Prime Minister then proposed that further consideration of the Bill be postponed for six months – which is a Parliamentary device for killing a measure. It was carried with acclamation. The Prime Minister in fact had no choice but to abandon the Bill, for it was quite evident that the Commons would have thrown it out entirely.

When the Bill of Pains and Penalties was abandoned London rejoiced, but the Queen's popularity was short-lived.

On 19 July, 1821, George IV was crowned with magnificent ceremony. Caroline claimed her right to be crowned with him but was ignored. She made several rather pathetic attempts to get into Westminster Abbey for the Coronation but was turned away from each door. She retreated disconsolately. London no longer supported her. The mob was more than just fickle. It had been whipped up and manipulated for political purposes. Now the politicians had no use for her.

Caroline died a mere fortnight later; as some said, of a broken heart. But although mortification concerning her treatment seems to have hastened her end, the cause of her death was a bowel obstruction. She met her end on 7 August, 1821 as bravely and defiantly as she had lived.

Her body was taken to Brunswick. There were disgraceful scenes during its last progress through London. She was buried among her illustrious ancestors, and on the lid of her coffin was written her own words: 'Here lies Caroline of Brunswick, the injured Queen of England.'

Injured, ill-used she certainly was, though it must be admitted that she had done everything she could to provoke her husband. She had been guilty of the worst possible indiscretions. She was foolish, arrogant, self-willed. But was she guilty of the offences for which she was tried? Most informed people at the time believed that she was.

On the other hand, it is very difficult to believe that anyone but a mad woman would have behaved as Caroline was alleged to have behaved with Pergami. She knew very well that she was being spied upon by the Regent's agents. She knew also what would be the penalty if she committed adultery, just as she knew she would inevitably become Queen of England upon the death of George III. Caroline was noted for her unwisdom, but she was not mad.

The witnesses who gave such evil-minded evidence against her were all suspect, and it is extremely doubtful whether her behaviour with Pergami amounted to anything more than gross indiscretion. Her levity of manner and laxity of habits, however, doubtless rendered her unfit to be the head of English society, and the measures which were taken to exclude her from it are understandable.

# Chapter 2
# Adelaide Bartlett

Throughout the snowy winter of 1886, England had been agog with the fantastic story of the Pimlico poisoning mystery. The Home Rule Bill, the fall of the Government, riots in the West End and in Belfast, crises in the Balkans and in the Empire, were of relatively minor interest compared with the fascinating Adelaide Bartlett and her strange husband, Edwin, whom she was alleged to have poisoned in the most remarkable and unprecedented manner in the early hours of New Year's Day.

Adelaide Bartlett was one of four very interesting women, each of whom has left an abiding question mark upon the gaslit scene of Victorian Britain. The other three, Madeleine Smith (1857), Florence Bravo (1876) and Florence Maybrick (1889) were each the centre of a lurid *cause célèbre*, after which the question of their guilt remained undecided.

Adelaide Bartlett's acquittal was certainly a controversial one. Everything in fact about the case was sensational and outrageous. It was like a piece of exotic fiction. If a novelist had written it he would have been accused of stretching credibility too far.

The origins of Adelaide Bartlett have always been obscure, as mysterious indeed as the heroine of a Gothic novel. The world had it on the authority of Sir Edward Clarke, Q.C., the man to whose brilliant defence at the Old Bailey Adelaide owed her life, that she was the illegitimate daughter of an Englishman of good family and fortune who had had an affair with an unknown Frenchwoman. She was born at Orléans in 1855 and was christened with the enchanting name of Adelaide Blanche de la Tremouille. She came to England at an early age and was introduced to Edwin Bartlett as his prospective bride when she was an attractive and graceful girl of nineteen. Her father, who refused to own her, bestowed upon her a dowry which, though modest, was greatly welcomed by Bartlett.

Edward Clarke may or may not have got this story from Adelaide herself who was no stickler for the truth. On her marriage certificate her father's name was given as Adolphe Collot de la Tremouille, Comte de Thouars d'Escury, a name which rolls straight out of the Gallic top drawer. It was at one time suggested that Adelaide was fathered by a member of Queen Victoria's entourage during the state visit to Napoleon III in August, 1855. But as Adelaide was born on 20 December, 1855, Her Britannic Majesty's visit can hardly be held responsible for her parentage. The most recent investigations seem to establish that her father's correct name was given on the marriage certificate, and that her mother was an obscure English girl named Clara Chamberlain. It is likely that Adelaide herself was not properly informed about her parentage.

She spent her childhood in France, and was then sent to England to stay with her mother's relatives. Her destiny was controlled by others, and she was always well provided with money. She took to accepting her life thus.

Illegitimacy was a matter for deep shame and disgrace in the nineteenth century. Ordinarily social life was difficult if not impossible for such outcasts. The stain, however, was considerably lightened if one's erring parent was an aristocrat, and particularly an English aristocrat, so great was the awe and reverence in which the upper classes were held. The

English milords of the day were gods and their right to seduce girls of the lower classes was barely questioned in a society steeped in puritanical hypocrisy. It was merely necessary to keep it as quiet as possible. Adelaide may well have fancied her father was an English lord. She had a ladylike grace and charm, and her origins were shrouded with the requisite mystery of absentee aristocracy.

At any event, 1875 found her at Kingston-upon-Thames staying with her maternal aunt and uncle, Mr and Mrs William Chamberlain. Among the Chamberlains' friends was Charles Bartlett who ran a removers' business in the town. One day Charles's brother, Edwin, came to visit him. Charles took him to the Chamberlains where Edwin instantly fell in love with Adelaide and wanted to marry her. She was an exceptionally attractive girl. Her dark, fascinating eyes were vibrant with expression. She had a full, beautiful mouth and a lovely complexion, an asset beyond price in the days when ladies were not supposed to use make-up.

Edwin was a prosperous grocer and provision dealer in partnership with Edward Baxter. He was about thirty years old. The marriage was quickly arranged. Adelaide's parents in Orléans, after making judicious inquiries concerning the prospective groom, gave their approval and the modest dowry. The marriage was arranged in typical French style. Afterwards, Adelaide herself said: 'My consent to my marriage was not asked, and I only saw my husband once before my wedding day.'

But the marriage was by no means an unhappy one. Adelaide was a charming and pliable girl, full of natural affection and anxious in every way to please her husband. Edwin, though a man of very strange ideas, loved her and was extremely loyal to her. As he was of lowly parentage and had had little education himself, he felt a deep respect for learning and was greatly impressed by Adelaide's aristocratic origins, even if they were on the wrong side of the blanket.

Adelaide, however, had been only sketchily educated, a fact of which Edwin was well aware and which he intended to remedy immediately. And so, instead of a honeymoon or, indeed, any kind of married life, he sent her off to a boarding school at Stoke Newington where she remained for two years, living with her husband only during the holidays. After that she went to a finishing school in Belgium. Adelaide submitted unquestioningly to this extraordinary beginning to her married life. The acquisition of learning and the accomplishments of finishing schools were greatly prized in those days and Adelaide may well have been pleased at the opportunity of filling the gaps in her education.

In 1878, her schooling completed, she went to live with her husband in the rooms above one of his shops in Station Road, Herne Hill. He had, very properly he considered, withheld the sexual side of married life from his schoolgirl wife. Edwin was either remarkably abstemious or slightly queer or, as some believed, he was having it off with the ladies of the town. Victorian London, according to the careful investigations of Henry Mayhew, contained 80,000 prostitutes. Brothels to suit all tastes, perversions and pockets abounded. Victorian sex life was lurid and to a large extent the result of the moralists' teaching that the enjoyment of sex was sinful.

Except for one celebrated occasion, the married life of Adelaide and Edwin apparently remained platonic. This at least was the general belief, fostered by Adelaide herself. Edwin treated Adelaide as though she was a piece of Dresden china. He was excessively proud of her and took great delight in showing her off to his friends who were, however, rather few. Adelaide was lonely. Her husband's time was wholly taken up by his business, now greatly enlarged and prospering mainly as the result of his wife's dowry which had been carefully invested in it. He bought Adelaide a couple of dogs upon which she lavished her pent-up affections.

The shadow in her life was her father-in-law and he was to remain so right to the end. Edwin Bartlett senior was a crafty old man whose animosity played a vital part in the tragic story of his son and Adelaide. He was antagonistic to Adelaide right from the start. To begin with, she was French and he disliked all foreigners, particularly the hated French.

Secondly she came between him and his son, off whom he had been sponging for some years.

At the time Adelaide went to live at Station Road, Bartlett *père* had become a widower and moved in with Edwin and his wife. The old man returned his son's abundant hospitality by being as unpleasant to Adelaide as he could. In 1878 he accused her of having an affair with his youngest son, Frederick.

This brought matters to a head. There was a great scene during which Edwin took his wife's part so strongly that he threatened to throw his father out unless he made a statement before a solicitor retracting his allegations against Adelaide. The old man complied, though with mental reservations, for he had no desire to quarrel with the son who provided him so munificently with the comforts of life. Bartlett senior remained on good terms with his son, visiting him at his places of business almost daily right to the end; but the quarrel with Adelaide was only mended on the surface. They continued to dislike each other as much as ever.

Adelaide Bartlett's sex life has become a matter of considerable importance in the annals of crime. On the surface, it would appear that in Edwin's eyes she stood high on her pedestal, and was too much of a lady to submit to the horrid indignity of physical sex. But there came a time when Adelaide, a warm affectionate creature, found herself very naturally wanting to have a child. That this could not be accomplished without the preliminary of copulation became obvious to her, after she had read a certain book she found in Edwin's library. It was eloquently entitled: *Esoteric Anthropology (The Mysteries of Man): A Comprehensive and Confidential Treatise on the Structure, Functions, Passionate Attractions and Perversions, True and False, Physical and Social Conditions and the Most Intimate Relations of Men and Women* by T. L. Nichols, M.D., F.A.S.

It is difficult to believe that a man who wished to protect his wife from the realities of sex should have put this book in her way. Such scandalous reading in a middle-class Victorian household was very unusual. That Adelaide read the book from cover to cover indicates a broadmindedness out of tune with her age, and has led some to believe that it was she who acquired the book herself in the first place, not Edwin.

She learned one vital thing from it : the precise moment in her lunar cycle in which copulation would most likely lead to pregnancy; and according to the Bartlett legend there was one Sunday afternoon, prudently chosen by Adelaide in conjunction with the knowledge she had acquired from Dr Nichols, during which she and Edwin were said to have had their one act of sex in their married life. It duly resulted in her pregnancy.

Certainly a married couple who copulated only once during their married life are deserving of some note. In the case of George IV and Caroline of Brunswick it seems likely enough. But as far as the Bartletts are concerned there is room for doubt; we have it only from Adelaide and her word was not always reliable. Indeed, the legend that Adelaide had fostered about her almost virginal marriage was later upset by Nurse Annie Walker who had the confidence of both Adelaide and Edwin. According to her, the Bartletts always slept together in the same bed; what 'the single act' meant was that they took precautions during sexual intercourse except on that one occasion which led to Adelaide's pregnancy. (A pocket full of french letters found in Edwin's clothes after his death seemed to confirm these statements.)

Nurse Annie Walker, a fully qualified midwife, was installed at Station Road about a month before the baby was due.

Edwin intended to take no chances with his precious wife during this difficult time. Annie Walker had been engaged through the good offices of Mrs Nichols, the wife of the author who had written the *Esoteric Anthropology*. She soon saw that Adelaide was going to have a difficult time, so she suggested to Edwin that a doctor should be called in.

Edwin was dead against this. He didn't want to have 'any man interfering with her'. Nurse Walker told him that it was the baby rather than the mother's life which would be in danger. Adelaide's confinement was so difficult and painful that a doctor was called in at the last minute, but he was too late to save the child. It was born dead.

Annie Walker stayed on for three more weeks until Adelaide was fully recovered. The two women became firm friends. Even after the nurse's professional services were no longer required, she used to visit the Bartletts staying, on at least one occasion, for several days.

She was on extremely friendly terms with both Adelaide and Edwin and was the recipient of many confidences, some of them on the most intimate subjects. Annie Walker later gave evidence at Adelaide's trial, and she said that she found the Bartletts a united and affectionate couple. Adelaide, however, did complain to her about the terms of her husband's will in which he had left everything to her, but only on condition that she did not remarry. In view of what happened later, an ominous interpretation was placed upon this; Adelaide has even been accused of forging the later will which removed the condition. However, she certainly had reason to complain about her husband's first will as his prosperity had been largely brought about by the infusion of her own dowry into his business.

In 1883 they left Station Road and went to live over another of Bartlett's shops in Lordship Lane, East Dulwich. There was no room for Bartlett senior. Much to Adelaide's relief the old man had to find lodgings of his own. He had no financial worries, however. His generous son saw to that.

It was in Lordship Lane that they met Mr and Mrs Matthews. Alice Matthews became an intimate friend of Adelaide's and remained so until her trial. George Matthews was a business associate of Edwin's and the two men also became close friends.

Then, in 1885, when the Bartletts had moved to Merton Abbey, near Wimbledon there was the fatal meeting with the Rev. George Dyson. Dyson, a graduate of Trinity College, Dublin, was the minister of the local Wesleyan chapel. He was about twenty-seven years old, had a heavy black moustache and closely trimmed whiskers and was not a man of either striking appearance or personality. He is said to have had dog-like eyes and a permanently wounded expression.

Dyson paid a duty call on the Bartletts. What impressed Edwin more than anything was the fact that the clergyman was a man of education, a university graduate. Edwin hoped that by encouraging the friendship he would be able to bask in culture. The Rev. Dyson's accomplishments in this direction were, as a matter of fact, slight. He was struggling along on a hundred pounds a year, and was envious of the Bartletts' opulence. The real attraction, however, was Mrs Bartlett, with her poise and fascinating accent. The three of them soon became fast friends and Dyson foolishly plunged headlong into a highly dangerous situation, one in which a clergyman should never find himself, for it was soon obvious to him that Edwin was more or less thrusting Adelaide into his arms and encouraging them to be together as much as possible.

It is not an unknown eccentricity for a man to thrust his wife into another man's arms. Watching one's wife being made love to and even copulating with someone else, is a form of masochism well-known to the sexologist. Edwin Bartlett was a strange man with strange ideas. Everyone who knew him said that. One of his favourite theories was that a man should have two wives, one for intelligent companionship and one for domestic purposes, and by the way he behaved over George Dyson, he gave the impression that a wife should have similar privileges.

Instead of being shocked at such un-Victorian notions, the Rev. Dyson pursued his intimacy with Edwin and his attractive wife unremittingly. There is little doubt that he became completely fascinated by Adelaide, but his friendship for Edwin remained strong right to the end. Edwin encouraged them to go out for walks together, and to kiss each other in his presence. They were soon kissing each other in secret, though no one knows how far their love-making went, or whether Adelaide became his mistress.

Edwin's remarkable attitude towards Adelaide's relationship with George Dyson was expressed in a letter written to him in September, 1885, when the Bartletts were spending a month at Dover. By then the three of them were on Christian name terms.

14 St James Street,
Dover, Monday.

Dear George – Permit me to say I feel great pleasure in thus addressing you for the first time. To me it is a privilege to think that I am allowed to feel towards you as a brother, and I hope our friendship may ripen as time goes on, without anything to mar its future brightness. Would that I could find words to express my thankfulness to you for the very loving letter you sent Adelaide today. It would have done anybody good to see her overflowing with joy as she read it whilst walking along the street, and afterwards as she read it to me. I felt my heart going out to you. I long to tell you how proud I feel at the thought I should soon be able to clasp the hand of the man who from his heart could pen such noble thoughts. Who can help loving you? I felt I must say two words: 'Thank you', and my desire to do so is my excuse for troubling you with this. Looking towards the future with joyfulness, I am yours affectionately,

Edwin.

The Freudian interpretation of this extraordinary letter might be that Edwin was a latent homosexual, and it is certainly possible that his curious make-up might have been complicated by such tendencies, and that he might not have been aware of them.

George's reply to Edwin's strange effusion was modestly naïve.

18 Parkfields, Putney,
September 23, 1885

My dear Edwin – Thank you very much for the brotherly letter you sent me yesterday. I am sure I respond from my heart to your wish that our friendship may ripen with the lapse of time, and I do so with confidence, for I feel that our friendship is founded on a firm, abiding basis – trust and esteem. I have from a boy been ever longing for the confidence and trust of others. I have never been so perfectly happy as when in possession of this. It is in this respect, among many others, that you have shown yourself a true friend. You have thanked me, and now I thank you; yet I ought to confess that I read your warm and generous letter with a kind of half fear – a fear lest you should ever be disappointed in me and find me a far more prosy, matter-of-fact creature than you expect. Thank you, moreover, for the telegram; it was very considerate to send it. I am looking forward with much pleasure to next week. Thus far I have been able to stave off any work and trust to be able to keep it clear. Good old Dover! It will ever possess a pleasant memory for me in my mind and a warm place in my heart. With very kind regards, believe me, yours affectionately,

George.

Taking full advantage of the liberal trust and confidence of his affectionate friend Edwin, George spent as much time as he could with Adelaide at the expense of his flock, and while Edwin was busy in London. He and Adelaide walked hand-in-hand along the sea shore. He knew that he was treading a very indiscreet path, though he did not dream that it would lead him to the dock at the Old Bailey.

George Dyson was a weak and selfish man and there is no doubt at all that he was after Adelaide; but as she was the stronger character of the two, she was no wife to be seduced without her full consent. Moreover, it was obvious that she was extremely fond of Edwin and remained loyal to him to the end, so the balance of probabilities is that Dyson didn't get his way with her.

Besides, a more interesting development took Dyson's attention and riveted him even more firmly to the Bartletts. Edwin made a new will, leaving everything unconditionally to Adelaide; and he appointed George co-executor with his solicitor. Not only was he made executor, but Edwin told

George that in the likely event of his death, he wished to give Adelaide to him, and there was apparently something like a betrothal between George and Adelaide.

Precisely how this extraordinary arrangement came about, Dyson himself who was thoroughly questioned about it later was a little vague. He said that his conscience began to smite him about his feelings for Adelaide and that he told both her and Edwin that he was getting too fond of her and that it was disturbing his work.

Edwin wouldn't hear of their friendship being discontinued. On the subject of George having Adelaide, Edwin may not have said more than just: 'If anything happens to me, you two may come together.' That would not have been an extraordinary thing to say by a hypochondriac who might have thought he had not very long to live. If Adelaide and George are to be believed, he very definitely bequeathed his wife to his friend, and the fact was taken for granted between them. There was for instance the occasion when Adelaide did or said something which neither man approved, and which drew the comment from George: 'When she comes under my care, I shall have to teach her differently.'

Adelaide went so far as to state specifically that her husband had given her to George Dyson whom she regarded as her fiancé. And according to her own words, she took her 'betrothal' to Dyson very seriously.

In the August of 1885 the Bartletts moved to London and took furnished rooms on the first floor of 85 Claverton Street, Pimlico, the house of Mr and Mrs Frederick Doggett. Mr Doggett, by some strange quirk of irony, was a Registrar of Births and Deaths.

George Dyson swallowing the rising tide of his conscience continued his delicious, if slightly frustrating affair with Adelaide. After all, it was Edwin's most ardent wish. During the last months of his life Edwin continued to enjoy his unhusbandly pleasure of watching Adelaide and George kissing each other. He encouraged them to spend days alone together, and to further this end he bought George a season ticket from Putney to Waterloo. George was supposed to be giving Adelaide instruction in such subjects as Latin, history, geography and mathematics. He stayed with her all day alone in the Claverton Street sitting-room, and his presence aroused considerable comment.

The Doggetts' maid surprised them in affectionate attitudes – on the sofa together, her head on his shoulder, him sitting on a low chair, her on the floor, her head on his knee. Once the maid surprised them on the floor together. The curtains were always pulled and there was never a sign of instruction of any intellectual nature going on.

Dyson's mind must have been simplicity itself. But Adelaide was no fool. It is difficult to know what went on in her mind to permit herself to be a party to this extraordinary affair. Even if she believed Edwin when he said he had not long to live, and if she had agreed that Dyson should have her next, why did she not have the delicacy to await the expected demise? Could she have been persuaded that she was filling Edwin's last months with pleasure by kissing and flirting with George in his presence? That Edwin looked upon her more as his daughter than his wife?

Whatever she thought, it seems that this curious exercise in voyeurism was having the effect of arousing – or re-arousing – Edwin's desire for Adelaide which was to have fatal consequences. Adelaide no longer shared his bed. She had insisted on sleeping separately. There was one simple reason. Edwin had for some years suffered greatly with his teeth. A quack dentist had sawn his bad teeth off at gum level and fixed him with a denture which naturally led to endless dental trouble. As a consequence of all this, his breath became extremely foul and offensive, so much so that his fastidious wife could not endure him coming close.

Edward, a hypochondriac, believed that he was suffering from some fearful disease. He was always dosing himself with pills and medicines, and among the things he took was mercury. It was never discovered why he took this particular toxic which was a standard cure for syphilis at the time. (Hence the theory that he had frequented prostitutes rather than soil his immaculate wife.) But although Bartlett actually suffered from the delusion that he had syphilis there was no post-mortem evidence for this disease later on.

Early in December he took to his bed with sickness and diarrhoea. Adelaide tenderly nursed him and summoned Dr Alfred Leach who found him suffering from a pain in his left side, diarrhoea and gastritis. Edwin received several visits from the dentist who removed bad teeth and stumps. This, combined with Dr Leach's treatment, brought about a rapid recovery in Edwin's health. Actually there was nothing much wrong with him, but he remained miserable and depressed. He suffered from delusions, had fits of hysteria and wept by the hour. All the time Adelaide performed the unpleasant tasks of the sick-room willingly and without complaint. Night after night she sat beside his bed on an easy chair, snatching what sleep she could and refusing to go to bed herself.

Edwin's malevolent father paid frequent visits but was admitted to the sick-room only three times by Adelaide who did not want Edwin disturbed by his father's ill-natured suspicions. She told the old man plainly that she had neither forgiven nor forgotten the quarrel at Station Road. She knew well enough that her father-in-law still believed the worst of her, mainly on the grounds that she was a foreigner. The evil-minded old man haunted Claverton Street, muttering vague and menacing accusations.

Although Dr Leach was satisfied with the progress of his patient, Mrs Bartlett suggested they should get another opinion. Edwin himself was firmly against this. He was quite content with Dr Leach's treatment.

But Adelaide insisted upon a second doctor being called in and gave the startling prophetic reason: 'If Mr Bartlett does not get better soon, his friends and relations will accuse me of poisoning him.' Edwin then agreed to the second opinion merely in order to protect Adelaide against his friends and relations, particularly his ill-natured father.

Dr Leach brought in a certain Dr Dudley who found Edwin depressed, complaining of lack of sleep. His gums were 'spongy and inflamed'. Otherwise there was nothing the matter with him. He told him he ought to get up and go out every day.

George Dyson was a constant, sympathetic visitor and there is no reason to think that the feeling between the two men had changed. But according to Adelaide a change came over Edwin about this time. His mental deterioration has already been noted. He became neurotic and hysterical and he suffered from delusions. He also developed a desire to reclaim his right of the marriage bed which to Adelaide was apparently incomprehensible – in view of the fact that she was betrothed to George – and nauseating on account of his fetid breath.

On 27 December Adelaide asked George Dyson to get her a quantity of chloroform privately. She told him that Edwin suffered from some painful internal complaint about which the doctor knew nothing, the spasms of which could only be soothed by the use of chloroform.

Edwin died on the last day of December. After a meal of half a dozen oysters, he went to have some teeth extracted under gas. Dr Leach and Adelaide accompanied him. In the cab Adelaide mentioned to the doctor that she and her husband were saying only that morning that they wished they were unmarried so that they could have the pleasure of getting married all over again. 'That is very flattering to you, Mr Bartlett,' remarked Leach. Edwin was all muffled up and his reply was inaudible.

The dentist drew Leach's attention to the state of necrosis in Edwin's gums. There is little doubt that Edwin heard the dread word necrosis. He took a long time – four minutes – before he became unconscious by the gas. Otherwise the operation was quickly and successfully performed.

Edwin and Adelaide returned to Claverton Street where there was a conversation with Mrs Doggett on the subject of taking chloroform. Mrs Doggett had had an operation some years previously – was not the sensation of taking chloroform 'nice and pleasant'? asked Adelaide. Mrs Doggett could not really agree that it was. Adelaide said that she was in the habit of administering sleeping drops to her husband.

Edwin, whatever else might have been the matter with him, was not off his food. For dinner he had jugged hare, for supper more oysters and several delicacies including chutney and he ordered a large haddock for breakfast.

Mr and Mrs Doggett had friends in to celebrate the New

Year with them. Upstairs Adelaide sat silently beside her husband's bed, listening to the sounds of the New Year celebrations below. At a quarter past midnight the Doggetts went to bed. The house was wrapped in silence until four o'clock in the morning when Adelaide awakened the Doggetts and told them that she thought her husband was dead. She had already sent the maid for Dr Leach.

Leach was completely confounded. He could find no reason for his patient's death. Adelaide said she awoke in her bedside chair to find Edwin lying twisted over on his side, face downwards. She said she had poured brandy down his throat in a vain effort to revive him. On the mantelpiece, within the dead man's reach, was a glass containing liquid, smelling like 'chloric ether'.

'Could he have taken poison?' asked Leach. Adelaide held that to be impossible, as he could not have got poison without her knowledge.

Leach declined to give a death certificate, saying there must be a post-mortem. Adelaide agreed to this and urged him to make the examination as soon as possible.

On the mantelpiece was a bottle of chlorodyne which, Adelaide assured the doctor, Edwin used to rub on his gums. Then he must have swallowed some, suggested Leach. If Adelaide had really murdered her husband, why did she not jump at this explanation which might have prompted the sympathetic Dr Leach, who had always been susceptible to her charms and the magnetism of her dark eyes, to sign the death certificate there and then? Instead, she positively insisted on the post-mortem examination. 'Spare no expense,' she said.

Dr Green, of Charing Cross Hospital, was unable to perform the autopsy until the following day. While Adelaide was distraught and chaffing at the delay, her father-in-law arrived at the house, bristling with suspicion. He kissed his son and ostentatiously smelt his mouth for signs of prussic-acid poisoning.

'We must have a post-mortem,' he said to Leach. 'This cannot pass.' The doctor informed him curtly that it had already been arranged. After looking round for signs of hidden poisons, the old curmudgeon kissed Adelaide good-bye and went off to make as much trouble for her as he possibly could.

The post-mortem took place on 2 January. The doctors were unable to discover any natural cause for death. They took the stomach away for examination.

With suspicions mounting around her – those of her father-in-law being the meanest and most persistent – Adelaide went to stay with her friends, the Matthews.

She kept her dignity and her head. The Rev. George Dyson, however, was in a state of panic. Though obviously Adelaide was the one under the deepest suspicion, he had no thought or consideration for anyone but himself. To give her the solace of his Christian office was the last thing in his mind.

As the days passed and the suspense mounted, his behaviour completely altered her feelings towards him. They had rows at the Matthews's house. Dyson found out that chloroform had been found in Edwin's stomach and he naturally enough wanted to know what Adelaide had done with the chloroform he had bought for her.

Adelaide was very angry. 'Oh damn the chloroform!' she exclaimed stamping her foot. Mrs Matthews – doubtless listening at the door – broke in on the scene to hear Dyson say, 'You did tell me that Edwin was going to die soon.' Adelaide denied that she had said anything of the kind. Dyson bowed his head, moaning, 'My God, I am a ruined man.' He warned her that he was determined to make a clean breast of the affair, although Adelaide asked him not to mention the chloroform.

In their more affectionate days Dyson had been in the habit of penning little verses to Adelaide. An example of his poetic powers has been handed down to posterity:

> *Who is it that hath burst the door,*
> *Unclosed the heart that shut before,*
> *And set her queen-like on her throne,*
> *And made its homage all her own?*
> *My Birdie*

Dyson now wanted the return of this deathless piece, and his 'Birdie' obliged him with fitting scorn.

On 16 January, she and Dyson had another interview. According to him, she told him that he was distressing himself unnecessarily – if he did not incriminate himself, *she* would not incriminate him.

Their last meeting before they appeared together in the dock at the Old Bailey was three days later at the Matthews's house where, according to him, she told him that she had retrieved the chloroform bottle from Claverton Street, had emptied the contents out of the railway carriage between Victoria and Peckham Rye, and thrown the bottle into a pond.

He said : 'Supposing it should be proved that you ——

'Don't mince matters,' she interrupted. 'Why not say I gave him the chloroform?'

Late in January the Home Office analyst found that a quantity of chloroform in the stomach had been the sole cause of Edwin Bartlett's death. When Dr Leach imparted this information to Adelaide expecting it to take a load off her mind, he was surprised to find her strangely agitated.

It was then that she confided in him about her husband's curious ideas of marriage and about the strange triangular relationship between herself, her husband and George Dyson.

During the latter stages of his illness, Adelaide said, Edwin wished to assert his marital rights. She had pointed out to him the impropriety of such conduct. 'Edwin,' she said, 'you have given me to Mr Dyson, and it is not right that you should now do what during all these years of our married life you have not done.' She had protested strongly against Edwin's behaviour, as it was 'a duty which she owed to her womanhood and to the man to whom she was practically affianced'. He apparently agreed with what she said, but when he got better, his desire for her became so urgent that she bought chloroform, intending to sprinkle some on a handkerchief and wave it in front of his face when he became too pressing. She did not, however, attempt to put this plan into action.

She never had any secrets from Edwin, she declared, and

the presence of the chloroform in the drawer so troubled her that, on New Year's Eve, she told him all about it. She gave him the bottle when he was in bed. 'He was not angry. He looked at it and placed it on the corner of the mantelpiece close to his bed.' She then went to sleep and awoke to find him dead.

Dr Leach made little comment when he heard the strange story which Adelaide imagined was made in complete confidence. But he assured her that the chloroform would not have had the effect on Edwin which she apparently expected.

The Coroner's inquest was held in February to the accompaniment of enormous public interest. Dr Leach recounted the story of Adelaide Bartlett's remarkable confidences. Medical evidence established that eleven and a quarter grains of alcohol were found in the deceased's stomach. Adelaide, on legal advice, declined to give evidence. But the Rev. George Dyson availed himself of the opportunity of 'making a clean breast of things'.

He told the story of the chloroform in detail. He had been deceived and duped by a wicked woman, so he claimed, deliberately thrown into her company by her husband, and as a consequence found himself 'attacked upon his weakest side'. His treachery to Adelaide and the way he tried to put all the blame on her resulted in her immediate arrest at the request of the Coroner's jury, but he failed to save his own reputation, for he was later arrested and charged as being an accessory before the fact. The Coroner's jury returned a verdict of wilful murder against Adelaide.

On 13 April, they both stood side by side in the dock at the Old Bailey before Mr Justice Wills. Dyson was nervous and uneasy and kept stealing glances at the woman with whom he had been so guiltily in love and whom he had so basely betrayed.

But Adelaide, drawn and composed, gazed straight ahead and did not give Dyson one glance. Her appearance in the dock caused something of a sensation. Her widow's weeds were gone and in defiance of the convention of the day she was hatless. Her hair had been cut short and was arranged in a halo of curls around her head. The v-line of her black, tightly-fitting dress was edged with white lace. Slender and poised, she looked pathetically appealing.

As soon as she had come under suspicion of causing the death of her husband, Adelaide's mysterious parent had come to her aid. Unlimited funds were placed at her disposal to provide her with the best legal advice and protection. Edward Clarke, Q.C., M.P., the greatest defence advocate of the day, had been briefed to defend her as early as 20 February, two days after the verdict of the Coroner's jury.

Although Adelaide Bartlett was perhaps the most interesting woman to be charged with murder in nineteenth-century England, the real hero of her trial was Edward Clarke. His defence of her has gone down in history as one of the greatest performances at the English bar.

He had an extremely difficult task. Public opinion was wholly against her. Everyone believed her guilty before the trial began, a state of affairs which naturally affects the minds of a jury. The circumstances of her married life were bizarre and greatly offensive to Victorian ideas. Her own story was not only scandalous, but difficult to believe. The fact that she was of foreign origin did not exactly help her case either.

Clarke was not a man who sought the limelight. He was a great humanitarian and Adelaide Bartlett aroused his deepest sympathy. Here was a woman, hounded by her relatives, abandoned by all her friends, including the Matthews, vilified by public opinion, condemned unheard.

When Adelaide stood in the box at the Old Bailey she had not a single visible friend in the world. The only humanity shown to her had been by the officials at Clerkenwell Prison and by her solicitor who handled her husband's and now her affairs. What she was to owe to Edward Clarke's single-minded devotion to her cause only transpired later.

In those days the defendant was not allowed to go into the witness-box and give evidence. Whether this was a good thing or a bad thing is an interesting legal argument. It is certain that Adelaide would have endured a terrible and agonizing cross-examination from Sir Charles Russell, the Attorney-General and the most deadly cross-examiner of his day, from which she would not have emerged unscathed.

Edward Clarke had the advocate's supreme gift – that of persuasion; and the task he set himself was to persuade the jury that Adelaide Bartlett's own story was true. He called no evidence himself. All the witnesses appeared for the Crown. Their evidence he brilliantly exploited in cross-examination. He was sometimes highly destructive, but more often and with amazing subtlety he turned the witness's own words to his client's advantage.

Clarke was one of the busiest counsel of the day and was greatly in demand. His desk was piled with lucrative briefs, but he dropped everything to defend Adelaide Bartlett. He spent days in the British Museum library studying the medical effects of chloroform. His whole mind concentrated on nothing but this one case – unlike the Attorney-General who was deeply involved in one of the great political issues of the day and did not bring the full force of his intelligence to bear upon the presentation of the prosecution.

Every day Edward Clarke arrived early in court, so that he was sitting there in his place when the prisoner was brought into the dock, and every day he gave this friendless and lonely woman a smile of encouragement. He knew what that meant to her. It was typical of the humanity of this great advocate. Adelaide was soon to discover what a great and powerful defender she had in court.

The trial began, as it continued and ended, in sensation. As soon as the charges were read, the Crown withdrew the case against George Dyson. He stepped from the dock a free man, and doubtless without a single thought for his former love whom he left alone to face the dread charge of murder.

Edward Clarke smiled encouragingly at the forlorn figure in the dock. He knew – she did not – that Dyson's acquittal could be turned to her advantage, for he would now have to give evidence for the Crown. Clarke wrote later: 'Having admitted that he was innocent, the Attorney-General could not help calling him as a witness, and so offering him for my cross-examination. That would not be hostile, but friendly and sympathetic, for the more closely I could associate his actions with those of Mrs Bartlett, the more I should strengthen the instinctive reluctance of the jury to send her to the hangman's cord, while he passed unrebuked to freedom.'

In his opening speech for the Crown the Attorney-General posed the vital question: How did the chloroform get into Edwin Bartlett's stomach? There were three alternatives, he said. Suicide, though there was nothing to suggest he would take his life. Accident, but no man would drink a liquid giving such agonizing pains without immediately perceiving the mistake he had made. The third alternative was deliberate administration by another person.

His theory was that Adelaide had first chloroformed her husband into insensibility and then poured the liquid chloroform down his throat.

Edwin Bartlett senior took the stand and gave his biased evidence against his daughter-in-law. He had worked hard to get her into the dock, yet his evidence had no real bearing on the prosecution's case. His object was to cover Adelaide with as much suspicion as possible. Calling him at all was not a very wise move on the part of the Crown, and old Bartlett's triumph was short-lived, for Edward Clarke thoroughly discredited him in his subsequent cross-examination.

Clarke soon made old Bartlett admit that he had disliked Adelaide from the start. He raked up the apology which the dead man had forced his father to sign concerning the allegations he had made against Adelaide. The old man admitted in court that even though he had signed the apology, he still believed his calumnies were true. He further admitted that he had entered a caveat against his son's will in order to try to get the money himself. The contemptible old man left the box with barely a shred of his character left.

Clarke dealt entirely differently with the Rev. George Dyson who gave evidence on the second day. He could easily have shown Dyson up for the weak, despicable creature he was – a man who was prepared to send the woman he said he loved to the gallows to save his own reputation. It was his statements more than anything which had placed Adelaide in the dock. He gave his evidence in a manner hostile and damaging to her. The temptation to annihilate

Dyson, as he had done old Bartlett, must have been great. But Edward Clarke's job was to persuade the jury of Adelaide's innocence, not to destroy the character of the man whose intimate association with her was presumed to be the motive for her guilt. By destroying Dyson's character, Clarke would also have destroyed that of his client.

He treated Dyson with kid gloves, perhaps rather to Dyson's surprise, for this curious man must surely have suffered in his conscience over what he was doing to Adelaide.

Skilfully Clarke got a number of valuable admissions out of Dyson. He said that Bartlett was a man of very strange ideas, a fact which Clarke used to support the truth of the extraordinary story which Adelaide had told Dr Leach. Dyson also admitted that Bartlett had believed he suffered from a terrible disease of which he would soon die. Clarke persuaded him to admit that Adelaide had not asked him to keep secret the purchase of the fatal chloroform. Dyson, too, had thrown away the bottles he had bought containing the chloroform, for fear of being associated with Bartlett's death. Adelaide had done the same. If Dyson's motives had not been incriminating – for the Crown had admitted him guiltless – why should similar acts of Adelaide be considered so? Clarke was thus skilfully building up the case for his client's innocence, brick by brick.

Dr Leach recounted the illness and death of Edwin Bartlett and read the notes which he had made at the post-mortem. Leach was a tiresome and self-conscious witness, who qualified almost every answer with uncalled-for explanations. He greatly tried the patience of both Judge and Counsel.

He spoke of the great devotion with which the accused nursed her husband. He explained that Edwin had been in an extremely neurotic state, hysterical, eccentric, unbalanced – so much so that Leach suspected at one time that he was insane. Clarke made much of the fact that Adelaide wanted the post-mortem as soon as possible, and also that the longer it was delayed the less likely was it that the true cause of death could be established.

Clarke finally got some important information out of Leach who had frequently administered chloroform. The effect of what Leach said was that, if Mrs Bartlett had made her husband inhale chloroform in order to render him unconscious, and then poured the liquid down his throat – which was the Crown's contention – then Bartlett would almost certainly have vomited, for he had recently had a large meal which included mango chutney. But no vomiting had taken place.

How then did the liquid chloroform get into his stomach?

The Crown now produced its expert medical witnesses. The chief of these was Dr Thomas Stevenson, Professor of Medical Jurisprudence at Guy's Hospital, London, a toxicologist of international standing. He said he knew of no recorded case of murder by the administration of liquid chloroform. It *was* possible to pour liquid chloroform down the throat of an unconscious person, but Clarke made him admit that it was an extremely ticklish and delicate operation – and one so difficult that he would be afraid of pouring it down the windpipe, should he perform it himself. The post-mortem had established that none of the chloroform had gone down Bartlett's windpipe, for it would have left traces behind if it had.

The Crown's case had closed. Edward Clarke offered no evidence. His defence was a magnificent speech, long remembered as a brilliant example of forensic eloquence and skilfully persuasive advocacy.

Before he dealt with the details of the evidence, he summed up the prosecution's case in devastating fashion.

'It is a marvellous thing that you are asked by the prosecution to accept. You are asked to believe that a woman who for years had lived in friendship and affection with her husband, who during the whole time of his illness had striven to tend him, to nurse him and help him, who had tended him by day, who had sacrificed her own rest to watch over him at night, had spent night after night without going to her restful bed, simply giving to herself sleep at the bottom of his couch that she might be ready by him to comfort him by her presence, who had called doctors, who had taken all the pains that the most tender and affectionate nurse possibly could, that by no possibility should any chance be lost of the doctors' ascertaining what his trouble was, and having the quickest means to cure it; you are asked to imagine that that woman on New Year's Eve was suddenly transformed into a murderess, committing crime not only without excuse, but absolutely without any object; you are asked to believe that by a sort of inspiration she succeeds in committing that crime by the execution of a delicate and difficult operation – an operation which would have been delicate and difficult to the highest trained doctors that this country has in it.'

Dealing with the prosecution's theory that the accused had first made her husband unconscious by inducing him to inhale chloroform, and then pouring it down his throat, he said that the expert evidence showed that an attempt to chloroform a sleeping person would cause him to wake up and resist, and that it was extremely unlikely that an unskilled person would be able to do it.

In similar manner Clarke went into great detail to discredit the other evidence presented against Adelaide. The packed court was hushed, listening avidly to his every word. Barristers crowded the benches to hear him. But no one listened to him more ardently than the slight, pale young woman in the dock, to whom his speech was the most important thing in her life. Clarke concluded in memorable style:

'This woman has not had the happiest of lives. She has been described to you as one who had no friends. But she had one friend – her husband. He did stand by her, strange as his ideas may have been, disordered as it would seem from some things that have been said, his intellect in some respects must have been. Yet in his strange way he stood by her and protected her. He was affectionate in manner, and when her reputation was assailed, he defended it as only the husband could defend it. And to her at this moment it may seem most strange that he to whom she had given this persistent affection, even during the years of such a life, should be the one of whose foul murder she now stands accused. And if he himself could know what passed among us here – how strange, how sorrowful it might seem to him – how strange that such an accusation should have been formulated and tried in court, in spite of the efforts which he endeavoured to make to prevent it – the precautions which perhaps by his own rash despairing act he too defeated.

'Gentlemen, that husband has gone. But she is not left without a friend. She will find that friend here today in the spirit which guides your judgement and clears your eyes upon this case. The spirit of justice is in this court today to comfort and protect her in the hour of her utmost need. It has strengthened, I hope, my voice. It will, I trust, clear your eyes and guide your judgement. It will speak with the evidence which I hope and believe has demolished and destroyed the suspicion which rests on her. And that spirit will speak in firm, unfaltering voice when your verdict tells the whole world that in your judgement Adelaide Bartlett is not guilty.'

Edward Clarke sat down to a thunder of applause which Judge and court officials tried sternly but in vain to quell.

The speech of the Attorney-General, who was not at his best owing to his political involvement, and the Judge's summing-up came as an anti-climax to Edward Clarke's brilliant oration.

Mr Justice Wills was a fanatical puritan. He had a thin, cruel mouth, and smouldering eyes which showed little understanding of his fellow human beings. He was boiling with indignation about the *Esoteric Anthropology*, the book which had enlightened Adelaide on sex matters, and he spent some time fulminating about it, expressing his shock and outrage that such 'garbage', such 'outpouring of impurity' should be permitted to corrupt the minds of the public. Indeed, he seemed more shocked about the book than the alleged murder of its owner.

The Judge believed in Adelaide's guilt, but the jury did not listen to him. The words of Edward Clarke were still in their ears when after two hours they found her not guilty, saying that 'although we think grave suspicion is attached to the prisoner, we do not think there is sufficient evidence to show how or by whom the chloroform was administered'.

Clarke had changed public opinion in favour of Adelaide's

innocence, and the verdict was greeted with roars of cheering and applause which the irritated Judge said was an outrage.

Overwhelmed, Edward Clarke broke down and wept while Adelaide passed silently out of the court. A week later she wrote him the following letter:

> 66 Gresham Street
> April 24th

Dear Sir – Forgive me for not earlier expressing my heartfelt gratitude to you. I feel that I owe my life to your earnest efforts, and though I cannot put into words the feelings that fill my heart, *you* will understand all that my pen fails to express to you.

Your kind looks towards me cheered me very much, for I felt that you believed me innocent. I have heard many eloquent Jesuits preach, but I never listened to anything finer than your speach (*sic*)

My story was a very painful one, but sadly true. My consent to my marriage was not asked, and I only saw my husband once before my wedding day

I am much gratified that Dr Stevenson has written to say that he concurs in the verdict, he wrote so kindly of Miss Wood who has been a true friend. I received great kindness at Clerkenwell from the Govenor (*sic*) to the lowest, they did their best to comfort me.

Assuring you that I shall always remember you with feelings of deepest gratitude, I am,

> Sincerely yours,
> Adelaide Bartlett.

The Miss Wood she referred to was the sister of her solicitor, Mr E. N. Wood, at whose home Adelaide stayed as a guest for several weeks after her acquittal. It has been said that while she was in Clerkenwell she enjoyed many privileges. The protecting hand was there all the time to give her help and ease her burden.

But many continued to believe that she was guilty and had

got away with it, among them Sir James Paget of St Barts Hospital, Queen Victoria's surgeon, who demanded that now the trial was over 'she should have told us in the interests of science how she did it'. There will always be those who question her innocence. Did she perhaps have some strange power over Edwin? He affirmed that he was able to draw currents of strength from her, and then there was a peculiar conversation with the doctor about mesmerism. Did she at the end persuade him, by some form of hypnotism, to drink the chloroform – overwhelmed perhaps at the prospect of having to endure him for the rest of his life? Some think he was in terror of Adelaide and that she completely dominated him.

Edward Clarke was firmly convinced that Edwin Bartlett had committed suicide, fearful of the dread word necrosis, which he might have thought meant that he had developed gangrene. Dr Leach, writing later in *The Lancet*, thought Edwin took the chloroform 'Out of sheer mischief, with the intention of alarming by his symptoms the wife who an hour or two before had talked about using it in an emergency'.

While the great controversy raged, Adelaide left them to it, stealing away, taking her mystery and her strange charm with her. She went to the obvious place, back to Orléans where she was born. Little of life remained, except Edwin's fortune and the great family who only half recognized her and to whom she had been an acute embarrassment.

# Chapter 3
# Warren Hastings

The impeachment and trial of Warren Hastings has been long condemned as an injustice to a great man who was the first Governor-General of India and a great administrator.

The fact that he was impeached by Edmund Burke, a political genius, has always been reckoned something of an anomaly. Burke was wrong about many things, and in view of Britain's imperialist role in India his impeachment of Hastings has until recently been regarded as his greatest mistake and failure.

But whatever are the currents of modern thought on the subject of imperialism and the British Raj, Warren Hastings's role in India was not as discreditable as his contemporary enemies alleged. Like Burke, he made mistakes. But Burke never had Hastings's awful responsibilities. He was not surrounded by relentless and powerful enemies, nor did he have to deal with Eastern potentates of fabulous wealth, immeasurable cunning, and living in voluptuous and demoralizing luxury. For two centuries the employees of the East India Company had been exploiting India. Warren Hastings

56

was the scapegoat for the Company's accumulated mismanagement, corruption and outrages.

Warren Hastings was born at Daylesford, Worcestershire, on 6 December, 1732, son of a country solicitor. He came from an old Oxfordshire family which had fallen into poverty. His mother died soon after his birth. His father deserted him and went to the West Indies. The boy was taken in charge by an uncle who educated him at Westminster where his contemporaries were the poet Cowper and Elijah Impey, later Chief Justice. Both were to become his life-long friends.

In 1750 Hastings went to Bengal as a writer in the East India Company. The affairs of the company were at a low ebb and Hastings, who thrived on troubles, rose rapidly. He was lucky to escape the horrors of the Black Hole, and when the company reasserted itself by force of arms, he became a member of the Council. Clive recognized his gifts and appointed him as Resident at the Court of Meer Jaffier.

There followed a time of scandalous misrule and corruption. Employees of the company despoiled and plundered Bengal in a manner which has been described as 'the most revolting page in our Indian history'. Clive returned to England and was violently attacked for the fabulous wealth he had amassed in India.

In 1764 Hastings resigned his seat and sailed home with, in contrast to contemporary practice, very little in the way of loot. During his first fourteen years in India he had gained little more than a reputation as a good administrator.

While at Fulta he had married the widow of an army officer. She died in 1759 after bearing him two children neither of whom survived childhood.

Hastings did not consider that his service in India had been either happy or successful. He was thirty-three, without either family or fortune. A man of some culture, he had a number of friends among the Georgian intelligentsia. He took to writing, had access to the best literary society of the day and made the personal acquaintance of Dr Johnson.

But in the eighteenth century it was very much more difficult to make a living out of writing than it is today, and he asked the East India Company if they could find employment for him again. In 1768 the company appointed him to the Council of Madras.

During the long voyage round the Cape his shipboard companions included Baron Imhoff, a portrait painter, and his fascinating and accomplished twenty-five-year-old wife, whose maiden name was Anna Maria Apollonia Chapusettin. There was little or no affection between the Baron and his wife. Hastings was instantly attracted to her, and she to him. Marian, as he called her, nursed him during a serious illness he had on the voyage, and by the time they landed at Madras she had become his mistress. Imhoff remained in India until 1773, but did not divorce his wife until 1777 when she and Hastings got married.

With her social charm, beauty and wit, Marian was both ornament and asset to Hastings. He was passionately in love with her and remained so throughout the long troublesome years which lay ahead.

In the 1770s the East India Company got into serious financial difficulties despite the enormous wealth flowing into its coffers and the fortunes being illicitly made by its employees. Reports of scandalous misrule and corruption caused an outcry in England. Lord North's Government was prepared to help the company, but at a price. In 1773 the Regulating Act was passed. This Act was a measure typical of the irresolute and hesitant administration which drafted it. It divested the company of much of its power and under its provisions Warren Hastings was appointed India's first Governor-General. This early attempt to frame administrative relations between England and her Indian dominions had many faults; its signal failure was the cause of the trial of Hastings. The principal mistake of the Regulating Act was that the Governor-General had no real power and could not select his officers. He was in fact little more than the Chairman of the Supreme Council of Bengal which could and often did overrule him.

The Council consisted of four members. They were General Clavering and Colonel Monson – third-rate politicians who had, however, considerable influence in the English Parliament – Philip Francis – reputed to be the author of *The Letters of Junius*, an accomplished politician and civil servant – and Barwell, a man who had long experience in India.

Warren Hastings's position was a difficult, almost impossible one. It was, to begin with, ill-defined legally. The Council were against him from the start. They did everything they could to reverse his decisions. Confusion was increased by the fact that the Indian rulers themselves had separate dealings with Company officials and ignored the Council at Calcutta. Others brought charges of corruption against Hastings which the Council eagerly took up, ordering him to refund money alleged to have been misappropriated.

Hastings sent his resignation to London. It was accepted. Clavering was appointed in his place.

Communication between London and Calcutta took many months, and in the long interval between his resignation and the notification of its acceptance Hastings changed his mind. There were a number of reasons for this. Colonel Monson died. With his casting vote Hastings now had a majority on the Council. Hastings refused to ratify his own resignation. When Clavering attempted to seize the governor-generalship, the Supreme Court ruled in Hastings's favour and the Army sided with him too. There was not much Clavering could do about it. He died two months later.

Hastings thus triumphed in his long battle with the Council. George III was indignant at his high-handed methods, but the East India Company did not object. With more trouble brewing in India, they considered Hastings the best man to have on the spot. And as England was now involved in war with America and with France, Hastings was left alone. He took on the whole military responsibility in India.

After a bitter campaign the French settlements in India were occupied. But French agents had stirred up the Indian princes and the British were drawn into the prolonged and exhausting Mahratta War. Haider Ali, Sultan of Mysore, invaded the Carnatic, and a French squadron were harrying the British on the high seas. The Peace of Versailles (1783) and the Treaty of Mangalore (1784) finally put an end to the hostilities.

It was these wars which took Hastings into such dangerous waters in India. They had to be financed, and so pressing was the demand for money that on one occasion he made a loan from his private purse. He reformed various government taxes and placed the monopolies of salt and opium on a more remunerative basis.

Hastings had been given supreme power in a country which had always been ruled by autocracy. He was dealing with Orientals who did not understand the ways of Western democracy and who would have regarded the high-minded principles of such men as Edmund Burke as weakness.

The Rajah of Benares was asked to contribute to the war. He refused and was fined half a million pounds; when he took to open revolt, he was arrested and deposed. There was also the ignoble affair of the Rajah of Tanjore, dethroned in favour of the Nabob of the Carnatic who had bribed the company's officials to use their troops to help him grab Tanjore. When Lord Pigot was sent from London to redress the wrong he was thrown in jail by the high-handed officials at Madras, where he died.

An even greater sensation was caused by the outrageous treatment of the Begums of Oudh, the wife and mother of the Nawab, Shuja-u-Dowlah, who had died leaving a fortune of over two million pounds, but owing large sums to the company. The Begums refused to pay the alleged debt; so more than a million pounds was extracted from them by force, mainly by rigorously ill-treating two eunuchs who were the Begums' agents. This was done apparently at Hastings's express orders. Hastings rightly anticipated that there would be trouble about this, and he secured documentary evidence that the Begums had rebellious intentions.

His conflict with members of the Council, particularly with Philip Francis, continued. In August, 1780 Hastings delivered a minute to the Council board in which he stated that 'he judged of the public conduct of Mr Francis by his experience of his private, which he found to be void of truth and honour. This is a severe charge but temperately and deliberately made.'

Francis's honour being thus called into question, a duel

was inevitable. It took place at Calcutta. Even though their seconds had baked their powder, Francis's pistol missed fire. Hastings waited for him to prime again. Francis then fired and missed. Hastings pulled his trigger and shot his opponent in his right side. Francis fell instantly and was invalided home to England.

This forthright method of dealing with political opponents was greatly admired in India and created something of a legend. But in England the incident only added more ammunition to the arsenal of Hastings's enemies, even though duelling between gentlemen was considered a right and proper way of settling disputes.

Indian affairs were very much occupying the attention of Parliament, and Hastings's enemies were hard at work trying to bring about his downfall. Francis who had reached England in 1781, with his accusations and evidence amply and skilfully prepared, found a formidable ally in Edmund Burke. Burke was a close friend of Admiral Pigot, Lord Pigot's brother, whose fatal imprisonment at Madras Hastings was supposed to have condoned. Moreover, his kinsman, William Burke, had served in India and his letters to Edmund were full of acrimony against Hastings.

But Burke was a great man and his enmity of Hastings was inspired by his abhorrence of the cruelty and injustices which were being perpetrated in India.

'Loaded for years as he has been with execrations of the natives,' cried Burke in Parliament, 'with the censures of the Court of Directors, and struck and blasted with the resolutions of this House, yet he still maintains the most despotic power ever known in India.'

On 30 May, 1782, the Commons resolved that Hastings should be recalled, but the company failed to do so. The following year Burke denounced him as 'the grand delinquent of all India', and the company reprimanded him for his conduct of affairs. Hastings replied in scornful terms.

Nevertheless he resigned. He had served thirteen years as Governor-General, had outlived or outlasted all his colleagues and ruined his health. He realized the importance of withdrawing from India before his enemies in England grew too strong.

Perhaps one of the most pressing things which forced his resignation was his wife whose health demanded that she leave India immediately. She sailed for England without him in January, 1784. Hastings himself left India the following year, arriving in England in June, 1785.

In England he was regarded with both interest and enthusiasm. He was fifty-two and was described as thin, of average height, 'very bald, with a countenance placid and thoughtful, but when animated full of intelligence'. He was pleased with his first reception in England, for he was given a formal expression of thanks from the company. His greatest pleasure was his reunion with his wife whose arrival in society had aroused much critical comment. Her diamonds were regarded with malevolent suspicion.

Hastings had been well received by the King and Queen, as had his wife before his arrival in England. He did not fully realize the entrenched power of his enemies. He was in fact anticipating a peerage and set about negotiating the purchase of Daylesford, the old family estate – quite unaware that Burke and Francis were busy forging the thunderbolts which were to shatter his dream.

The clouds began to gather early in 1787. In May, Burke formally impeached Warren Hastings at the bar of the House of Lords. He was taken into custody by the sergeant-at-arms and granted bail for twenty thousand pounds.

The trial itself was held in Westminster Hall and did not begin until 13 February, 1788. When Warren Hastings was summoned and appeared at the bar he looked, as Macaulay described him, 'very infirm and much indisposed. He was dressed in a plain, poppy-coloured suit of clothes.'

Fanny Burney, the diarist, was at his trial. She was at that time Lady-in-Waiting to Queen Charlote, consort to George III; the royal family's support of Warren Hastings at first incurred their unpopularity. Fanny Burney herself, as the youngest member of Dr Johnson's circle, was very much on Hastings's side. She wrote of Warren Hastings's appearance at the first day of the trial: 'Pale looked his face – pale, ill and altered. I was much affected by the sight of that dreadful harass which was written on his countenance. Had I looked at him without restraint, it could not have been without tears. I felt shocked, too shocked and ashamed to be seen by him in that place.' According to her, he wore a green coat, not a 'poppy-coloured suit of clothes'.

Fanny Burney, a literary and social personage of some consequence whose opinion could not be ignored, put up a spirited defence of Hastings to one of his detractors. She told William Wyndham, a Parliamentary friend of Burke, that she had found Hastings mild, pleasing and his manners were gentle to the point of humility – which came as something of a surprise to Wyndham, considering the ferocious despotism of which Hastings was accused.

It took the clerks of the court two days to read the charges against Hastings. On the third day Burke rose to deliver his opening speech which occupied four whole days. It is considered one of history's greatest orations.

The effect of Burke's speech was such as had scarcely ever been witnessed in a court of justice before. As he detailed the horrors alleged to have been practised by Hastings on the princes and the peoples of India, 'both the orator and his audience were convulsed with terror and agitation'. One spectator wrote:

'Ladies fainted away in the galleries. Mrs Sheridan, amongst others, had to be carried out insensible. The faces of the strongest men, as well as of the more sensitive women, were flushed with emotion or bathed with tears.'

More than once Hastings audibly protested against the enormities with which Burke accused him. But nothing could stop Burke's spellbinding flight of grandiloquence, in which his audience loyally played their part by their swoons, groans and sobs of readily-stirred passion. Of Burke it was said that 'he appeared raised, enlarged into something ethereal by his subject, and his voice seemed to shake the very walls of that ancient court'. On 18 February, he came to his famous climax:

'I charge Mr Hastings with having destroyed for private

purposes the whole system of government by the six provincial councils which he had no right to destroy.

'I charge him with having delegated away from himself that power which the Act of Parliament had directed him to preserve inalienably within himself.

'I charge him with having formed a committee to be mere instruments and tools at the enormous expense of £62,000 per annum.

'I charge him with taking bribes of Gunga Gowind Singh.

'I charge him with not having done that bribe service fidelity, even in iniquity, required at the hands of the worst of men.

'I charge him with having robbed these people of whom he took the bribes.

'I charge him with having fraudulently alienated the fortunes of widows.

'I charge him with having, without right of title or purchase, taken the lands of orphans and given them to wicked persons under him.

'I charge him with having removed the natural guardians of a minor Raja and given his zamindary to that wicked person Deby Singh.

'I charge him – his wickedness being known to himself and all the world – with having committed to Deby Singh the management of three great provinces; and with having thereby wasted the country, destroyed the landed interest, cruelly harassed the peasants, burned their houses, seized their crops, tortured and degraded their persons and destroyed the honour of the whole female race of that country.

'In the name of the Commons of England, I charge all this villainy on Warren Hastings, in the last moment of my supplication to you.

'I impeach Warren Hastings Esquire of high crimes and misdemeanours.

'I impeach him in the name of all the Commons of Great Britain in Parliament assembled whose national character he has dishonoured.

'I impeach him in the name of the people of India, whose laws, rights and liberties he has subverted, whose properties

Queen Caroline (*above*), consort of
George IV, was accused of immoral
conduct unbecoming to a queen. A
contemporary drawing (*below*)
shows her trial in the House of
Lords. Public interest was great.

In 1886 Adelaide Bartlett was acquitted of the murder of her husband, Edwin, after a memorable defence at the Old Bailey by Edward Clarke, Q.C., seen in this drawing (*top*) cross-examining Edwin Bartlett, the dead man's father. Warren Hastings was the scapegoat for all the accumulated wrongdoings of the East India Company. His trial lasted for seven years. Hastings is portrayed here (*above*) as 'Saviour of India' in a contemporary cartoon. Hastings was impeached by one of Britain's great statesmen, Edmund Burke (*right*). From a painting by Sir Joshua Reynolds.

he has destroyed, whose country he has laid waste and desolate.

'I impeach him in the name and by virtue of those eternal laws of justice which he has violated.

'I impeach him in the name of human nature itself which he has cruelly outraged, injured and oppressed in both sexes, of every age, rank, situation and condition of life.'

Hastings remarked later that he was hypnotized by Burke's incomparable oratory into believing, for a moment, that all the things he said about him were true.

But, as the first Lord Birkenhead said of this famous occasion, 'it is one thing to deliver a philippic, another to manage a prosecution'.

There was some argument about the method in which the trial should be conducted. Burke and Fox wanted each charge to be taken separately. The defence protested and requested, 'Prove all your allegations, then we will defend them.' The Lords decided in favour of the defence.

Fox opened the Benares case which Grey continued the next day. Several days were taken up reading papers and hearing witnesses. The Court then adjourned to 15 April, when the case of the Begums of Oudh was opened by Adam, and Sheridan summed up in a three-day speech of great drama. At the end of it Sheridan fell back into the arms of Burke as though overcome by his own emotions.

This sort of thing, though vastly entertaining to the public, some of whom had paid as much as fifty guineas a seat to see the show, was strongly criticized, as was Burke's unlawyerlike style and intemperance of language which brought down upon him the censure of the Lord Chancellor and even of the House of Commons.

Public opinion was still more critical when at the end of the session the trial was adjourned for a whole year. Its expense and the great length to which it threatened to run excited much comment. Hastings himself was naturally full of complaints at the delay and the legal expenses which he had to bear personally. When the session opened in February, 1789, he demanded that the trial should proceed more quickly. But the Regency Bill was absorbing the attention of Parliament, and it was not until 21 April that the trial resumed.

In 1789 the hearing occupied only seventeen days. In answer to Hasting's complaints, Burke retorted that a man who had amassed an immense fortune by bribes would hardly feel the loss of £30,000. One would have thought that such a comment would have disqualified Burke from continuing to conduct the prosecution.

In his resumption Burke made allegations against Hastings which he was not entitled to make under his brief from the Commons; the Commons ordered him to withdraw them. Burke was forced to submit, but made it plain that he would pursue the trial to the end. Burke's illegal conduct of the prosecution brought him several rebukes from the Lords.

When the session ended on 8 July, Hastings made another protest and asked their Lordships to consider that 'not one-tenth part of one single article of the twenty which compose the charge had been brought to a conclusion on the part of the prosecution', and that he had every prospect of passing the remainder of his life under impeachment and of suffering far more severely than if he had pleaded guilty at first.

Many members of the Upper House were sympathetic with him, the Earl of Camden pointed out that not only the accused, but their Lordships should be considered, 'who were bound to sit out the trial, although many of them would be dead before it ended'.

Nevertheless in the following year, 1790, the Lords sat no longer than a fortnight which was taken up by Fox's speech on the charges of internal maladministration and corruption, and with endless disputes about admissibility of evidence.

Burke and his friends were beginning to be alarmed at the inordinate length of the trial and at the undoubted fact that the public was turning against them. An appeal was made to the Commons to expedite matters – without result. The session ended in June, and the case was postponed for the rest of the year.

In December, 1790, Parliament was dissolved. When the new Parliament met, the question was raised whether an impeachment did not end with dissolution of Parliament. It was a difficult legal question and one on which eminent judges and lawyers took opposite views. It was finally decided, however, that dissolution did not end an impeachment. Consequently, after nearly a year's interval the trial was again set in motion in May, 1791 when speeches were delivered and evidence given on the charges of prodigality, corruption and favouritism in the award of contracts.

Again Hastings complained to the court. He reminded them that he was now sixty years of age and had been four years their prisoner, 'loaded and tortured by the most virulent accusations, and that at the rate of progress hitherto made, he had no human expectation of living to make his defence, or to hear their Lordships' judgement'. Burke and Fox replied saying, not untruthfully, that the delay was not of their making.

The prosecution closed at the end of May. Then Hastings read a long statement of his defence – a dull piece of prose compared with the fiery magnificence of his opponents' oratory. But he made some important points, among them being the fact that of the 34 witnesses he originally wished to call, some were dead, others had left for India or to distant parts of England or Europe 'after an annual, but fruitless and disheartening attendance'.

For this and other reasons he complained of the unparalleled injury which he had suffered 'by the extension of a criminal trial beyond the chances of a life's duration'.

But another seven months elapsed before the trial was resumed in February, 1792 when Law, afterwards Lord Ellenborough, opened the defence. After speeches lasting eight days, witnesses were called.

The interminable proceedings continued for only twenty-two days in 1792, then being adjourned until February of the following year. The case began to bore everybody including the Lords and was heard before very thin houses. By October, 1793 one-hundred-and-twenty-seven changes in the peerage had occurred, and many of the Lords had not heard the beginning of the case. The whole thing was becoming a farce. Apart from that the French Revolutionary War had broken out which not only diverted the attention of the nation from the case, but caused a split between Burke and Fox.

The case against Hastings finally began to crumble when Burke made a series of legal errors and when the defence called some effective evidence. A number of important Indian residents spoke warmly in Hastings's favour. Officials and soldiers who returned from India all added their voices to the turn of the tide.

Despite Hastings's renewed appeal for an immediate verdict, however, the trial was adjourned until February, 1794, to the accompaniment of some sharp recriminations in both Houses as to the responsibility for the delay and increased criticism of the immense costs.

At the resumption, Burke summed up the case against Hastings in a speech which lasted nine days. Once more he lashed the accused with the barbs of his eloquence, and defended his use of strong words in describing Hastings's alleged conduct. In the words of Sir Alfred Lyall, Hastings's biographer, 'It must be admitted that the display of such ever-burning animosity, and such constant use of figurative execration were unworthy of a great statesman and splendid orator, a man of lofty patriotism and political genius, kindly hearted and beloved in private life. But he was suffering from public disgust and private anxieties.'

In June Burke applied for the Chiltern Hundreds and left Parliament for ever.

In 1795 came the eighth and last session of the trial. The House of Lords resolved themselves into Committee. After several days' discussion they gave judgement in Westminster Hall, in April. Warren Hastings was found innocent by a large majority, on each of the sixteen questions that were put to the vote. After a trial lasting eight years he was formally acquitted. The following year Burke wrote: 'As to the acquittal, that it was total, I was surprised at; that it should be so in a good measure I expected from the incredible corruption of the time.'

Hastings's costs amounted to over £70,000. The expenses of the prosecution were originally billed at £61,695, of which £16,996 was disallowed. After some discussion about the payment of Hastings's costs. The East India Company granted him an annuity of £4,000, paying the first ten years outright, and in addition an interest-free loan of £50,000. He finally purchased Daylesford estate where he lived in retirement and comparative obscurity until his death in 1818, outliving his great enemy, Edmund Burke, by twenty years. His devoted wife survived him by some years and was over ninety when she died.

The trial of Warren Hastings has been called a blot on English judicial history. Sir James Stephen in *History of Criminal Law*, has criticized it sharply: 'It was monstrous that a man should be tortured at irregular intervals for seven years in order that a singularly incompetent tribunal might be addressed before an excited audience by Burke and Sheridan in language far removed from the calmness with which an advocate for the prosecution ought to address a criminal court.'

Warren Hastings had his faults, but he was treated as a scapegoat for the centuries of abuse perpetrated by the East India Company. Burke and Sheridan did their reputations considerable harm by their vindictive attacks. They would have been greater men if they had observed a true perspective.

The Prince Regent summed Warren Hastings up best when he called him, in 1814, 'the most deserving and at the same time one of the worst used men in the Empire'.

# Chapter 4
# The Marquess of
# Queensberry

'It is one of the tragedies that will live
always in romantic history.'
Max Beerbohm on Oscar Wilde's sentence.

Oscar Wilde's contemporaries, both friends and enemies,
were too obsessed with his so-called crimes to be able to
separate the man from the artist. One of the good things
about this permissive age is that Wilde the poet and playwright can be fully appreciated with no one caring much
about how he lived his private life.

Today the society which loathed and condemned him is
regarded with curiosity and contempt, and the judge who
sentenced him as no ornament to the English bar. Only Wilde
himself emerges with credit from the sordid business. He is
seen not only as one of the greatest dramatists of the nineteenth century, but as a martyr and a man of courage.

It was the most famous acquittal of the nineties which
launched Wilde on the road to ruin, a path he could easily

have avoided. He had only himself and Lord Alfred Douglas to blame. He would not listen to the advice of his true friends.

Wilde's homosexual relationship with Lord Alfred Douglas, third son of John Sholto Douglas, the eighth Marquess of Queensberry, caused his downfall. Homosexuality was widespread in Victorian London where the police knew of no less than twenty thousand persons in connection with it.

There had been a number of scandals. In 1889 a house at 19 Cleveland Street, off Tottenham Court Road, was raided by the police and discovered to be a brothel used by certain members of the aristocracy for homosexual purposes. A number of peers hastily fled the country, including Lord Arthur Somerset, a son of the Duke of Beaufort and a close friend of the Prince of Wales, who persuaded Lord Salisbury to permit him to pay visits to his parents quietly in the country 'without fear of being apprehended on this awful charge'.

Oscar Wilde turned to homosexuality in middle life. He was born in 1856, son of Sir William Wilde, a famous Irish surgeon, and went to Trinity College, Dublin, and Magdalen College, Oxford. In 1884 he married Miss Constance Lloyd by whom he had two sons.

He was therefore a man perfectly capable of living a normal married life. At Oxford he had contracted syphilis, but before his marriage he had been assured by his doctor that all traces of the disease had gone. However, shortly after his marriage signs of syphilis reappeared, and he immediately ceased sexual relations with his wife. It is believed that he took mercury which was the usual treatment for the disease in those days and this had the effect of turning his teeth black.

He was thirty-two when he was introduced to homosexual practices by a seventeen-year-old youth, Robert Ross, the son of the Honourable John Ross, Q.C., Attorney-General for Upper Canada. Ross became a journalist and later was Wilde's literary executor. Ross, who died in 1918, boasted to Frank Harris that he was 'the first boy Oscar ever had'. Their love-affair began in 1886. After Wilde's death there was some dispute among his queer friends as to which of them had the dubious distinction of introducing him to homosexuality, Ross or Lord Alfred Douglas.

Wilde, however, did not meet Douglas until 1891 by which time he had acquired a decided taste for homosexual practices. He became extremely fond of Douglas who was a beautiful young man of Adonis-like appearance. He was known to his friends as Bosie Douglas, which comes from the nickname Boysie given to him in his childhood by his doting mother.

Apart from his extraordinary good looks and appearance of eternal youth Alfred Douglas was a man of culture and intelligence and later distinguished himself as a poet. Wilde doted on him for years and, though Douglas's affection for Wilde was a more selfish one, there was doubtless a genuine bond between them.

Alfred Douglas became a Roman Catholic convert and died in 1945. He never lived down the scandal and the inglorious part he played in it. In later years he tried to make out that his relationship with Wilde was more spiritual than sexual. He said that for a short time there did occur between them 'certain familiarities' of the sort that go on in English public schools, and he added that 'of the sin which takes its name from one of the cities of the Plain, there was never the slightest question. I give this as my solemn word before God as I hope to be saved.'

He need not have brought the Almighty into it, for Oscar Wilde was never accused of sodomy and did not practise it. Relatively few homosexuals do, despite the popular image. There is in fact so much misinformation about a subject which could until recently be discussed only in medico-legal textbooks, that the precise method in which Wilde practised his perversion is worth mentioning briefly. He would make love to the youth to the accompaniment of mutual sexual fondling and masturbation. Finally Wilde would perform fellatio upon his partner.* As everyone who has been to an

* Wilde was wont to excuse his passion for fellatio by offering the curious belief that the consumption of human sperm nourished his brain cells.

English public school knows, these are the kind of 'familiarities' which to a greater or lesser extent go on. Bosie was as addicted to them as much as Oscar and just as guilty of transgressing the law, as it then stood and remained until quite recently.

The attraction between the two men, however, was certainly more than physical. Oscar Wilde was the most brilliant and entertaining conversationalist of his day. Douglas, like so many, revelled in his sparkling company and never-failing wit. It greatly flattered his vanity to be seen with Wilde, now rich and famous, at the very height of his success. Wilde himself became infatuated with the young Adonis, both physically and spiritually. They had much in common. Douglas was something of an intellectual, and his company was very much to Wilde's taste. They were soon the closest of friends, were seen everywhere in each other's company and went on trips abroad together.

During these years Wilde wrote his best plays. He also indulged his homosexual desires with a variety of other youths, most of them well below him in the social scale. He got to know Alfred Taylor, a notorious homosexual who procured youths for him. All of these youths were themselves experienced homosexuals, male prostitutes or blackmailers. It was never suggested that Wilde corrupted an innocent youth.

His relations with these unsavoury individuals was incidental, though much was made of it at the trials which ended in his imprisonment. His friendship with Lord Alfred Douglas continued uninterruptedly. How long it remained on the physical plane is not really known. According to Douglas it only lasted a short time. Wilde was certainly as promiscuous as it was possible to be.

It was Wilde's company and the magic of his conversation which enchanted Douglas. 'I have never known anyone to come anywhere near him,' he told H. Montgomery Hyde thirty years after Wilde's death.* 'One sat and listened to him

* In *The Trials of Oscar Wilde* (edited by H. Montgomery Hyde) Notable British Trials Series (William Hodge)

enthralled. It appeared to be Wisdom and Power and Beauty and Enchantment. It was indeed enchantment and nothing else.' Robert Ross claimed that Wilde's extraordinary magnetism would always be difficult to convey to those who never knew him: 'To talk to him was to be translated to an enchanted island or to the palaces of the *Fata Morgana.* You could not tell what flowers were at your feet or what fantastic architecture was silhouetted against the purple atmosphere of his conversation.'

Not everyone was fascinated by Wilde. The late Victorians flocked to his plays in which they found something of the wit and vitality of Sheridan. Yet Wilde's artistic arrogance and extravagant aesthetic poses, his withdrawal from life into a dream-world of art was an attack on their precious values.

Although his homosexual activities were discreetly concealed even from his most intimate friends, his excesses and uncontrolled appetites made him fat and gross. 'All his bad qualities began to show in his face,' a friend said of him. During his American tour of 1882 when Wilde's eccentric appearance caused a great sensation the New York gourmet and wit, Sam Ward, described him thus:

'His make-up is very extraordinary – long black hair hanging to the shoulders, brown eyes, a huge white face like a pale moon, a white waistcoat, black coat and knee breeches, black silk stockings, shoes with buckles. Until he speaks, you think him as uncanny as a vampire.'*

Wilde wrote extravagant, highly-coloured letters to Douglas which, though not improper, were certainly suggestive of a homosexual relationship. The most famous was this one:

My Own Boy,

Your sonnet is quite lovely, and it is a marvel that those red rose-leaf lips of yours should have been made

* Ward was the brother-in-law of Mrs William Astor. His sister was the poet, Julia Ward Howe (1819–1910) who wrote the famous *Battle Hymn of the Republic* which begins "Mine eyes have seen the glory of the coming of the Lord."

no less for music of song than for madness of kisses. Your slim gilt soul walks between passion and poetry. I know Hyacinthus, whom Apollo loved so madly, was you in Greek days.

Why are you alone in London, and when do you go to Salisbury? Do go there to cool your hands in the grey twilight of Gothic things, and come here whenever you like. It is a lovely place – it only lacks you; but go to Salisbury first.

Always, with undying love,

Yours
Oscar.

As Wilde's counsel, Sir Edward Clarke, remarked later in court, it was a letter the terms of which might appear extravagant to those in the habit of writing commercial correspondence. Sir Edward's understatement caused a gale of laughter in the Old Bailey and the mirth of the court was barely quenched by his assertion that Oscar Wilde, as a poet, considered his letter a prose sonnet. Most people regarded it as little else than a pretty letter to a pansy boy.

Alfred Douglas received a whole collection of these poetically loving effusions from Oscar and thought so highly of them that, when he sold an old suit to an unemployed clerk named Wood, he left a number of the letters in a pocket.

Alfred Wood's real occupation was that of a male prostitute, and his association with Douglas was no coincidence. Douglas introduced him to the insatiable Oscar who wined and dined him at the Café Royal and then took him home where Wood hired out his body to Wilde for the sum of £3 an hour. But he was more interested in blackmailing his lover over the letters he had found in Alfred Douglas's old suit, and this he promptly proceeded to do. It was a far more profitable business.

Wood returned all the letters except one for £35 which Wilde gave him on the pretext of paying for Wood to go to America to start a new life. But Wood was soon back. Blackmail was a better proposition in Victorian England where a job as valet to a gentleman with certain tendencies could be turned to very profitable account. Wood was in business with two professional blackmailers named Allen and Clibborn.

Already a copy of the 'My Own Boy, your sonnet is quite lovely'-letter had been sent to actor-manager Beerbohm Tree who was then rehearsing Wilde's latest play *A Woman of No Importance* at the Haymarket Theatre. Tree could hardly have been less interested. He just handed the letter back to Wilde with the remark that it might be open to misconstruction.

When Allen turned up at Wilde's house confident of getting a goodly sum out of him for the return of the letter, he was greatly taken aback at his reception.

'I suppose,' said Wilde, 'that you have come about my beautiful letter to Lord Alfred Douglas. If you had not been so foolish as to send a copy of it to Mr Beerbohm Tree, I would gladly have paid you a very large sum of money for the letter, as I consider it to be a work of art.'

'A very curious construction can be put on that letter,' warned Allen.

'Art is rarely intelligible to the criminal classes,' Wilde told him.

'A man has offered me £60 for it.'

'If you take my advice you will go to that man and sell my letter to him for £60. I myself have never received so large a sum for any prose work of that length. I am glad to find that there is someone in England who considers a letter of mine worth £60.'

'The man is out of town,' said Allen rather taken aback.

'He is sure to come back. Take my advice. Sell it to him.'

Completely non-plussed, the blackmailer changed his tune and began to whine that he was broke. The smiling and magnanimous Oscar thereupon gave him a half-sovereign. Allen departed almost in tears. What could you do with a man like that? A few minutes later his partner Clibborn turned up and handed the letter to Wilde, saying it was no good trying to blackmail a man who only laughed at them.

Wilde gave Clibborn a half-sovereign too with the remark: 'I'm afraid you are leading a wonderfully wicked life.'

Clibborn shrugged. 'There is good and bad in every one of us.'

'You are a born philosopher,' Wilde told him.

But that was by no means the end of the matter. In fact it was the beginning of the end for Oscar Wilde, for a copy of the letter had fallen into the hands of the recipient's father, the Marquess of Queensberry. The Marquess viewed a phrase like 'it is a marvel that those rose-red lips of yours should have been made no less for music of song than for the madness of kisses' in a somewhat different manner to the way the tolerant Beerbohm Tree had done.

The eighth Marquess of Queensberry was a well-known figure in sporting circles. He had been an amateur lightweight boxing champion and he was the author of the Queensberry Rules which govern amateur boxing to this day.

Queensberry was a coarse, violent man with a filthy mind and an unpleasant temper. He hated and ill-treated all his family and was hated by them in return. He was an insignificant-looking undersized individual with red whiskers and a drooping lower lip. Wilde described him as having an ape-like face, a bestial, half-witted grin, twitching hands and of having the gait and dress of a stable-man. Queensberry neither looked nor behaved like an aristocrat. He preferred the company of toughs, thugs and prostitutes to people of his own class. Without doubt he was mentally disturbed, as his family recognized, though they never managed to get him certified.

Queensberry had already made himself ridiculous over his eldest son, Lord Drumlanrig, and Lord Rosebery who became Prime Minister in 1894. Drumlanrig was Rosebery's private secretary and had been made an English peer, Lord Kelhead. This infuriated Queensberry. He created an absurd scene by going after the Prime Minister with a dog whip.

There was no doubt, however, that Queensberry was on to something in his objection to the association of his young son Alfred with Oscar Wilde. He had them watched and told Alfred that Wilde was not a fit man for him to associate with. In 1894 father and son exchanged a series of communications which were later to become celebrated.

Writing from Carter's Hotel, Albemarle Street, W.1, Queensberry, after accusing his son of leaving Oxford with discredit and then spending his time 'loafing and lolling about doing nothing', threatened that if he did not cease his intimacy with 'this man Wilde', he would disown him and cut off his allowance. 'I am not going to try and analyse this intimacy, and I make no charge; but to my mind to pose as a thing is as bad as to be it. With my own eyes I saw you both in the most loathsome and disgusting relationship as expressed in your manner and expression. Never in my experience have I seen such a sight as that in your horrible features. No wonder people are talking as they are.' He added that he had heard on good authority that Mrs Wilde was petitioning to divorce her husband for sodomy 'and other crimes'. If he thought that was true he would be 'quite justified in shooting him on sight'. He concluded by saying he declined to receive a letter in return, 'in view of your recent hysterical and impertinent ones'.

Alfred Douglas replied briefly by telegram: 'What a funny little man you are.'

'You impertinent young jackanapes!' fumed Queensberry by letter. 'I request that you will not send such messages to me by telegraph.' If he did, he would get the thrashing he deserved. If he caught him with Wilde again, he would make a public scandal.

Queensberry then tore up every communication he received from Alfred, but continued to write him insulting letters calling him a reptile and a miserable creature and denying that he was his father, saying 'in this Christian country' – Queensberry was an atheist – 'with these hypocrites, 'tis a wise father who knows his own child'.

Alfred Douglas took up the war against his father with alacrity and enthusiasm. When Queensberry went to the restaurants frequented by Wilde and Douglas and warned the managements that he would thrash them both if he found them together on the premises, Douglas replied by giving his father details of their dining-out arrangements and challenging him to come and see what happened to him if he started any of his 'ruffianly tricks'.

Though Bosie plainly welcomed this contest with his hated father, Oscar was worried. This sort of thing wasn't good for his work. He couldn't write with this Queensberry tumult going on around him. He thought he might stop Queensberry by bringing an action against him for the libel in the letter containing the suggestion that his wife was trying to divorce him for sodomy, which was quite untrue. But he was dissuaded from doing this by Alfred Douglas's cousin, George Wyndham, M.P., who wanted to avoid a family scandal.

Actually Wilde had a good case for criminal libel here, and he might well have won if he had brought it instead of waiting another year during which Queensberry's investigators had dug up some damning evidence against him.

Wilde retreated to Worthing to escape the persecution, and here he wrote *The Importance of Being Earnest*, perhaps his best play and certainly his most successful. On one of his rare visits to London on business Queensberry called unexpectedly upon him, accompanied by a thug. Queensberry accused Wilde of being thrown out of the Savoy Hotel for 'disgusting conduct', and said if he saw him with Alfred again he would thrash him. Wilde threatened to call the police and Queensberry left.

Alfred continued the war against his father with zest and informed him: 'If you try to assault me, I shall defend myself with a loaded revolver which I always carry, and if I shoot you, or he shoots you, we should be completely justified, as we should be acting in self defence against a violent and dangerous rough, and I think if you were dead not many people would miss you.'

Queensberry found out that his former wife, Alfred's mother, was keeping her son supplied with money and this infuriated him. He wrote an insulting letter to Lady Queensberry's father, Alred Montgomery: 'Your daughter must be mad the way she is behaving. She evidently wants to make out that I want to make out a case against my son. It is nothing of the kind. I have made out a case against Oscar Wilde, and I have to his face accused him of it. If I was quite certain of the thing, I would shoot the fellow on sight, but I can only accuse him of posing. It now lies in the hands of the two whether they will further defy me. Your daughter appears now to be encouraging them, although she can hardly intend this. I don't believe Wilde will now dare defy me. He plainly showed the white feather the other day when I tackled him – damned cur and coward of the Rosebery type. As for this so-called son of mine, he is no son of mine, and I will have nothing to do with him. He may starve as far as I am concerned after his behaviour to me.'

Oscar and Bosie escaped the persecution during the winter of 1894 by going to France and North Africa. *The Importance of Being Earnest* was finished and was going into rehearsal during the winter, and the play was planned to open at the St James's Theatre in February, 1895.

In Algiers they met André Gide who told Wilde that he did not think he put the best of himself into his plays. Wilde replied by talking about the greater drama of his life.

'I have put my genius into my life,' he exclaimed. 'I have put only my talent into my works.' He spoke of the 'scarlet Marquess' who was persecuting him. 'My friends are extraordinary. They beg me to be careful. Careful? But how can I be careful? That would be a backward step. I must go on as far as possible. I cannot go much further. Something is bound to happen – something else.'

With these ominous and prophetic words, Wilde left for England with his young companion for the opening night of *The Importance of Being Earnest* on 14 February.

They found their malevolent old enemy still on the warpath. Accompanied by his tough bodyguard, Queensberry had booked a seat for the opening night with the object of making a scene, but his ticket was cancelled and his money returned to him. The police were warned to keep an eye on him. After prowling threateningly around the theatre entrances, the 'scarlet Marquess' left a large bouquet of vegetables arranged in a grotesquely suggestive manner addressed to Oscar Wilde.

'This makes his conduct idiotic,' remarked Wilde. 'Robs it of all dignity.'

Queensberry's next step was to call at the Albemarle Club to which Wilde belonged, on 18 February. He handed a card to the hall porter, saying: 'Give that to Oscar Wilde.' On the card was written: 'To Oscar Wilde posing as a somdomite' (*sic*). The porter looked at the card, but he did not understand the meaning of the misspelt word and placed it in an envelope.

Wilde collected the card on 28 February and immediately went with Lord Alfred Douglas and Robert Ross to consult his solicitors, the senior member of which was Charles Octavius Humphreys, an experienced criminal lawyer, who asked Wilde on his solemn oath whether there was any truth in the libel. Wilde said on his oath that he was innocent. Both Douglas and Ross knew this to be a lie, and if they had any private reservations in their minds that their own homosexual activities with Wilde had not been precisely sodomical, they were well aware that they were splitting hairs.

'If you are innocent,' Humphreys said to Wilde, 'you should succeed.'

The question of the considerable costs of the contemplated action against Queensberry was brought up at the conference. Wilde said he was heavily in debt and had no funds available.

The expression on Humphreys's face changed. No firm of solicitors could undertake such an action unless the costs were guaranteed. When Alfred Douglas saw the possibility of the case against his hated father falling through owing to Wilde's lack of funds, he immediately promised that his own family would be only too pleased to pay the costs. The Marquess had caused them all so much trouble and suffering that they had often talked of getting him certified and shut away in an asylum.

Douglas's promise that the Queensberry family would foot the bill seemed to satisfy Humphreys who doubtless considered the word of a titled gentleman good enough for anyone. But Douglas had no authority at all to make such a promise and his family in fact never made any attempt to pay the costs. Wilde instead was made bankrupt, and later he bitterly reproached Douglas for misleading Humphreys and rushing him (Wilde) into the fatal action against Queensberry.

Douglas imagined that, if the case were won, his father would get seven years' penal servitude, which very improbable result would have given his son the liveliest pleasure and satisfaction. Douglas didn't seem to appreciate that it made little difference in law whether he and Wilde had committed sodomy or not. Any kind of sexual misbehaviour between two males was subject to the same draconian punishment. Certainly neither he nor Wilde realized that the unforgivable thing was to draw public attention to the unspeakable by bringing the action in the first place. Only a totally innocent man could have got away with it, and Wilde knew well enough that however beautiful was his relationship with Alfred Douglas, there was nothing innocent about it.

On 2 March, 1895, Queensberry was arrested and charged with criminal libel. He appeared before the magistrate at Great Marlborough Street where his solicitor intimated that he had acted as a father under great indignation and that he had a perfect answer to the charge. Queensberry was granted bail and both sides then began to prepare for the action which was to have such dramatic, and for Wilde, tragic consequences.

Queensberry's solicitor, Charles Russell of Day and Russell, realized from the start that the libel would be hard to justify in court despite his client's anxiety to bring it into the open. Queensberry had flatly refused to withdraw or make any apology. Instead he had employed detectives who were digging out the facts about Wilde's homosexual practices with a variety of youths of evil reputation.

Russell wanted to brief Edward Carson, Q.C. – later Lord Carson – to defend Queensberry, but Carson was reluctant. He had been at Trinity College with Wilde in the seventies, and did not relish the idea of appearing in court against a fellow classmate in such a case. But he changed his mind after he had discussed the matter with the Lord Chancellor, Lord Halsbury, who told him that the most important thing was to arrive at justice. When Carson saw the evidence which the probing detectives had dredged up against Wilde, he realized Queensberry would win the case. There was no more hesitation on his part.

Wilde, on hearing that he would be cross-examined by Carson, remarked characteristically: 'No doubt he will do so with the added bitterness of an old friend.'

Carson appeared at the police court hearing on 9 March, and admitted that his client sent the letters. 'Lord Queensberry thought it was as well for the morality of his son to put a stop to the relations between the parties,' he said.

In answer to the charge, the prisoner replied: 'I have simply this to say, your worship. I wrote that card simply with the intention of bringing matters to a head, having been unable to meet Mr Wilde otherwise and to save my son, and I abide by what I wrote.'

Queensberry was then committed for trial on bail.

Humphreys wanted to brief Sir Edward Clarke, Q.C., who had so brilliantly defended Adelaide Bartlett. Before he accepted the brief, Clarke had an interview with Oscar Wilde in his chambers in which he earnestly demanded: 'I can only accept this brief, Mr Wilde, if you can assure me upon your honour as an English gentleman that there is not and never has been any foundation for the charges that are made against you.' Wilde gave him this assurance, though apparently nobody pointed out to Clarke that Wilde was an Irish, not an English, gentleman which may or may not have made a difference. The celebrated Oscar Wilde was Clarke's most embarrassing client and had himself to blame for embarking on this highly dangerous legislation with a lie on his lips.

Meanwhile Queensberry's investigators were reaping a rich harvest of muck. A number of employees at the Savoy had highly compromising stories to tell of Wilde's homosexual adventures in that exclusive hotel. Lord Alfred Douglas also featured embarrassingly in these squalid romances with low-born pansy boys, but it wasn't in Queensberry's interest to vilify a member of his own precious family, and the result was that Oscar often got the blame for Bosie's salacious adventures. Prostitutes and their associates were all willing to assist in the downfall of Wilde, for they attributed a falling off in business to the spread of homosexuality made fashionable by Wilde and Douglas.

The case naturally caused a great sensation abroad, particularly when it was discovered that a French journalist who had lived for many years in London had been empanelled in error on the Grand Jury which had to consider the evidence against Queensberry before the prosecution could proceed. The journalist should have pointed out the mistake to the authorities, but he could not resist the temptation of sitting on the Grand Jury and listening to the evidence which included Queensberry's scandalous references to Lord Roseberry and his eldest son.

The Grand Jury's deliberations were supposed to be secret, but the French journalist reported them fully in the Paris Press and all the continental papers followed suit. Although the British Press were inhibited from mentioning it, the fact that the Prime Minister's name was connected with the case was the talk of London. There was much embarrassment in Whitehall and Downing Street. If Oscar Wilde persisted in his action against Queensberry, it was obvious to informed circles that nothing could save him from the dire consequences of it, for to have hushed it up would have provoked an even greater scandal.

Just before the case, Wilde's friends urged him strongly to drop the prosecution and go abroad. In particular George Bernard Shaw and Frank Harris, at a luncheon at the Café Royal, put great pressure upon him. Harris told him bluntly that he was going to lose the case against Queensberry.

'You don't realize what is going to happen to you,' said Harris. 'It is not going to be a matter of clever talk about your books. They are going to bring up a string of witnesses that will put art and literature out of the question. Clarke will throw up his brief.'

Bernard Shaw agreed with the force of Harris's argument. Alfred Douglas who was also there listened in sulky intransigence to what Harris was saying. When he saw that Wilde was impressed by Harris the young man jumped petulantly to his feet.

'Your telling him to run away shows you are no friend of Oscar's,' he exclaimed. He hurried Wilde out of the restaurant with scant regard for good manners.

Douglas considered Wilde's case against Queensberry as part of his own private war with his father. Even though he was well aware of the kind of evidence which Queensberry had against Wilde, he was determined that his friend should not be persuaded to drop the case. Douglas had a great influence over Wilde. It was not until later that Wilde realized the young man's selfishness and treachery, and from the misery of his prison cell he bitterly reproached him for it.

And so, urged on recklessly by his spoilt and selfish young companion, Oscar Wilde embarked on one of the most foolish and ill-conceived libel suits in legal history. It opened at the Old Bailey on 3 April, 1895 before Mr Justice Henn Collins. In support of Sir Edward Clarke for the prosecution were Mr Charles W. Mathews and Mr Travers Humphreys. The defending counsel, apart from Edward Carson, were Mr Charles F. Gill and Mr Arthur Gill. Representing Lord Alfred Douglas and his elder brother Lord Douglas of Hawick were Mr Edward Besley, Q.C., and Mr John Lionel Monckton.

The tone of Sir Edward Clarke's opening speech for the prosecution was moderate, but like all his performances at the bar, highly effective. It was greatly admired in particular by his leading opponent, Edward Carson. But it was not at all to the taste of Lord Alfred Douglas who wanted to hear a devastating attack on his father's character.

There were only two witnesses at the trial – the porter of the Albemarle Club who gave formal evidence of being handed the offending card by Lord Queensberry, and Oscar Wilde himself. Wilde's evidence was a brilliant, if fatal performance. His cross-examination by Edward Carson was one of the most famous in the history of jurisprudence and a memorable occasion in the Old Bailey.

During his examination-in-chief by Clarke, Wilde recounted his friendship with Douglas, told of the attempt to blackmail him over the letters, and of Queensberry's abuse of him over the friendship with Douglas. He denied the accusations of indecency which had been made against him.

Carson began his cross-examination in deceptively mild fashion.

'You stated that your age was thirty-nine. I think you are over forty. You were born on 16 October, 1854?'

'I have no wish to pose as being young,' replied Wilde. 'I

am thirty-nine or forty. You have my certificate and that settles the matter.'

'But being born in 1854 makes you more than forty?' pursued Carson smoothly.

'Ah, very well,' agreed Wilde, as though it didn't matter.

But it did. Carson had caught him out telling a lie in the first minute. A quite unimportant lie perhaps, but a lie nevertheless, and a lie in the witness box always has a bad effect on the jury.

After accentuating the fact of Lord Alfred Douglas being so much younger and that the two of them had stayed together at various places, Carson then turned the questioning to the subject of literary matters, and here he was at a decided disadvantage compared with his sparkling opponent.

Carson referred to a story with homosexual overtones called 'The Priest and the Acolyte' published in an Oxford undergraduate magazine, *The Chameleon*, to which Wilde had contributed an article, 'Phrases and Philosophies for the Use of the Young'.

'The Priest and the Acolyte' was about a priest who fell in love with a boy who served him at the altar. Carson asked Wilde whether he did not think the story blasphemous.

'I think it violated every artistic canon of beauty,' was the reply.

'That is not an answer.'

'It is the only one I can give.'

'I want to see the position you pose in,' was Carson's next question, and to this Wilde was a little sensitive.

'I do not think you should say that.'

Carson raised his eyebrows mildly. 'I have said nothing out of the way. I wish to know whether you thought the story blasphemous.' Considering what was written on Queensberry's card which provoked the action, for Carson to talk about the position Wilde was posing in can only be interpreted as provocative.

'The story filled me with disgust,' replied Wilde. 'The end was wrong.'

'Answer the question, sir,' rapped out Carson. 'I wish to know whether you thought the story was blasphemous.'

Wilde shrugged. Blasphemy didn't enter into it so far as he was concerned. 'I thought it was disgusting,' he replied. Carson then read an extract from the story and Wilde dismissed the passage as 'disgusting – perfect twaddle'.

'So far as your works are concerned,' pursued Carson, 'you pose as not being concerned about morality or immorality?'

'I do not know whether you use the word "pose" in any particular sense.'

'It is a favourite word of your own?'

'Is it? I have no pose in this matter. In writing a play or a book, I am concerned entirely with literature, that is with art. I aim not at doing good or evil, but in trying to make a thing that will have some quality of beauty.'

'Listen, sir.' Carson picked up the magazine and quoted. 'Here is one of the "Phrases and Philosophies for the Use of the Young" which you contributed: "Wickedness is a myth invented by good people to account for the curious attractiveness of others." You think that true?'

'I rarely think that anything I write is true,' was the baffling answer.

When the titters had died down Carson took refuge in another quotation. ' "Religions die when they are proved to be true." Is that true?'

Wilde nodded. 'Oh yes, I hold that. It is a suggestion towards a philosophy of the absorption of religions by science. But it is too big a question to go into now.'

'Do you think that was a safe axiom to put forward for the philosophy of the young?'

'Most stimulating,' replied Wilde.

Carson got nowhere by trying to pull 'Phrases and Philosophies' to pieces, so he turned to Wilde's book *The Picture of Dorian Gray*. From Wilde's introduction he quoted: 'There is no such thing as a moral or immoral book. Books are well written or badly written.' Wilde agreed: that expressed his view on art. An immoral book could be a good book if it produced a sense of beauty, but if it were badly written it would produce a sense of disgust.

'Then,' said Carson, 'a well-written book putting forward perverted moral views may be a good book?'

Wilde corrected him. 'No work of art ever puts forward views. Views belong to people who are not artists.'

'Then a perverted novel might be a good book?' asked Carson, thinking he had him in a corner.

'I do not know what you mean by a perverted novel,' replied Wilde distantly.

'Then I will suggest that *Dorian Gray* is open to the interpretation of being such a novel?'

Wilde was unimpressed. 'That could only be to brutes and illiterates,' he told Carson. 'The views of Philistines on art are incalculably stupid.'

Carson could hardly avoid the cross-examination of such an opponent as Oscar Wilde becoming more of the nature of a discussion. But he continued patiently, treading ground where the witness was more confident and familiar than he was, but fully conscious that he had some deadly arrows up his sleeve with which to deflate the enormous self-confidence of his quick-witted opponent.

He presently began to read extensive extracts from *The Picture of Dorian Gray* in which a man addresses a youth in the following terms: 'It is quite true that I have worshipped you with far more romance of feeling than a man usually gives to a friend. Somehow I have never loved a woman. . . . I quite admit that I adored you madly, extravagantly, absurdly.'

Carson asked Wilde if he thought that described the natural feeling of one man towards another.

'It would be the influence produced by a beautiful personality,' replied Wilde.

'A beautiful person?' Carson almost sneered.

'I said "beautiful personality". You can describe it as you like. Dorian Gray's was a most remarkable personality.'

'May I take it that you, as an artist, have never known the feeling described here?' Carson's voice was rich with irony.

Wilde was not to be drawn on that one. 'I have never allowed any personality to dominate my art,' he replied.

'Then you have never known the feeling you describe?' pursued Carson.

'No,' replied Wilde shortly. 'It is a work of fiction.'

'So far as you are concerned you have no experience as to its being a natural feeling?'

'I think it is perfectly natural for any artist to admire intensely and love a young man. It is an incident in the life of almost every artist.'

Carson wanted a more embarrassing admission than that.

'Let us go over it phrase by phrase,' he said. ' "I quite admit that I adored you madly". What do you say to that? Have you ever adored a young man madly?'

'No, not madly. I prefer love. That is a higher form.'

'Never mind about that,' said Carson pushing the question a little rashly. 'Let us keep down to the level we are at now.'

Wilde looked at him imperturbably. 'I have never given adoration to anybody but myself.'

This was greeted with roars of laughter in which Carson did not join, but stood there biting his lip.

'I suppose you think that is a very smart thing,' he said when he could finally make himself heard.

'Not at all,' replied the witness blandly.

Carson didn't leave the point. He was quite content for Wilde to have his fun. He was ready to turn the tables on him at any moment.

'Then you have never had that feeling?' he asked.

'No, the whole idea was borrowed from Shakespeare, I regret to say – yes, from Shakespeare's sonnets.'

'I believe you have written an article to show that Shakespeare's sonnets were suggestive of unnatural vice?'

'On the contrary,' replied Wilde, 'I have written an article to show that they are not. I objected to such a perversion being put upon Shakespeare.'

Carson left the matter there and returned to his quotations from *Dorian Gray*.

' "I have adored you extravagantly"?' he read and looked up questioningly at the witness.

'Do you mean financially?' asked Wilde innocently.

'Oh, yes, financially! Do you think we are talking about finance?'

Oscar Wilde sighed. 'I don't know what you are talking about.'

Carson then read another long passage from *Dorian Gray* and asked whether it did not suggest unnatural vice.

Wilde replied: 'It described Dorian Gray as a man of very corrupt influence, though there is no statement as to the nature of the influence. But as a matter of fact, I do not think that one person influences another. Nor do I think there is any bad influence in the world.'

'A man never corrupts a youth?' asked Carson.

'I think not.'

'You don't think that flattering a young man, making love to him in fact, would be likely to corrupt him?'

'No.'

Carson then turned to the letters Wilde had written to Alfred Douglas.

'Why should a man of your age address a boy nearly twenty years younger as "My Own Boy"?'

'I was fond of him. I have always been fond of him.'

'Do you adore him?'

'No, but I have always liked him. I think it is a beautiful letter. It is a poem. I was not writing an ordinary letter. You might as well cross-examine me as to whether *King Lear* or a sonnet of Shakespeare was proper.'

'Apart from art, Mr Wilde?'

'I can't answer apart from art.'

Carson tried another tack. 'Supposing a man who was not an artist had written this letter, would you say it was a proper letter?'

'A man who was not an artist could not have written that letter,' replied Wilde uncompromisingly.

'I can suggest for the sake of your reputation that there is nothing very wonderful in this "red rose-leaf lips of yours",' said Carson a little sneeringly.

'A great deal depends on the way it is read,' Wilde told him contemptuously.

' "Your slim gilt soul walks between passion and purity". Is that a beautiful phrase?'

'Not the way you read it, Mr Carson. You read it very badly.'

This considerably needled Carson who replied with some

heat: 'I do not profess to be an artist, and when I hear you give evidence, I am glad I am not.'

Sir Edward Clarke then rose with superb dignity to intervene in the row between his client and Edward Carson.

'I do not think my learned friend should talk like that,' he said. He then turned to Oscar Wilde. 'Pray do not criticize my friend's reading again,' he rebuked.

Carson swallowed his anger and continued the cross-examination on the subject of the 'love-letters' Wilde had written to Alfred Douglas. Wilde said he had never written to another young man in this fashion.

Carson produced another of these letters and invited Wilde to read it in view of the criticism his own reading had been subjected to.

'No, I decline,' said Wilde. 'I don't see why I should.'

'Then I will.' Carson read it out to the fascinated court.

> Savoy Hotel,
> Victoria Embankment,
> London

Dearest of all Boys

Your letter was delightful, red and yellow wine to me; but I am sad and out of sorts. Bosie, you must not make scenes with me. They kill me, they wreck the loveliness of life. I cannot see you, so Greek and gracious, distorted with passion. I cannot listen to your curved lips saying hideous things to me. I would sooner – than have you bitter, unjust, hating . . . I must see you soon. You are the divine thing I want, the thing of grace and beauty; but I don't know how to do it. Shall I come to Salisbury? My bill here is £49 for a week. I have also got a new sitting-room . . . Why are you not here, my dear, my wonderful boy? I fear I must leave – no money, no credit, and a heart of lead.

> Your own Oscar.

'Is that an ordinary letter?' asked Carson.

'Everything I write is extraordinary,' replied Wilde. 'I do

not pose as being ordinary, great heavens. Ask me any question you like about it.'

'Is this the kind of letter a man writes to another?'

'It was a tender expression of my great admiration for Lord Alfred Douglas,' declared Wilde. 'It was not, like the other, a prose poem.'

Carson suddenly moved on from a realm where Wilde was able to explain his actions, perhaps plausibly, from the standpoint of the slightly decadent *fin de siècle* artist and man of letters. Carson had a quiverful of black evidence about Wilde's personal life and he now pulled out some of his deadly arrows.

He asked about Wood, the homosexual youth Douglas had introduced him to and who tried to blackmail him over the letters he had found in Douglas's old suit. Wilde denied he had had immoral relations with Wood.

Other names came up – the blackmailers Allen and Clibborn. Then there was a youth named Shelley employed at the offices of John Lane, his publishers, whom he dined at the Albemarle Hotel.

'Was that for the purpose of having an intellectual treat?' asked Carson sarcastically.

'Well, for him, yes,' said Wilde, perhaps with some truth. 'We dined in my own sitting-room and there was one other gentleman there.'

The name of this mysterious gentleman was not given in court, but Wilde wrote it down. It happened to be Maurice Schwabe, the nephew of Sir Frank Lockwood, the Solicitor-General, who turned out to be another member of the homosexual circle, to the increasing embarrassment of the authorities.

Wilde admitted that his sitting-room led into the bedroom, but he denied that Shelley stayed all night. He did not embrace him, nor indulge in any improper conduct with him. But he took him to theatres, restaurants and exhibitions and gave him money.

'Did you think this young man of eighteen was a proper and natural companion for you?' asked Carson.

'Certainly,' replied Wilde.

He also admitted to a similar intimacy with a lad named Alphonse Conway who sold newspapers on Worthing pier. He took him to Brighton and gave him presents, but denied kissing him and indulging in familiarities with him. He did not even know he sold newspapers.

'It is the first I have heard of his connection with literature,' he said humorously.

The Court adjourned until the next day. It was obvious from the expression on the faces of most of the jury that Mr Oscar Wilde no longer amused them. They were all men of the world, and they knew perfectly well what his admissions of friendship with these various youths meant.

The following day Carson pressed Wilde about his association with certain young men, beginning with the notorious Alfred Taylor who kept a kind of brothel and procured youths for various perverts including Wilde. Here Wilde had met a number of youths, though he strenuously denied that there was anything improper. Carson asked him about his association with Sidney Mavor, Fred Atkins, Charles Parker and his equally notorious brother William, all young men in lowly occupations whose enjoyment of Wilde's sparkling company, not to say his bounty, was a very remarkable thing, implied Carson, if it was innocent.

What enjoyment was it to him, asked Carson, to entertain grooms, coachmen and valets?

'The pleasure to me,' declared Wilde, 'was being with those who are young, bright, careless and free. I do not like the sensible and I do not like the old.' Besides, he said, he had a passion to civilize the community.

Carson recalled the occasion when Taylor brought the two Parker brothers to dine with him. One was a valet, the other a groom. They dined in a private room at Kettner's.

'You did the honours to the valet and the groom?' said Carson, deeply sarcastic.

'I entertained Taylor and his two guests.'

'Did you give them an intellectual treat?'

'They seemed deeply impressed.'

'During the dinner did you become more intimate with Charles than the other?' asked Carson.

'I liked him better,' admitted Wilde, though, contrary to what Charles Parker later alleged, he denied to have taken him back to the Savoy for a homosexual interlude.

Carson asked about the whiskies and sodas and iced champagne he bought for his boy friends, but Wilde couldn't remember what they drank.

'Do you drink champagne yourself?'

'Yes,' replied Wilde expansively. 'Iced champagne is a favourite drink of mine – strongly against my doctor's orders.'

'Never mind your doctor's orders, sir,' exclaimed Carson a little testily.

'I never do,' came the answer as quick as a flash to the accompaniment of delighted titters in court.

He saw Parker several times, and gave him presents, but no improprieties took place.

'What was there in common between this young man and yourself?' demanded Carson. 'What attraction had he for you?' Carson was thinking what everybody else in the court was thinking. Did Oscar Wilde take them all for fools? Apparently he did, judging by his answer.

'I delight in the society of people much younger than myself. I like those who may be called idle and careless. I recognize no social distinctions at all of any kind; and to me youth, the mere fact of youth, is so wonderful that I would sooner talk to a young man for half an hour than be – well cross-examined in Court.'

Carson smiled faintly. He could believe that. 'Do I understand,' he pursued, 'that even a young boy you might pick up in the street would be a pleasing companion?'

'I would talk to a street arab with pleasure,' declared Wilde.

'You would talk to a street arab?' Carson made it sound incredible. Remember, this was 1895.

'If he would talk to me – yes, with pleasure.'

'And take him to your rooms?'

'Be it so,' replied Wilde.

There was a strange feeling in court now. This was all very different from the literary wit and wisdom of the previous day. The jury were distinctly hostile. Sir Edward Clarke was uneasy, for his client had sworn that there was never any truth in these allegations against him.

Carson asked Wilde if he had written any 'beautiful letters' to Charles Parker as he had written to Douglas. Wilde answered that he did not think he had written any letters to Parker.

'Have you any letters of his?' asked Carson.

'Only one.'

Carson read the following letter from Parker: 'Am I to have the pleasure of dining with you this evening? If so, kindly reply by messenger or wire to the above address. I trust you can, and we can spend a pleasant evening.'

Clarke, a little alarmed, jumped to his feet. 'I should like to see the handwriting,' he said.

'We will see about that,' Carson told him. 'Parker himself will be here, which will be better.'

Clarke sat down in silence, seeing his case collapsing around him.

Carson continued the relentless cross-examination. Wilde had lost some of his confidence, though his wit had not deserted him. He denied visiting Parker at 50 Park Walk in the spring of the previous year. Carson then asked him if Park Walk was not ten minutes' walk from his house in Tite Street.

'I don't know,' replied Wilde. 'I never walk.'

But that sally did nothing to alleviate the deadly effect of the information which was elucidated from Carson's next questions. It seemed that Taylor and Parker were among those arrested during a police raid at a club at Fitzroy Street where a number of men were found to be wearing female clothing.

More questions about his relations with youths followed. The strain was now beginning to tell on Oscar Wilde. He then made a fatal and devastating mistake from which he tried in vain to extricate himself.

Carson was asking him about a sixteen-year-old youth named Grainger who was a servant at Alfred Douglas's rooms at Oxford. Grainger waited at table, Wilde replied, anticipating the usual question. He had never dined with him. He added a spontaneous epigram: 'If it is one's duty to serve, it is one's duty to serve; if it is one's pleasure to dine, it is one's pleasure to dine.'

Carson instead asked him the unexpected question.

'Did you ever kiss him?'

'Oh, dear no. He was a peculiarly plain boy. He was unfortunately extremely ugly. I pitied him for it.'

Wilde could hardly have made a worse reply. Carson jumped on him.

'Was that the reason why you did not kiss him?' he snapped.

Wilde recoiled. 'Oh, Mr Carson, you are pertinently insolent.'

Carson followed up his tremendous advantage by rapping out question after question. Why had he mentioned his ugliness? Why had he put it forward as the reason he had not kissed the boy?

Wilde was not lost for words, but he was confused. He knew he had blundered badly.

'If I were asked why I did not kiss a doormat, I should say because I do not like to kiss doormats. I do not know why I mentioned that he was ugly, except that I was stung by the insolent question you put to me and the way you have insulted me throughout this hearing. Am I to be cross-examined – because I do not like it?'

'Why did you mention his ugliness?' persisted Carson. 'Why did you mention his ugliness?'

Wilde became almost inarticulate under Carson's verbal assault, finally gathering his thoughts sufficiently to say:

'You sting me and insult me and try to unnerve me. And at times one says things flippantly when one ought to speak more seriously. I admit it.'

'Then you said it flippantly?'

'Yes, it was a flippant answer.'

Whether the court believed him or not, it did his case untold harm. Carson had done what he had set out to do. He had cast serious doubt on the truth of Wilde's denials that he

Oscar Wilde (*left*), whose lost libel case against the Marquess of Queensberry brought about his own downfall. Sir Thomas Picton (*below*), tried in 1806 for unlawfully torturing an accused girl in Trinidad. Aimee Semple McPherson (*bottom*), the Hot Gospeller, tried for conspiring to obstruct justice.

The trial of Marie Besnard ranks
with the Dreyfus case as one of
France's great judicial scandals. On
the flimsiest evidence, mostly gossip
and tittle-tattle, she was put on trial
for murdering by poison eleven
people, including her own husband.
The case lasted twelve years, five of
which she spent in prison. She is
seen here (*right*) at her first trial at
Poitiers, in 1952, during a relentless
examination by the President of the
Court, after which she broke down
in a storm of weeping, believing that
there was no justice for her. After
this, devoted lawyers fought her
case in the French courts for years.
They caused uproar by the manner
in which they exposed the ineptitude
of the scientific experts who
appeared for the prosecution. This
picture (*below*), taken at her second
trial, in 1954, shows her with her
lawyers, Maitre Hayot (*on the left*)
and Maitre Gautrat.

had committed indecencies with this collection of unpleasant young men.

Sir Edward Clarke, in his re-examination of Oscar Wilde, adopted a course most damaging to the Marquess of Queensberry. The way Carson had treated Wilde in the box made this inevitable. When one's client is attacked in this way, it is considered right and proper to strike back. Carson took this calculated risk. No one liked Queensberry anyway.

Clarke read out in detail the insulting and unpleasant letters Queensberry had written to his son and other members of his family. These letters, with the evil malice they showed towards his family and the doubtful light on his son Alfred's legitimacy, caused an enormous sensation. They obviously upset Queensberry who stood up in the dock grinding his teeth and shaking his head like the maniac he was.

Nevertheless Clarke was full of foreboding which was increased when Wilde came to him during the luncheon interval and asked him if the defence could examine him about anything and everything they chose. When Clarke asked Wilde what was on his mind, he replied: 'Well, some time ago I was turned out of the Albemarle Hotel in the middle of the night, and a boy was with me. It might be awkward if they found out about that.'

This was not a great shock for Edward Clarke. It had become clear to him during the latter part of Carson's cross-examination that his client had deceived him and had told him a deliberate lie when he said he was not guilty of the practices Queensberry accused him of. Clarke would not have undertaken the case had he known this.

When the court reassembled after lunch Oscar Wilde was not there. Rumours were going round that he had already fled the country, but he turned up a quarter of an hour late with the apology that the clock in the hotel where he was lunching was wrong.

After more questions which endeavoured to show that Wilde in his association with the various youths whose names had been mentioned was only prompted by the highest motives, Clarke declared the case for the prosecution closed.

This in itself caused much speculation, for everyone expected that Clarke would put Lord Alfred Douglas in the box to give evidence against his father, and this Douglas was extremely anxious to do. Many believed that great pressure had been brought to bear on Clarke to prevent this, for Douglas was prepared to reveal scandalous things about his blackguardly father. But such evidence would not have been relevant at this point in the trial. If Queensberry had gone into the box and alleged immoral conduct between his son and Wilde, then Douglas could have given evidence in rebuttal. But Queensberry did not go into the box. The case against him was about to collapse.

Carson in his opening speech for the defence played upon the jury's parental feelings by saying that all Queensberry wanted to do was to save his son from being corrupted. He announced that he was going to put into the box the various young men with whom Wilde had had homosexual relations. On this note of sensational expectancy, the court adjourned until the following day.

Clarke knew that his case was lost. But what he feared more than that was that his client might be arrested in the court if the evidence of the youths were heard. He told Oscar Wilde that night that he hadn't a hope of persuading the jury to find Queensberry guilty, and that if the case went its full course he was certain that the Judge would order his arrest. He advised Wilde to agree to the prosecution being withdrawn before Carson called any of his evidence, and he told him that there was no necessity for him to be in court.

Privately Clarke hoped that Wilde would take the opportunity of leaving the country immediately to escape the consequences of his actions, and there is little doubt that at this point he would have been allowed to do so.

Wilde accepted his counsel's advice about withdrawing the prosecution, but he did not take the hint about being out of court, much less of leaving the country.

The following day Clarke told the Judge that his client wished to withdraw the prosecution, saying that the evidence might induce the jury to come to the conclusion that 'Lord Queensberry in using the word "posing" was using a word for which there was sufficient justification to entitle the father who used those words under these circumstances to the utmost consideration, and to be relieved of a criminal charge in respect of his statement.'

Sir Edward Clarke asked for a verdict of not guilty. Mr Justice Collins pointed out to the jury that this meant that justification was proved, and that it was true in substance and in fact that Oscar Wilde had 'posed' as a sodomite, and that Queensberry's statement was published in such a manner 'as to be for the public benefit'.

This was the verdict of the jury and the result of the case which put Oscar Wilde in a very serious position indeed. It was greeted with prolonged cheering in court.

Outside the Old Bailey there were uproarious scenes of popular approval. Prostitutes lifted their skirts and danced on the pavement.

Clarke and Carson left the court together. 'I shall not feel clean for weeks,' said Clarke. Wilde left by a side entrance, and received the following message from Queensberry: 'If the country allows you to leave, all the better for the country. But if you take my son with you, I will follow you wherever you go and shoot you.' Queensberry's solicitors immediately sent copies of all their witnesses' statements to the Director of Public Prosecutions who had no option but to bring charges of gross indecency against Wilde.

There is good reason for saying that the authorities did not want to prosecute Wilde and would have been quite willing for him to have gone abroad. The warrant for his arrest was delayed to allow him to do this. His failure to avail himself of the delay was due to his inability to make up his mind.

The statute under which he was charged had only come into force in 1886. Before that the law did not concern itself with indecencies which took place in private between consenting male or female adults. The law only punished acts against public indecency or conduct which might corrupt youth.

In 1885 the Criminal Law Amendment Act was introduced into the House of Lords. Its object was to protect females and suppress brothels. When the Bill was going through the Commons Committee an M.P. named Labouchere introduced a new clause, Section 11, which created an entirely new offence – that of indecency between male persons in public or private. The clause was not debated and it was added to the Bill almost by chance, without the House recognizing that the words 'in public or private' had completely altered the law.

This notorious Clause 11 was strongly criticized by the legal profession and a learned Recorder dubbed it 'the blackmailer's charter'. It remained on the statute book for over eighty years during which a rich harvest of blackmail and misery was reaped from it. Only recently has the law been altered. Feeling on the subject is so sensitive that even in these comparatively enlightened times, the law which abolished 'the blackmailer's charter' was called 'the pansy's charter' in some intolerant circles.

The warrant for Oscar Wilde's arrest was issued late in the afternoon of the day on which the case against Queensberry finished. He was at the Cadogan Hotel in Sloane Street with Alfred Douglas and there his friends, with the conspicuous exception of Douglas, were imploring him to leave the country before the police came for him.

His wife, dumbfounded with amazement and horror at the appalling scandal which had broken over them, said between her sobs: 'I hope Oscar is going away – abroad.' She was in total ignorance about such matters as homosexuality.

As for Wilde himself, he simply could not make up his mind to flee or not. In England he was a great success. He was aware that the exceptional merit of his plays stood out brilliantly against the almost unrelieved mediocrity of what had been produced on the English stage for a whole century. Abroad he was nothing. If to stay meant ruin, to flee meant ruin too.

In this state of agonizing indecision he was arrested at half past six on the evening of 5 April, 1895 by Inspector Richards of Scotland Yard. Alfred Taylor was arrested with him and both were charged with committing acts of gross indecency with other male persons.

In Victorian England there was undisguised delight. The newspapers gloated in terms of vulgarity and with a contempt for justice which in these days would have landed all their editors in prison.

The two trials which followed were not acquittals, but were certainly among the most famous held at the Old Bailey.

As soon as Oscar Wilde was arrested all his plays were taken off, and his books disappeared from the bookshops – which meant that his source of income dried up immediately. He found himself heavily in debt.

Sir Edward Clarke, despite being deceived by Wilde in the first place, unhesitatingly offered to defend him and to do so without fee or reward. The same offer was made also by his juniors, Mr Charles W. Mathews and Mr Travers Humphreys (later to become one of the most distinguished judges to sit upon the English bench, one of his last trials being that of John George Haigh, the acid bath murderer at Lewes Assizes in 1949).

Wilde was deserted by all his friends with the exception of Alfred Douglas who paid him regular visits in prison while he was awaiting trial. Many of Wilde's cronies fled the country, afraid of being arrested on similar charges. It has been said that after Wilde's arrest there was a mass exodus of terrified homosexuals who left England for France. Some were people in important social positions, and rumour had it that they included an ex-Cabinet Minister, a one-time President of the Royal Society, a recently-ennobled millionaire and a famous General.

Clarke told Lord Alfred Douglas that his continued presence in London was prejudicial to his client and urgently requested him to leave the country, which he did. Clarke flatly refused to call Douglas as a witness, fearing that a cross-examination of Douglas would do Wilde's case great harm.

Wilde's first trial began on 2 April, 1895 and lasted five days. It also was held at the Old Bailey. The Judge was Mr Justice Charles. The main witnesses for the prosecution were a wretched band of homosexual youths and blackmailers, the very scum of Victorian society. As Crown witnesses, they could admit to the same offences as Oscar Wilde had committed, without fear of punishment. They were ruthlessly attacked in cross-examination and made to admit blackmail, but though they got off scot-free their later activities did not escape the attention of the police.

Wilde gave evidence denying the charges. It was not a sparkling performance as his evidence had been in the Queensberry trial. But his description of 'the love that dare not speak its name' drew loud applause in court.

Among the prosecution's witnesses was Edward Shelley, aged twenty-one, a clerk employed at the offices of John Lane and the Bodley Head, Wilde's publishers, who admitted spending two consecutive nights in bed with Wilde at the Albemarle Hotel in 1892. Afterwards he was stricken with conscience. John Lane was highly embarrassed by this. Shelley had to leave the firm after being endlessly tormented by members of the staff who knew very well what was going on and called him 'Mrs Wilde' and 'Miss Oscar'.

The jury disagreed following a notable speech by Clarke and a summing up in which the Judge was if anything favourable to Wilde. It is thought that the jury might have been repulsed by the despicable creatures which the Crown produced as witnesses against the brilliant man who was being destroyed in the dock. Juries in those days did not like Section 11 of the 1885 Criminal Law Amendment Act and were notoriously reluctant to convict victims of the 'blackmailer's charter'.

Sir Edward Clarke's attempts, however, to turn the jury's disagreement into a not guilty verdict were in vain, and Wilde was forced to face another trial. He was granted bail of £5,000 by a judge in chambers. One of his sureties was Lord Douglas of Hawick, the heir to the Marquess of Queensberry, following the death of his elder brother, Lord Drumlanrig.

As soon as Wilde was released on bail, he was hounded by a gang of thugs hired by Queensberry who followed him around to ensure that he did not get admission into any hotel in London. Wilde finally took refuge in his mother's house at Chelsea, gasping, 'Let me lie on the floor, or I shall die in the streets.' He collapsed across the threshold 'like a wounded stag', as his brother put it.

The authorities immediately went ahead with plans for

another trial. The prosecution this time was to be led by Sir Frank Lockwood, the Solicitor-General. Edward Carson who had defended Queensberry refused to be briefed against Wilde.

'Can't you let up on the fellow now?' he said to Lockwood. 'He has suffered a great deal.'

'I would,' Lockwood said. 'But we cannot. We dare not. It would at once be said, both in England and abroad, that owing to the names mentioned in the Queensberry letters, we were forced to abandon it.' As mentioned before, Lockwood's own nephew on his wife's side had been frequently mentioned in the trials as being mixed up in the unsavoury scandal.

Travers Humphreys said fifty years later that Oscar Wilde again could easily have left the country at this point. Humphreys had been told that, even though the £5,000 bail had been put up in cash, Wilde's sureties would not have suffered if he had absconded. The authorities, even though they felt themselves bound to continue the prosecution for the reasons put forward by Lockwood, to say nothing of the pressure of public opinion, would have preferred their quarry to have escaped.

Great pressure was put on Wilde to do this. Frank Harris had a yacht ready to take him to the Continent, and Mrs Wilde begged him to go. Lord Douglas of Hawick told him he would be prepared to pay the whole £5,000 surety.

But Wilde refused to run away and hide. 'I cannot see myself slinking about the Continent, a fugitive from justice.' He showed some courage in deciding to remain and face the music.

His true character and his loyalty towards Douglas was revealed during a lunch with Frank Harris when they discussed the case.

Wilde thought he had a good chance of acquittal. Harris pointed out that the evidence which would weigh most against him were the statements of the Savoy Hotel employees, but Wilde declared that the hotel employees were wrong. 'It was not I they spoke about at the Savoy. It was Bosie Douglas. I was never bold enough.' He told Harris that Sir Edward Clarke knew this, but he refused to let him bring it out in court. 'He wanted to, but I would not let him. I told him he must not. I must be true to Bosie. I would not let him.'

When Frank Harris told him that he was determined that the truth should come out, Wilde said it was useless. He was guilty, anyway, of the things they alleged against him. Frank Harris was said to have been surprised at this confession of guilt, although this point hardly squares with his words at the lunch at the Café Royal, mentioned above, when in the presence of George Bernard Shaw, Oscar Wilde and Bosie Douglas, he tried to persuade Wilde to abandon the suit against Queensberry.

The fact that the evidence of the Savoy staff applied to Douglas, not to Wilde, was not revealed until after Douglas's death in 1945, for Douglas would have taken anyone to law who had repeated Wilde's revelation to Frank Harris in 1895.

Oscar Wilde's second trial began on 20 May. It lasted four days. The Judge was Justice Wills, the fanatical puritan with the cold-blooded legal mind who presided over the trial of Adelaide Bartlett and who plainly disapproved of the fact that she had escaped the attentions of the hangman.

At his second trial the case was pressed ruthlessly against Wilde. The wretched gang of blackmailers and pansy boys whose immunity from prosecution was further extended in exchange for their evidence once more told their craven stories. Literary matters were not discussed with the exception of the two foolish letters Wilde had written to Alfred Douglas, and these were put with such force, not only by Lockwood, but by Wills in his summing-up, as being evidence of guilty passion between the two men that the foreman of the jury intervened to ask the Judge why in that case was not Lord Alfred Douglas also in the box?

The Judge of course had no answer. After all Oscar Wilde was the quarry. Victorian England did not hound members of the aristocracy. They were likely to enjoy the protection of royalty as in the case of Lord Arthur Somerset. Justice Wills did not say that of course. He just waffled and told the foreman of the jury testily: 'I think you should deal with the matter upon the evidence before you.'

The foreman disagreed – and what foreman of any jury would dare to argue with a judge in the Old Bailey these days?

'It seems to us,' said the foreman, 'that if we are to consider these letters as evidence of guilt, and if we adduce any guilt from these letters, it applies as much to Lord Alfred Douglas as to the defendant.'

The Judge knew very well what was going through the mind of the jury, and he agreed with them – as a puritan he could hardly approve of Lord Alfred Douglas's conduct. 'But how does that relieve the defendant?' he requested. 'Our present inquiry is whether guilt is brought home to the man in the dock.'

Perfectly true. But why wasn't Lord Alfred Douglas on trial? Wills dealt with that problem too.

'There is a natural disposition to ask why should this man stand in the dock and not Lord Alfred Douglas? But the supposition that Lord Alfred Douglas will be spared because he *is* Lord Alfred Douglas is one of the wildest injustice. The thing is utterly and hopelessly impossible. I must remind you that anything that can be said for or against Lord Alfred Douglas must not be allowed to prejudice the prisoner. And you must remember that no prosecution would be possible on the mere production of Wilde's letters to Lord Alfred Douglas. Lord Alfred Douglas, as you all know, went to Paris at the request of the defendant, and there he has stayed, and I know absolutely nothing more about him. I am as ignorant in this respect as you are. It may be there is no evidence against Lord Alfred Douglas – but even about that I know nothing. It is a thing we cannot discuss, and to entertain any such considerations as I have mentioned would be a prejudice of the worst possible kind.'

Mr Justice Wills left it at that, and of course the Judge always has the last word. He was perfectly right in law – he always was – but he hadn't answered the foreman's question.

The jury took three hours to find Wilde and Taylor guilty. Justice Wills sentenced them with hard words:

'People who can do these things must be dead to all sense of shame, and one cannot hope to produce any effect upon them. That you, Taylor, kept a kind of male brothel it is impossible to doubt. And that you, Wilde, have been the centre of a circle of extensive corruption of the most hideous kind among young men, it is equally impossible to doubt. I shall under such circumstances be expected to pass the severest sentence that the law allows. In my judgement it is totally inadequate for such a case as this. The sentence of the court is that each of you be imprisoned and kept to hard labour for two years.'

There were cries of 'Shame!' in court, but outside the mob cheered, the women of the streets pranced with glee, and the harlot Press rejoiced that justice had at last been done to the unspeakable Oscar Wilde.

But the story didn't end there. Wilde's friends and so-called friends argued and squabbled over him not only for the rest of his life but for the rest of theirs as well.

Prison conditions in the 1890s were appalling, and Oscar Wilde served Mr Justice Wills's savage and vindictive sentence with courage and dignity. What he wrote about his prison experiences did much to bring about the improvement in penal conditions in the early twentieth century. 'The Ballad of Reading Gaol', which he wrote in Reading prison, is a powerful and moving poem which stands unique in English literature.

But Wilde wrote nothing else. Prison broke him. When he was released he went to live on the Continent. His friends said that he devoted the rest of his life to his homosexual passions. The crime for which he was so brutally punished was not a crime in Continental countries and is no longer a crime in England.

He died in Paris in 1900. Two years previously Queensberry, sunk in his miserable paranoia, imagining to the last that he was being pursued by the 'Oscar Wilders', was laid to rest among his rather more illustrious forefathers.

Bernard Shaw blamed Wilde for wasting the final years of his life, saying that it was not plain living or high thinking that prevented him writing in Paris.

But Shaw didn't understand Wilde or why England should have such a tormented conscience about him. Wilde's private life was his own affair. He was no debaucher of youth. Mr Justice Wills was quite wrong when he suggested that he was. Wilde's accomplices including Lord Alfred Douglas were all practising homosexuals, and two of them at least were notorious blackmailers. He was sentenced under an immoral law which came accidentally on the statute book in 1885 in the face of strong criticism from the legal profession, and which has only recently been altered in the face of even stronger criticism from people who have inherited something of the mentality of the eighth Marquess of Queensberry.

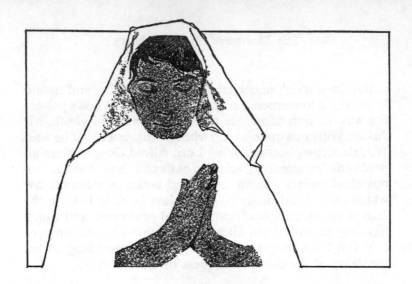

# Chapter 5
# Aimee Semple McPherson

They called her the Hot Gospeller. She was gay, dynamic, sexy, the kind of evangelist which only the twenties could have produced. Her career was surrounded by unprecedented publicity, created mainly by herself and her extraordinary organization. At the Angelus Temple, Los Angeles, which was described as one of the world's most ugly buildings she conducted a vast religious circus, the extravagances and show-biz style of which was one of the wonders of the frenzied world of the Aspirin Age.

Aimee Semple McPherson's life reached its peak of high melodrama in the year 1926 when her alleged kidnapping was followed by one of the most extraordinary trials in American history.

She was a Canadian, born Aimee Elizabeth Kennedy at Ingersol, Ontario, on 9 October, 1890. Her mother, Minnie Kennedy, later known to millions as 'Ma' Kennedy, was a Salvation Army stalwart. Mrs Kennedy was, like her daughter, strong-willed and obstinate and there was often much friction between them.

After a teenage flirtation with the Devil, the gay Aimee

was among those called sternly to account by a six-foot travelling evangelist named Robert Semple. Aimee was more than converted. She was infatuated. So was Semple. They married, were united together in the Lord, and they set off to China to free the inhabitants of the world's most ancient civilization from their heathen thraldom. Unfortunately for the souls of China's millions, Semple died of fever at Hong-Kong, with his unborn child in Aimee's womb.

After bearing Roberta Starr in 1909, nineteen-year-old Aimee returned to New York where her parents had removed, and there she married a grocery clerk, Harold McPherson, by whom she had another child, Rolf. The marriage failed. Aimee, with the Semple fire burning fiercely in her heart, thought only of revival meetings. Her husband, in the divorce proceedings which inevitably followed, said that at home 'she had wild-cat habits' and described her as 'a great actress who could throw herself into a fit at any time'.

Aimee Semple McPherson was indeed a complex personality. She was a good and sincere woman for all the natural faults and failings which brought scandal upon her name. She taught and believed a simple and joyful form of Christianity, using all the tricks in the world of vaudeville to further the work of her Four Square Gospel movement. She was haunted all her life by Robert Semple, the man with whom she had set out at the age of seventeen into the unknown to fight the great battle for the Lord, and whom she had lost so tragically before her twentieth birthday.

That Aimee was sexy, there is little doubt. Everything about her suggested sex, and she became known as the world's most pulchritudinous evangelist. It was not that she was particularly attractive. There was a certain heaviness about her features and her body. Her legs were straight and she had thick ankles during an age when women first revealed their legs to public view. But she had a finely shaped head, Titian hair, a good skin, a remarkable physical vitality and a vibrant, husky voice.

It has been said of her that she emanated sex without being sexually attractive. There is no doubt that she needed a man in her life, both physically and emotionally. It was this need which brought on her tragedy. Like so many people in the limelight who are the centre of interest and adulation, she was lonely, frustrated and lacked personal happiness.

So far as marriage was concerned, she had set for herself and her followers a standard. Divorce was not recognized. Marriage was only dissoluble at death. So she could not marry again while Harold McPherson lived.

She threw all her unbounded energies into the evangelical movement and, in her own words, 'answering the clarion call that brooks no denial' she set off to Southern California to achieve astonishing fame and undreamed-of fortune – to become 'the great Sarah Bernhardt of the pulpit'.

In 1917 she was travelling across America with a car and a tent, accompanied by her mother and her two children. During these years she developed both her technique and her Four Square Gospel creed.

By 1923 she had forsaken the life of the itinerant evangelist and was the enthroned Sister-in-the-Lord in the Angelus Temple, in Los Angeles, beneath the electrically illuminated rotating cross at the top of the Temple which she and her mother owned exclusively between them in two equal shares. It cost one million and a half dollars and had a payroll of $7,000 a week, which was some measure of her earthly, if not spiritual, success. Here Aimee conducted her vast religious circus which became famous for its evangelical extravaganzas.

Her phenomenal success was due to several things. She made religion as exciting as a variety show and very much more emotional. She never used the hell-fire techniques with which the evangelists of the nineteenth century bludgeoned the unbelievers into the fold. Aimee knew that times had changed. People wouldn't take hell-fire any more: so she preached universal love and brought religion into the jazz age.

By 1926 she was a millionairess and world famous, surrounded by adoring crowds of sycophants. But by that time she was getting bored with it all. Though the central figure of this great organization, she was a lonely and sad woman.

Her faith burnt as brightly as ever and she believed that she was doing a great work for the Lord, yet her secret desire was to escape from it.

Then she fell in love. He was Kenneth G. Ormiston, the radio operator of the Angelus Temple. He was not a member of the Four Square cult, but a man of some sophistication. They soon became close friends, despite the fact that he had a jealous wife while Aimee was pledged to the celibate life so long as her second husband lived – and McPherson was hale and healthy in New York.

The affair between Aimee and Ormiston blossomed. It was soon the subject of rumours, gossip and scandal. A maid and the house detective of the Ambassador Hotel saw Ormiston going into her room a number of times in compromising circumstances. In 1926 Aimee went to London and Paris where her short skirts and night-club visits were the subject of much unfavourable comment, though naturally enough her antics and sartorial splendour made her very popular with the Press. Later she went to the Holy Land. Ormiston was absent from California at this time and many believed that he secretly accompanied her.

When she returned to Los Angeles she began to talk mysteriously about the possibility of her disappearance. Those who really knew her believed that she had intended to vanish permanently. Ormiston was seen less and less, though the pair of them were caught out on more than one occasion meeting at hotels, if one is to believe testimony given later at the trial.

On 9 May, 1926, Ormiston went to Carmel, a quiet and exclusive seaside place between Los Angeles and San Francisco, and under the name George McIntyre rented a cottage from Henry Benedict. The scene was set for the decade's most sensational disappearance.

On 18 May, Aimee spent the day on the beach at Venice, near Los Angeles, accompanied by her secretary Emma Schaeffer. She was a splendid swimmer and in between riding the Pacific rollers, she made notes for the Sunday night sermon which she knew she would not preach, and which she prosaically entitled 'Light and Darkness'.

After a while she despatched Emma Schaeffer on a point-less errand, and when that lady returned the evangelist had vanished.

By evening when she still failed to turn up, her disappear-ance was a nation-wide sensation. A great search began with planes, motorboats and deep-sea divers. Thousands gathered on the shore at Venice, searching the sky for divine omens while Mrs Kennedy prematurely announced: 'She is with Jesus.'

The cynics believed that Aimee was frolicking with Ormis-ton rather than singing with the angels. Ormiston had given up his job at the Temple and his wife had added his name to the list of missing persons at the sheriff's office.

But the thousands of Aimee's followers would not have the purity of their beloved Sister called into question. A great collection was started for a Sister Aimee McPherson Mem-orial, and at one meeting $36,000 was taken for this purpose. Even when it was plain that Aimee was alive, money was still collected for the memorial. None of this money was ever returned – a plain case of fraud, as Assistant U.S. Attorney Simpson said later.

Aimee's plan to vanish completely foundered in the storm of publicity which her disappearance caused. When the news-papers hinted plainly enough that she and Ormiston had run off together, Aimee realized that her naïve scheme was im-possible. The Press was too powerful for her, and her enemies too many and too vocal. The foolish dream of ever-lasting love with Kenneth Ormiston in some secret undis-coverable haven had to be abandoned.

Aimee disappeared on 18 May. On 25 May a letter was received at Angelus Temple mailed the previous day in San Francisco. It was signed 'The Avengers' and it stated that they held Aimee prisoner and demanded half a million dollars for her release. Aimee's mother, Mrs Kennedy, in-formed the police but paid little attention to the letter. The police waited at the proposed rendezvous but in vain.

In the early hours of 23 June Aimee made her memorable reappearance at the Mexican border town of Agua Prieta with the story that she had just escaped from her kidnappers whose names were Rose, Steve and Jake. Her story, which made the front page of nearly every newspaper in the world, was that she was lured into a car near the beach at Venice by Rose who asked her help for her dying baby. A sponge was pressed on her nostrils and she passed out. She came to in a hut where she was held prisoner, bound hand and foot for most of the time. Finally, when she was left on her own, she managed to free herself and escape. She walked all day through the blazing sun, finally reaching Agua Prieta after midnight.

When Aimee returned to the Angelus Temple she received the kind of welcome only accorded queens, presidents and movie stars. The world at large, however, greeted her arrival with cynicism and ribald laughter. Only her most devout followers believed her incredible story. Everyone else was of the opinion that she had been on a month-long sex jaunt with her married boy-friend and that she had broken every rule in the evangelist's book.

Deputy District Attorney Joseph Ryan was ordered by the Los Angeles District Attorney, Asa Keyes, to investigate the story. Ryan was immediately suspicious. To him Aimee's account of being chloroformed in the kidnapping car was not credible. She alleged that she had been kept unconscious for fourteen hours while in a wet bathing costume. Medical opinion declared such a thing impossible without permanent ill-effects. When she arrived at Agua Prieta, her clothing was untorn and had no dust or perspiration marks – despite the fact that she maintained to have walked in the heat of the day through a semi-desert where temperatures reached 120 degrees at that time of the year.

Ryan met Aimee's two children, Roberta and Rolf. Their bland indifference about what was supposed to have happened to their mother struck him as being very odd. They had lived in this fantastic religious circus all their lives, the centre of daily drama, dominated by two fanatical and strong-willed women. When asked what they intended to be when grown up, Roberta replied disinterestedly: 'I suppose we'll be evangelists. But we don't want to be.'

Though Aimee declared that before God her kidnapping

story was true, the police were unconvinced and proposed to drop the inquiry. This resulted in such a chorus of derision that Aimee rashly issued a public challenge to the authorities to take action.

The Grand Jury was then instructed to investigate. Aimee arrived at the Hall of Justice to give evidence on 8 July, 1926. She was attended by her Temple Guard of Honour like a queen with her ladies in waiting. During the hearing the Guard of Honour dutifully prayed in an adjoining room.

Aimee in the witness-box was a match for the District Attorney and his deputy. They were quite unable to shake her story. On the question of her perspiration-free clothing, she coolly replied that she very rarely perspired, though during her walk of escape she was hot and her forehead was moist. It was pointed out that water was not her first thought, on arriving at the Mexican border town.

'Don't you know,' inquired the District Attorney, 'that it is practically impossible for anyone, particularly a woman, to walk over the desert in Mexico in the broiling sun from noon to practically midnight without water?'

Aimee got out of that one by offering to repeat the journey.

When asked if she handled the finances of her church, she said that she did not. 'If I want any money, they give it to me like a child.' But she was no child in the witness-box. She got the better of all her questioners and ended by addressing the Grand Jury in a masterly and persuasive speech.

She would not blame anyone who doubted her story. 'But it did happen, ladies and gentlemen. I would not work hard for seventeen years, and, just as I saw my dearest dream coming true, sweep it over.'

District Attorney Keyes subpœna'd Kenneth Ormiston to appear before the Grand Jury, as being 'the key to the entire mystery'. Ormiston was apparently located in Norfolk, Virginia, thousands of miles away on the other side of the continent. He sent a telegram to Keyes with the reply that it was quite out of the question for him to come all the way to Los Angeles. He had no knowledge of the affair, and he could afford neither the money nor the time to cross the

American continent on 'what would be nothing else than a worthless errand'. This was cool enough; but as no one could subsequently trace Ormiston there was nothing Keyes could do about it.

Meanwhile Sunday came and Aimee, angel-sweet in the Temple before her adoring followers, promised her kidnappers forgiveness, which, thought the District Attorney's office, was a hell of a nerve considering that these kidnappers did not exist. As for herself – 'blessed are they which are persecuted for righteousness sake'.

On the Monday Mrs Kennedy took the stand and the District Attorney asked her about the letters from 'The Avengers' demanding money for Aimee's release. 'Did it not strike you that the general tone of this letter sounded like your daughter?' Mrs Kennedy said no. She had to admit, however, that it gave the impression of someone trying to impersonate Aimee. She denied that just before her daughter's disappearance, she and Aimee had a number of quarrels about money.

The District Attorney produced a witness who identified Aimee as a woman he saw in a car on 20 June, at Agua Prieta, three days before her re-appearance.

On 20 July the Grand Jury found that the evidence for her having been kidnapped was insufficient.

Her bitterest enemies were among the Press. They didn't let the story rest and were soon on to a sensational development. Two days after the Grand Jury's findings the love nest at Carmel was discovered. Four very trustworthy witnesses identified Aimee as the Mrs McIntyre who shared the cottage rented by Ormiston from Henry Benedict. The couple had arrived on 19 May, the day following Aimee's supposed kidnapping, and departed hastily ten days later when local interest in them became embarrassing. They left behind books containing passages Aimee quoted in her sermons, and also a grocery slip in writing identified as hers. The quiet community of Carmel considered themselves very exclusive and were reluctant to become involved in the distasteful Aimee McPherson scandal. This was the reason given why the news had taken so long in leaking out.

To this feast of scandal was added the rumour that the real reason for her disappearance was to have an abortion.

Aimee stood defiantly against the storm of public opprobrium. She refused to go to Carmel to face the witnesses. She also refused to supply specimens of her handwriting or to be fingerprinted. Instead she appealed to Ormiston, still ungallantly lying low and leaving her to face the music alone. He finally responded with an affidavit in which he admitted renting the Carmel cottage, but declaring that the lady who stayed with him was not Aimee, but a Miss X.

This apparent vindication from an admittedly interested source served to increase Aimee's defiance. She easily rebutted the abortion rumour by producing medical evidence which proved that the complications caused by the birth of her second child precluded her ever having another. But this was a side issue.

A Mrs Lorraine Wiseman now appeared upon the scene. This lady claimed to be the sister of Ormiston's Miss X. She claimed that she had stayed at the Carmel cottage at the time when Aimee was supposed to have been there. Mrs Wiseman had a certain resemblance to Aimee, and much was made of this. But her story was somewhat discredited when it turned out that she was wanted by the police on a number of charges.

The situation was threatening to get out of hand. Once more the Grand Jury sat to investigate it. The entire evidence, both material and spoken, was placed upon a table before the Jury. One of its members, a woman named Mrs Holmes, got hold of the vital grocery slip found in the Carmel cottage when no one was looking. Quietly excusing herself, she went to the ladies' room and flushed it down the toilet as coolly as you please.

This thoroughly outraged public opinion, and when the Grand Jury declined to take action against Mrs Holmes the outcry was such that the Jury itself was summarily discharged by Judge Keetch, much to their indignation.

The clamour was so great now that the District Attorney had no alternative but to file a criminal complaint against Aimee, Mrs Kennedy, Ormiston and Mrs Lorraine Wiseman.

The complaint charged them with conspiracy to obstruct justice and giving false evidence before the Grand Jury. The counts carried punishment of up to fourteen years' imprisonment.

Before the trial opened, both sides as usual jockeyed for position. There was an uninhibited discussion of all the evidence. It was conceded that, however reprehensible Mrs McPherson's conduct had been, she had not actually committed a crime.

Then a new witness came upon the scene with a curious story. She was a young woman named Bernice Morris who had been secretary to a blind attorney named McKinley. Aimee and her mother had employed McKinley to try and trace the alleged kidnappers, or at least to establish their existence by fair means or foul. During his investigation McKinley had been killed in a road accident – Aimee appeared to have gone to great lengths to prove the existence of her non-existent kidnappers.

Meanwhile the religious circus went on non-stop at the Angelus Temple. Between the Hallelujahs, Praise the Lords, and cries of Sweet Jesus and Fight the Devil, it seemed more concerned to save Aimee's reputation than to save souls for Jesus, though nothing stopped the endless clink of money being extracted from the faithful.

The trial which began before Judge Blake on Monday, 27 September, 1926 was a preliminary hearing to decide whether there was sufficient evidence against the defendants for them to be sent for trial before a higher court.

The world expected their share of scandal. Reporters arrived from every corner of the globe. The correspondent of the London *Daily Mail* was instructed to cable at least a thousand words daily.

In his opening District Attorney Keyes stated he was prepared to prove that the kidnapping story was a fabrication, and that to support it Mrs McPherson and Mrs Kennedy had conspired to commit acts injurious to public morals and to obstruct justice. He claimed evidence that Mrs McPherson had hidden at Carmel with Kenneth Ormiston with the knowledge and consent of her mother, and then tried to get other

117

persons indicted for the fictitious kidnapping; that Mrs McPherson had hired and paid Mrs Wiseman to produce a false Miss X, that she prepared and signed false affidavits, and finally that she hired and paid McKinley to manufacture false evidence.

Five witnesses then went into the box and identified Aimee as the woman who occupied the Carmel cottage with Ormiston.

After the first day's hearing Aimee introduced a new and startling element into the proceedings. She discussed the day's events in court in her Temple and on the radio and said a lot of derisive things about those who had given evidence against her, calling them 'a fine little bunch of parrots who recited their pieces just as they were schooled to do for months'.

The case proceeded on these lines. When evidence of immorality between Aimee and Ormiston was given by hotel employees, Aimee furiously called the District Attorney 'a dirty, lecherous libertine' in her jeering radio commentary on the proceedings that night.

Daily the evidence mounted against her. Deputy District Attorney Ryan continued to affirm that his investigations utterly refuted her kidnapping story. He was savagely mauled in cross-examination, but gave as good as he got.

Despite protests from the prosecution Aimee's attorney, Gilbert, maintained that Ryan was prejudiced against Aimee from the start, and had taken a venomous and 'unholy interest' in the prosecution.

'I took no unholy interest in this case,' retorted Ryan. 'This has been the most atrocious thing that ever transpired.'

'You batted a woman's name around because your curiosity was aroused?'

'No, sir. I didn't bat her name around. She batted her name around.'

'I want you to tell the court when you made up your mind that Aimee Semple McPherson's story of her kidnapping was false,' demanded Gilbert amid a storm of objections which the Judge overruled.

'I made up my mind,' replied Ryan unruffled, 'when I saw

that Kenneth G. Ormiston was up there at Carmel, and when I examined those grocery slips, and when I compared the handwriting with the "Light and Darkness" sermon notes written by Mrs McPherson, and when I had an opportunity to trace down Ormiston's movements step by step.'

As Gilbert's questioning became more belligerent, so did Ryan's answers. He maintained that he went to Douglas, Arizona, where Mrs McPherson was in hospital after her reappearance on 23 June, with an open mind. But there were some parts of her story he didn't believe.

'What parts of her story didn't you believe?'

'What didn't I believe? You want everything?'

'You heard my question,' snapped Gilbert.

'All right. I'll give it all to you. I didn't believe in the existence of the shack. I didn't believe in Rose and Steve. I didn't believe she was bound. I don't believe she was ever incarcerated. I don't believe she walked that distance. And that's that.'

'Didn't you say you were going to Douglas to break Mrs McPherson?'

'Absolutely not.'

Gilbert questioned him about the behaviour of Aimee's children. 'The little children were not involved in this gigantic conspiracy, were they? They hadn't seen her while she was away, had they?'

Ryan smiled cynically. 'I'm not so sure. They showed a total lack of emotion, and were unmoved when they first met their mother in hospital.' He said that Aimee kissed them and asked: 'Are you glad your mother is alive?' and then immediately afterwards said: 'Let's have our pictures taken.'

'Weren't the children embarrassed by all the cameramen?' asked Gilbert.

'No, they had had too many rehearsals.'

'And when did you first make up your mind that Mrs McPherson's story was a fake?'

'When I returned from Carmel,' replied Ryan. 'Then I knew she was a fake and a hypocrite.'

This was strong stuff. Ryan wasn't the kind of stumbling, hesitant witness Aimee liked to see in the box and make fun of later on her radio show. Salacious stories about her without number were going the rounds, and someone said, referring to the absence of sweat on her clothes after her alleged desert walk, 'Had Aimee sweated more then, she might be sweating less now.'

But everything in this strange case didn't go entirely against Aimee. Right in the middle of the trial District Attorney Keyes was arraigned in an adjoining court on criminal charges of conspiracy to defraud. This most embarrassing action was adjourned until he had disposed of his duties as prosecutor in the McPherson case, and it hardly added to his stature in court.

Mrs Lorraine Wiseman presently went into the box and entirely reversed her original story. Aimee, she now explained, had admitted to her to have stayed with Ormiston at Carmel, and subsequently they had cooked up the Miss X hoax between them. To put the story across they had considered it essential that she, Mrs Wiseman, should look as much like Aimee as possible, and Aimee had assisted her to this end.

A blistering cross-examination did not shake her story, though in view of her reputation with the police and the fact that she had spent time in a mental hospital, it was not difficult for the defence to discredit her.

Rather more difficult to discredit was the highly respectable Bernice Morris, a law student, with her story of how Aimee and her mother hired her late employer, Attorney McKinley, to manufacture false evidence about the alleged kidnapping.

Among the defence witnesses were two judges. Judge Bardin declared that a Mrs Kimball had signed an affidavit in his office to the effect that she was the mysterious Miss X. Superior Judge Carlos S. Hardy was a friend of Aimee and her mother, and such a distinguished witness was calculated to do much in her favour.

Cross-examination was conducted by Attorney Dennison who addressed the judge in a quiet, respectful voice.

'Did you believe the story of McKinley?'

'Yes, I believed it.'

'Do you believe that Mrs McPherson was kidnapped?'

The judge hedged. 'I have no reason to believe otherwise.'

'I didn't ask you that,' said Dennison speaking softly in the hushed silence. 'I asked you whether you still believe that Mrs McPherson was kidnapped.'

The judge hesitated, fatally perhaps, then replied: 'Yes, I do.' The impression was created that he could hardly have made any other reply.

Judge Blake gave his decision on 3 November. He found that there was sufficient cause to believe the defendants guilty. He ordered them to be held for trial on three counts, each count carrying a penalty of one to fourteen years in prison.

Aimee was stunned, but the worst was perhaps to come, when the newshounds in their relentless pursuit of titbits for the sex-hungry public, unearthed a trunk in New York, said to have been left in a hotel by Ormiston. It was crammed with frilly women's clothes, both intimate and otherwise, all bought in Los Angeles, all Aimee's size and some bearing the marks of Aimee's laundry.

Also found were sloppy love letters which Aimee had written to Ormiston. The whole precious load was entrained under guard to Los Angeles for the final undoing and humiliation of Sister McPherson who remained obstinately defiant and continued preaching in the Temple such sermons as 'The Greatest Liar in Los Angeles'.

Then all of a sudden District Attorney Keyes announced that the trial would not continue. On 10 January he asked the court to dismiss all the charges on the ground that it would be impossible to get a conviction.

The court assented. Aimee fainted.

According to rumour, there was no reason for her to be surprised, for it was said that a $30,000 pay-off was involved, and the fact that the District Attorney later went to prison for corruption lends substance to the rumour.

The elusive Ormiston finally turned up, but no one was interested in him now, least of all Aimee who celebrated her great acquittal by going on a national 'rehabilitation tour'. She discovered to her sorrow and disappointment that the public weren't half as interested in the rehabilitated Aimee as in the notorious one. It was sex, not sermons they wanted. In any case not many people believed in her innocence.

Ormiston returned to his radio business and was a popular chief engineer of a Los Angeles radio station when he died in 1937 at the age of 41. District Attorney Keyes, after serving nineteenth months in San Quentin prison, was released in 1931 and three years later died of a stroke at his Beverly Hills home. Joseph Ryan resigned as his deputy in 1927 after accusing Keyes of irregularities in his office, adding that during the McPherson affair, the District Attorney never drew a sober breath. Ryan left politics and went back to law. He died of a heart attack in 1951. Judge Hardy was impeached in 1928 for accepting money from Aimee McPherson. He died in 1948.

Aimee herself lived on until 1944, sinking into obscurity. The end of her case was the end of her era. She belonged to the twenties and when the twenties were finished the world had finished with her.

# Chapter 6
# Thomas Picton

The island of Trinidad became part of the British Empire on 18 February, 1797 as a consequence of Sir Ralph Abercromby's military expedition which drove the Spanish out of the West Indies.

Abercromby appointed Lieutenant-Colonel Thomas Picton as Trinidad's first Governor.

He could hardly have made a worse choice. Picton was a brave and ruthless soldier with neither experience nor qualifications for administration. Discipline was his god and discipline, in the British Army at the end of the eighteenth century was brutally enforced.

Abercromby had agreed with the inhabitants of Trinidad that their own laws should continue to be administered until such time as His Britannic Majesty should grant to his new subjects the sacred privileges of the laws of England.

Picton was duly instructed, and Abercromby left the Trinidadians to his tender mercies.

Ruthless military discipline was immediately imposed. At first the inhabitants of the island welcomed this iron hand, for it was applied to innumerable criminals and outlaws who had flocked there before the British came. Picton put them down with great ferocity and restored order to Trinidad. For such excellent work in the imperial cause he was made a Brigadier-General.

But Picton didn't stop there. Having eliminated the malefactors, he applied the iron hand to the inhabitants in general. There was soon a great outcry. Stories of dark deeds and cruel injustices reached England with such persistence that the Government sent out a Commission under Colonel William Fullarton to investigate. Fullarton who reached Trinidad early in 1803 found that the rumours were by no means exaggerated.

Among the crimes attributed to Governor Picton was the flogging to death of a slave, Goliath, who was owned by a planter named Dawson, noted for his humanity towards his human cattle. Goliath had a pass to go to church every Sunday, despite of which he was arrested and thrown into jail. Many white people were against Negro slaves going to church, for fear they might learn there something about the equality and brotherhood of man and thus become discontented with their lot. When Dawson made a personal protest to Picton about the imprisonment of Goliath, the Governor upbraided him for allowing his slaves too much freedom. 'I will humble them!' he exclaimed. Later Goliath was found dying at the gates of his master's plantation. All the flesh had been torn off his back by prolonged and merciless flogging.

Soldiers had been hanged for alleged crimes without any form of trial. Slaves had been unlawfully seized. Two West Indians had been burnt at the stake for trifling offences.

Although Picton tried to discredit Fullarton with accusations of jealousy, even insanity, he found himself in an impossible position. The rest of the Commission were solidly behind Fullarton. Picton was forced to resign his governorship. He sailed secretly from Port of Spain at dead of night.

When he arrived in England in December, 1803 he was astonished and dismayed to find public hostility towards him as strong as it had been in Trinidad. There was a great public clamour that he should be brought to trial. Doubtless the authorities would have preferred not to have taken any proceedings as Picton was a good and brave soldier and soldiers were urgently wanted for the war with Napoleon.

But the wave of liberalism and humanitarianism, inspired by the principles which had brought about the French Revolution, was impossible to resist. Some action had to be taken against Picton whose inhumanities were somehow causing more public concern than Napoleon's career of aggression in Europe.

It was politically desirable therefore to bring Picton to trial. But the authorities chose none of the enormities with which he was accused in Trinidad and which could have been used to frame a capital charge against him. He was charged with the more or less technical offence of permitting the application of torture under the Spanish law he had to administer.

The case centred around an immoral half-caste girl of eleven years old named Luisa Calderon. As is often the case in countries where the climate brings females to the flower of womanhood before they reach their teens, Luisa, though of tender age, was no child. She may of course have been innocent when her mother came to an agreement with a Trinidad businessman named Don Pedro Rouis, whereby she would do his housework and share his bed in return for their joint keep. This kind of domestic arrangement was not unusual in those days.

Under Don Pedro's tutelage Luisa seems to have developed into a sexy little minx and she was presently having an intrigue with a scoundrel by the name of Carlos Gonzales, a so-called friend of Don Pedro. Not content with stealing the favours of Don Pedro's young mistress, Gonzales broke into the house and robbed him of £2,000. Some said that Luisa knew nothing of Gonzales's intention, others alleged that she and her mother let Gonzales in during Don Pedro's absence and facilitated his getaway.

In any event they were both arrested and charged with complicity in the robbery. Luisa was taken before the magistrate. She denied that she knew anything about her lover's crime. The magistrate, though he did not believe her, had no power to take further action against her without the authority of the Governor. Picton, when appealed to, replied with a signed note which read: 'Inflict the torture on Luisa Calderon.'

The terrified child, still protesting her innocence, was then taken to a cell and picketed, a form of punishment used on British soldiers. Her left wrist was tied to a rope which passed over a pulley fixed in the ceiling. Her right hand was lashed to her left foot. She was then suspended on the rope in such a manner that the entire weight of her body rested on her other foot which was placed on a sharp wooden stake.

Picton was arrested by order of the Privy Council and tried before Lord Ellenborough at the Court of King's Bench on 24 February, 1806. Mr Garrow prosecuted for the Crown. Mr Dallas appeared for the defendant.

Thomas Picton himself did not go into the courtroom to hear the trial. During the proceedings which lasted from nine in the morning until seven at night he paced up and down the hall of the courts, accompanied by several civil officers from Trinidad. He was forty-eight at this time, a tall, sallow-complexioned man dressed in black and doubtless enduring a greater ordeal than anything he experienced on the field of battle.

Opening the case for the prosecution, Garrow, while expressing the strongest desire for condign punishment for the perpetrator of so flagrant an offence, said no one would be more happy than he if the facts justified the jury finding the accused innocent. He made this rather curious opening because it was so repugnant to think that the British character could be stained by such a thing as the torture of a suspected criminal. (The fact that this precise form of torture was regularly inflicted upon recalcitrant British soldiers made nonsense not only of what counsel was saying, but of the whole trial.)

Garrow proceeded: 'The case is that a representative of the King in one of the dependencies of this country, bound to protect the subjects of it against all species of vileness, has abused his situation and discredited the country to which he belongs by inflicting what, in England, few have ever heard of, and have only read of with detestation and horror – the torture of one of His Majesty's subjects without the least pretence of law, the least justification. He has gratified on a helpless girl his tyrannical disposition to oppress, and the benignant code of laws which had prevailed in the island were unhappily cruelly innovated under his administration.'

Counsel then outlined the events which led to the arrest of Luisa Calderon whose abundant sex life at the age of eleven was a source of wonderment to the English jury and had to be explained as the normal thing in Trinidad where girls became mothers at twelve and lived in concubinage, 'if from their condition they could not form a more honourable connection'.

Garrow recounted young Luisa's immoralities in as sympathetic a manner as possible – after all, he was calling her as his chief witness – and then dilated upon her terrible sufferings.

He produced a drawing in watercolours representing Luisa under the torture, her sufferings being administered by a brute-faced looking Negro. Garrow handed the drawing to Lord Ellenborough. When the Judge had examined it he advised that it should not be shown to the jury if the defence objected. Strangely enough, defence counsel Dallas made no objection and the picture was passed to the jury.

The prosecuting counsel pointed out that even if – as he anticipated the defence would maintain – under the laws of Spain torture could be used in Trinidad, there was still no justification for a British governor to apply it. The Governor ought to have been aware that torture was not known in England, and that it never would be, never could be, tolerated.

Garrow held, however, that torture had actually never been used in Trinidad – and he claimed to be prepared to support such a statement with evidence – 'until the defendant cursed the island with its production'.

Luisa Calderon then gave evidence. She had been brought to England with other witnesses by Colonel Fullarton when he heard her story. Luisa was now sixteen. Her appearance caused something of a sensation in court. She was a slim, delicate girl, exceedingly pretty, and she moved with a natural grace. She wore a white muslin gown and a dazzling white turban from which protruded curly wisps of her raven hair. She was described as being 'of a very genteel appearance'. She spoke little English and gave her evidence through a Spanish interpreter in a soft voice which fascinated all who heard it.

It was obvious that the Crown had an extremely appealing witness – despite her morals for which she could hardly be held responsible.

She told the court that in 1801 she was living in the house of Don Pedro Ruiz. She remembered the robbery. She recollected that she and her mother were arrested on suspicion and brought before Governor Picton who threatened her that, unless she did confess who had stolen the money, the hangman would have to deal with her. (According to the story told to Fullarton's Commission, she had been taken before a magistrate and not the Governor.)

Luisa explained that she had then been taken to the jail and threatened: She would be spared if she confessed; if not, she would be tortured. When she persisted in her innocence a Negro was brought in and tortured before her eyes.

Though terrified, she still refused to say anything. She was then tortured herself. The picture which had been introduced into the court was shown to her. She looked at it and shuddered with horror – reaction which Garrow described as accidental, but conclusive, evidence of the fact.

Luisa related that she had remained upon the spike in this agonizing state of torment for three-quarters of an hour. Eventually she had not been able to stand the pain any longer and screamed out that she was guilty. But as soon as she had been released and further questioned, she retracted and again maintained her innocence. Put once more to the torture, she had remained on the spike for twenty-two minutes. When she was taken down she fainted.

Afterwards she was taken to a cell and put into grillos. The grillo was a long piece of iron which was fastened to the wall. There were two rings for the feet. Her arms were bound. In this miserable and painful position she remained for eight months. Her wrists bore the marks of her punishment to that day. She displayed them to the court.

Don Rafael Shandoz, a police officer on the island, recounted that he saw the girl immediately after she had been tortured. She was confined in a kind of garret with a low sloping roof. The grillos were placed in such a position in the low room that she could hardly raise herself up. She had no advocate to advise her and no surgeon to attend her. Her jailer was the Negro who had tortured her.

Don Rafael claimed that he had in fact never known torture to be inflicted in Trinidad until the arrival of Governor Picton – a point that was substantiated by Don Juan Montes later on during the trial. The first time Don Rafael had seen such an instrument as the picket was in the barracks of the English soldiers. It had been in use in the jail about six months before Luisa Calderon was tortured on it. The first torture he witnessed in Trinidad had been by the direction of Governor Picton who had instructed the jailer: 'Go and fetch the black man to the picket guard and put him to the torture.'

The order for the application of the torture – *'applicase la question a Luisa Calderon'* – was produced in the handwriting of the accused.

This completed the case for the prosecution.

Mr Dallas for the defence attempted to put a different light on the case. When the late Sir Ralph Abercromby – Abercromby had died in active service in Egypt, in 1801 – appointed Picton Governor of Trinidad, Dallas reminded the court, he had ordered him to abide by the existing laws of the island, until otherwise instructed from London.

'Now the law was Spanish law,' Dallas emphasized, 'and in the neighbouring island of St Vincent, it was a well-known fact that torture existed.'

The Judge intervened. 'The question is, Mr Dallas, whether torture existed in Trinidad. Was the punishment unlawful, in which case the law infers malice, or was it authorized by the law of Spain? If so, the case should be transferred to a special verdict.'

Dallas then called the Attorney-General of Trinidad who

produced various legal books of the Spanish West Indian islands. Certain passages were translated for the purpose of showing that torture was permitted in such circumstances as those before the court.

The Crown produced evidence in rebuttal and called Don Pedro de Vargass, a lawyer who had practised in the Spanish colonial law courts. He said that there was nothing in Spanish law to justify the infliction of torture, and to his knowledge torture was never resorted to. A law of Old Castile dated 1260 permitted torture in certain cases, but he understood that it was never extended to the West Indies, and it was so much abhorred in Spain that it was either repealed or had fallen entirely into disuse.

After counsel had addressed the jury, Lord Ellenborough summed up rather in favour of the accused. It was for the jury to say, in the absence of all positive proof on the subject and in the face of so much negative evidence, whether the law of Spain was so fully and completely established in Trinidad as to make torture a part of the law of that island. Without going through the authorities, he thought the jury might take it to be the existing law of Old Spain that torture could be inflicted.

The jury did not share Lord Ellenborough's opinion on the matter. They concluded that there was no such law existing in Trinidad as that of torture at the time of the surrender of the island to the British. The accused was pronounced guilty.

But a new trial was moved on various grounds which included 'the infamous character' of Luisa Calderon and the fact that Picton did not proceed from any motives of malice, but from a conviction that the right of torture was sanctioned by the laws of Trinidad which he had been ordered to enforce.

Picton was allowed bail for £40,000 and in 1808 a re-trial was held before Lord Ellenborough at which the verdict of guilty was superseded by a special verdict which did not give any judgement, and so the proceedings against Picton were dropped. Despite the evidence of the first trial, the court apparently was satisfied that the law of Spain permitted the existence of torture in Trinidad at the time of its cession to Great Britain.

The fact that the same torture which Luisa Calderon suffered was freely inflicted upon the soldiers of His Britannic Majesty's forces at the time may have had something to do with the decision.

The inhabitants of Trinidad were not entirely against their former governor. They presented him with a sword of honour and subscribed £4,000 towards his legal expenses. Picton returned the money to them asking that it be used for the relief of suffering caused by a widespread fire in Port of Spain.

Picton's supporters in England were both forthright and vocal. One wrote in a monthly periodical of the time:

'In an evil hour the Governor associated with him, in the government of the island, the British naval commander on the station, and Colonel Fullarton. This was, as might naturally have been expected and as certainly was designed by one of the parties, the origin of dispute and the source of anarchy. It is well known that Fullarton on his return to England preferred charges against Picton, which were taken into consideration by the Privy Council, and gave rise to a prosecution that lasted for several years. No pains were spared to sully his character, to ruin his fortunes, and to render him an object of public indignation.

'A little strumpet by name Louisa Calderon, who cohabited with a petty tradesman in the capital of Trinidad, let another paramour into his house (of which she had the charge) during his absence, who robbed him, with her knowledge and privity, of all he was worth in the world. The girl was taken before the regular judges of the place; who, in the course of their investigation, ascertained the fact that she was privy to the robbery, and therefore sentenced her, in conformity with the laws of Spain, then prevalent in the island, to undergo the punishment of the *picket* (the same as is adopted in our own regiments of horse).

'But as it was necessary that this sentence should receive the governor's confirmation before it could be carried into effect, a paper stating the necessity of it was sent to the government-house, and the governor, by his signature, conveyed his assent to the judges. The girl was accordingly picketed, when she acknowledged the facts above stated and discovered her accomplice.

'That the life of this girl was forfeited by the laws of every civilized country is a fact that will not admit of dispute. Yet clemency was extended to her, and she was released, having suffered only the punishment above stated, which was so slight that she walked a considerable distance to the prison without the least appearance of suffering, immediately after it was inflicted.

'But what was the return for the leniency of the governor? He was accused by Colonel Fullarton of having put this girl (whom he had never even seen) to the torture, contrary to law; and the caricaturists of England were enlisted in the service of persecution. After a trial which seemed to have no end, after an expense of seven thousand pounds (which must have completed his ruin, had not his venerable uncle, General Picton, defrayed the whole costs of the suit, while the expenses of his prosecutor were all paid by the government) his honour and justice were established on the firmest basis, and to the perfect satisfaction of every upright mind.'

This account of the affair considerably differs from that given in court. But whatever the truth is, the unfortunate girl received harsh treatment, even though the early nineteenth-century writer reckoned that her life should have been forfeited 'by the laws of every civilized country'.

As for Picton, he rejoined the army which he should never have left. In 1810 he was appointed to command a division in Spain at Wellington's express request. He was wounded at Badajoz in 1812 but refused to leave the ramparts. He had just inherited a fortune and he gave every surviving member of his command a guinea. The following year he was invalided home to England.

In 1815 he was knighted for his services during the war and received the especial thanks from the Commons for his great services. During the Hundred Days he was severely wounded at Quatre Bras. But he concealed his injury and despite considerable pain insisted upon leading his men into battle at Waterloo where in the thickest part of the action he was shot in the head by a musket ball and killed instantly. His body was brought home to London and interred in the family vault at St George's, Hanover Square. Parliament ordered a monument to be erected to his memory in St Paul's Cathedral.

# Chapter 7
# Marie Besnard

Some people think that Marie Besnard suffered one of the greatest wrongs at the ponderous hand of French justice since Dreyfus.

Marie Besnard was known alternately as the Black Widow or Good Lady of Loudun, and in 1949 was accused of murdering by poison eleven people including her husband. Whatever one's views on this case, it certainly showed French criminal administration at its worst. The case lasted twelve years, five of which Marie Besnard spent in prison.

She had three trials. The first one exposed the weakness of the scientific evidence in such a manner that under Anglo-Saxon justice all proceedings against her would have been dismissed or abandoned.

In the accusatorial system of justice which is practised in England and America it is the prosecution which has to prove the guilt of the accused. Guilt must be proved beyond a shadow of doubt: the accused is presumed innocent until proved guilty. In France and many Continental countries, however, the inquisitorial system is in force; here the innocence of the accused person is not automatically taken for granted until guilt is proved.

The two systems, though fundamentally different in procedure, have their advantages and disadvantages. Grave miscarriages of justice can occur, and indeed have taken place under either.

Marie Besnard suffered the full disadvantage of the inquisitorial system, one of which is the prolongation of the criminal prosecution – in her case to twelve years. This is considered inhuman under the English system which insists upon a speedy trial. Guilt must not only be proved beyond reasonable doubt, but within reasonable time.

Marie Joséphine Philippine Besnard was born in 1896 of a family of farmers and landowners who represent the cream of French agricultural prosperity. In 1919 she married her cousin Auguste Antigy who died in 1927. In 1929 she married Léon Besnard who owned a shop in Loudun which sold rope. Besnard died on 25 October, 1947 of heart disease.

The Second World War and the Occupation had brought out the best in some French people and the worst in others. After the Germans left, there was an orgy of denunciations against those alleged to have fraternized with the Germans. At the end of the war a German prisoner named Dietz worked for the Besnards. Marie was suspected of having an affair with him. After her husband's death the gossips accused her of murdering Léon. A letter was sent to the local police alleging she had poisoned him because of his jealousy. Marie was all for bringing a libel case, but her lawyer persuaded her not to.

The police, however, listened avidly to all the scandal and gossip which was retailed to them. There also were suggestions that she had poisoned other members of her husband's family in order to get hold of the family property. On 11 May, 1949, Léon Besnard's body was exhumed, and the analyst reported large quantities of arsenic in his remains.

On 21 July, Mme Besnard was arrested by two policemen whose names were Nocquet and Chaumier. According to her, they were most offensive when she declined to confess her guilt.

They threatened: 'It will be much more serious for you if you're obstinate, whereas if you tell the truth we'll get you off easily.'

Dietz was also questioned. Apparently he was told that Marie had confessed in a manner which implicated him; while she was told that Dietz had not only admitted being her lover, but had given away Marie's confidence that she had poisoned her husband.

Marie Besnard was not easily taken in. In fact, during the whole of her twelve-years' ordeal she kept her head in the most remarkable manner. Her stolid obstinacy and her iron-clad resistance to prolonged police pressure obviously led her prosecutors to assume that no innocent person would present such a flintlike face to the pressure they put upon her. It did not occur to them that Marie might have been just a determined, strong-minded woman refusing to submit to a monstrous injustice.

They took her to Poitiers prison where she was examined by the *juge d'instruction*, M. Roger, who informed her that Dr Béroud, the famous Marseilles police toxicologist, had detected an abnormal quantity of arsenic in Léon Besnard's internal organs. When Marie and her legal advisers requested an examination of the remains by another expert, the judge very sharply put them in their place.

'A man of Dr Béroud's competence and reputation is never wrong.' The thing for Mme Besnard to do was to confess, rather than question the competence of renowned experts. This was put to her even more strongly by the police in the seclusion of her prison cell.

'You'd better confess now, you old witch,' they told her. 'The analysis was positive. You stuffed your husband full of arsenic.' When she still refused to admit to a crime she had not committed, they threatened: 'Do we have to knock you about to make you confess? If you were a man, you'd see what you'd get.' She told them that she did not believe her husband died of poison. 'You won't escape, you old bitch,' they continued to threaten. 'They'll cut your head off.'

Judge Roger treated her more politely, though he informed her brusquely that she didn't know what she was talking about when she suggested that Dr Béroud had made a mistake. The Judge declared that Béroud's decisions could not be disputed and she had better accept them, for there would be no second examination. The Judge further pointed out that Béroud was chosen to make the examination because he did not know her and was unaware of the local rumours circulating about her. His examination therefore, apart from being expert and indisputable, would have been totally unbiased.

The Judge regarded Marie with such suspicion and took the stories circulating about her in Loudun so seriously that he ordered the exhumation of the bodies of every member of her family who had died within the last twenty-five years. Boxes containing the remains of ten more people were sent to Marseilles where Béroud in the course of time reported quantities of arsenic present in all of them.

Consequently Marie Besnard was accused of poisoning ten other people who included her own father and mother and her husband's father, mother and sister. The motive was ascribed as personal gain, for the whole of the considerable family property had fallen to her.

She had been arrested in July, 1949, but was not brought to trial until February, 1952. In the meantime the evidence against her appeared to accumulate overwhelmingly. She was represented in the Press as a monster, an ogre, to be compared with Landru and Petiot. In France it was a time for revenge. War and defeat required scapegoats rather than heroes.

In prison tremendous pressure by the police was brought to bear upon the obstinate Marie. Her lawyer, Maître Hayot, intervened in this tough, and quite unauthorized police inquisition, and forbade her to answer any questions except in the presence of her lawyers.

But this did not stop the war of nerves which went on in the prison. She shared cells with other prisoners who, acting under police orders, told her that her defence was hopeless, that her lawyers had given the case up, that unless she confessed she would either spend her life in prison or have her head cut off. Everything was done to shake her confidence and undermine her faith. The women who co-operated with the police in this contemptible work were let out of prison or given very light sentences for their own crimes.

The prosecution, despite their apparently overwhelming evidence, had their difficulties. Their case was by no means as conclusive as it was made out to be. The presence of arsenic in the bodies, even if it could be proved to have been the cause of the deaths involved, amounted to no more than suspicion against the accused woman. The rest of the evidence was little more than ill-natured gossip and hearsay. No one had seen Marie administer poison to any of her alleged victims. Hence the desperate attempts to make Marie confess.

Again and again the trial was postponed in the hope that fresh evidence of Marie's guilt would turn up, or that she would finally break down and confess as the result of the relentless campaign which was being waged upon her in prison. But there was no new evidence and Marie obstinately persisted in her innocence.

As the trial approached Maître Hayot suggested that the well-known Parisian lawyer, Maître Gautrat, should assist in the defence. Gautrat was undecided. But when he visited Marie at the prison and put her through an even more searching examination than her *juge d'instruction* he finally agreed to defend her.

The trial eventually opened at Poitiers on 20 February, 1952. It began with an examination of the accused by the Judge, President Favart. She was a diminutive figure standing in the box, dressed completely in black against which her face was greyish-white from her two and a half years in prison. She wore thick-lensed glasses. She was not a good witness. Her vagueness on many important points told in favour of the prosecution. During the afternoon interval, she broke down and wept uncontrollably, as she realized that everything had gone against her in that relentless examination.

But things began to turn more in her favour at the resumption when Maître Hayot strongly criticized both the examining judge and the police officer Nocquet for the manner in which the accused had been treated in prison.

The famous Dr Béroud, of Marseilles, then gave evidence.

He could not, of course, say that a criminal hand had administered the arsenic, but there could be, or so he stated himself, no possible doubt about his findings.

Maître Gautrat, however, soon made it clear that he had scant respect either for Dr Béroud or his findings. He had already established, much to the astonishment of the *Avocat-Général*, that when the jars containing the essential parts of the exhumed bodies were sent from Poitiers to Marseilles, they seemed in some strange way to multiply. More jars arrived at Marseilles than left Poitiers. The various lists were examined in the court, and there was no doubt about the truth of Gautrat's revelation. There could be only two explanations, Gautrat pointed out. Either extra jars were added during the journey or the jars had been added in the Marseilles laboratory.

While the reporters rushed to the phones to report this latest sensation, the President invited Dr Béroud to explain the mystery.

This the highly embarrassed Béroud was unable to do. Gautrat, suavely and cunningly came to his rescue. Of course such a thing could easily happen in a big laboratory as his. 'You are a great expert and receive many such jars a day. And as these jars are put on the shelves, they may get muddled.' Such a thing must often happen, Gautrat wickedly concluded – so, when Béroud reported that he found arsenic in the intestines, he must have analysed the intestines of a body unconnected with the Besnard case. Outraged at such a suggestion, Béroud took off his spectacles, and wiped the sweat from his face, as Gautrat reminded him that he had once analysed an eye from a body which had been in its grave for five years, although, as Gautrat told him, an eye decomposes within five weeks.

This was all highly embarrassing not only for Dr Béroud who was having his much-prized reputation seriously deflated but also for the *Avocat-Général*, and indeed the court itself which was accustomed to lean heavily upon the authority of such an expert.

But Gautrat had not finished yet. His intention was utterly to discredit the far-famed Béroud. After getting Béroud to admit his usual assertion that he could clearly distinguish the arsenic rings in a glass tube, he handed him six glass tubes and asked him to tell the court which of these contained arsenic. After carefully examining them, Béroud returned three of the tubes to counsel.

Gautrat informed him in wounding terms, heavy with sarcasm, that none of the tubes contained arsenic. He had the written guarantee of the laboratory which had provided them.

The court collapsed in uproar. Gales of laughter swept around the infuriated Dr Béroud who sat slumped in his chair. Even the President hid his smiles in the sleeves of his judicial gown.

When silence was restored Maître Hayot jumped to his feet. He read to the court the letter which Béroud had written to the *juge d'instruction*, claiming that it was not necessary to examine scientifically what was in the tube, for a clever and experienced eye could not be mistaken.

'You have just put that to the test, Dr Béroud,' he said. 'You have been proved wrong.'

Tumult broke out again. There were some who did not like this turn of events in Marie Besnard's favour. President Favart promptly suspended the hearing.

After such a rout, a prosecution would ordinarily have reconsidered its position, and even withdrawn capital charges based upon 'scientific' evidence so easily discredited. But the *Avocat-Général* indicated no such move.

Following his slip-up in court, Dr Béroud slipped up also on leaving the Palais. He had a heavy fall and was unable to appear in court the following day. He sent his assistant, Dr Médaille, in his place. Médaille too had a bad time at the hands of the defence counsel who established without difficulty that the Marseilles laboratory had got the bodies all thoroughly mixed up and didn't know whose viscera matched whose muscles – in one instance they had found an eye in a skeleton.

Other experts went into the box. According to their statements, the muddle among the cadavers at Marseilles had been so great that all the work would have to be done again.

Professor Perperot, the chemistry expert to the Paris Court of Appeal, mentioned that Béroud's methods of work would not have enabled him to find arsenic, even if there had been any; they were the methods of an ignoramus.

Béroud, injured both in body and reputation, turned up at the last day of the hearing. He leaned heavily on two gendarmes and refused to answer any more questions.

'I am not here to pass an examination,' he declared. 'I proceeded in the way my masters taught me. That is all.'

The case was hurriedly adjourned to enable other experts to get to work on the evidence.

Marie had manifestly won the first round, but she was still kept in prison while the experts tried to sort out the muddled remains of her exhumed relatives.

The charges were reduced from eleven to five. The second trial began at Bordeaux on 15 March, 1954. To Marie Besnard's counsel was now added Maître Jacqueline Favreau-Colombier, an attractive young woman barrister who not only assisted her in her defence in court, but came to see her every day in prison and looked after her interests and personal problems as only a woman could.

The devotion of Madame Favreau-Colombier, wrote Marie Besnard* afterwards, 'who was defending me as she would have defended herself, was a miracle, like Christmas. She could have been my daughter, and it was she who was protecting me.'

The second trial was before President Pourquery de Boisserin. There was a different *Avocat-Général* prosecuting.

After the customary examination of the accused, the psychiatrist who had examined Marie gave evidence. He expressed the opinion that Marie was 'abnormally normal', and he protested against stool pigeons being placed in her cell in an attempt to demoralize her into making a confession. One of these stool pigeons gave evidence and admitted that she had been freed by the *juge d'instruction* immediately afterwards.

* In *The Trial of Marie Besnard* (transl. by Denise Folliot), William Heinemann Ltd, 1963

Marie's enemies then trooped into the box and repeated their malicious accusations against her, though with perhaps less conviction than before. To one of them Maître Gautrat put the question: 'Now you know the Béroud report was false, do you still believe that your friend Marie is guilty?' The answer was: 'No, I don't believe it.'

There was a dramatic silence and Gautrat turned to the *Avocat-Général* and said: 'Do you not have the impression that the accusation has crumbled?'

But the evidence of the experts had yet to be dealt with. They had been working on the specimens with the help of an atomic pile and a Geiger counter. Once again Gautrat confounded them, accusing them of incompetence, of even falsifying the results. In particular he attacked M. Griffon, Director of the Toxicological Laboratory of the Police Prefecture in Paris, the inventor of the nuclear-physics text for finding arsenic in hair.

At first Griffon refused to give the details of his methods. When Marie's lawyers prodded him he merely exclaimed: 'Ah, I found arsenic, and you don't like that!' But Gautrat didn't let him get away with that. He discussed Griffon's work on the atomic pile and suggested that his calculations were not done properly. Gautrat drew attention to the fact that English nuclear physicists disagreed with Griffon's methods. 'Your results cannot be admitted as they allow for an error of eighty per cent. That is what they think of your method in England at the atomic centre, whose authority no one will contest.' He plainly told him that this method – washing the hair of dead bodies – could not remove the arsenic.

This criticism infuriated Griffon who claimed that the English did not know how to use the atomic pile. Gautrat in turn suggested that Griffon had better go to England and give them lessons.

'Are you an expert?' shouted Griffon, banging the witness-box.

'No,' replied Gautrat. 'But doctors Lebreton and Derobert do not agree with you. Neither does Smith in England. And they are experts.' He read out documents to substantiate his words.

After dealing very roughly with Griffon, Gautrat called expert witnesses of his own who called the scientific methods of the prosecution's experts dubious and old-fashioned.

So much doubt and discredit was cast upon the prosecution's case against Marie that immediate acquittal seemed the obvious and just result of the second trial. But in France reasonable doubt does not necessarily lead to acquittal.

The trial was once more adjourned which the President tried to justify by saying that the court and jury had not sufficient data upon which to pronounce judgement. This time, however, Marie Besnard was granted bail.

It took another seven years before the final trial. During this time Marie Besnard who had become known as the Black Widow lived under a deep cloud of suspicion. The delay was partly due to the difficulty in getting the scientific evidence re-assessed. Several of the experts including Professor Frédéric Joliot-Curie died during the course of the investigations, and so the whole thing had to start all over again.

The case had developed into a great judicial scandal when the final trial opened on 20 November, 1961 under President Nussy Saint-Saens. The prosecution now only wanted a nominal conviction which would save the face of the state authorities which had pursued what was obviously a hopeless case for so many years, and with such lack of charity.

But Marie's lawyers now scented complete victory and would have nothing but unconditional acquittal for their client. Maître Hayot quoted the late Professor Joliot-Curie's opinion that M. Griffon had falsified his results to make them fit the case. Maître Gautrat produced Griffon's laboratory forms – he had got hold of them only with great difficulty – which contained many scratched-out and altered figures.

'Here is the proof of a veritable fake!' he cried, waving it before the court.

The outraged Professor Griffon rushed to court to defend his scientific honour, but the President told him coolly: 'I must confess that a report like yours leaves a disagreeable impression.'

The defence now had little difficulty in demonstrating, with the assistance of scientific witnesses of their own, that all the expert evidence against Marie was worthless. Such arsenic as had been found in the bodies had come from the cemetery soil which – as Professor Perperot had proved and told the court earlier on – did contain arsenic; and another scientist had explained how buried bodies absorb arsenic.

Commissaire Nocquet was publicly accused of stirring up the case against Marie Besnard in order to acquire promotion and reputation. Jacqueline Favreau-Colombier said in ringing and scornful tones: 'The Marie Besnard they tried to show you was created by Commissaire Nocquet. Ah, if she had been guilty, what a fine career lay ahead of him!'

Marie Besnard was finally acquitted of all the counts against her. But her life was shattered, her health ruined, her mind filled with bitterness and scarred with awful memories. For that she has had no compensation.

# Chapter 8
# Henriette Caillaux

Every country has its judicial skeletons – England, Slater and Evans; America, Chessman and the Rosenbergs; France, Dreyfus and Besnard, and perhaps Caillaux.

Henriette Caillaux is one of the few people in history who literally got away with murder. She committed the crime before witnesses, but a jury acquitted her and she left the court triumphant over justice, with no penalty to pay, and theoretically without a stain on her character. Marie Besnard, though plainly innocent, endured infinitely more. Adelaide Bartlett, though the case against her was unproved, suffered the obloquy of the jury's doubts and escaped infamy only by vanishing into complete obscurity.

Henriette Caillaux is best compared with Charlotte Corday who also murdered in high places with the same magnificent aplomb and conviction that she was doing the right thing. But Corday did not get away with it, for the society in which she lived, though it begat modern France, was rougher with justice and unimpressed by the pretensions of outraged females who took the law into their own hands.

Madame Caillaux's victim was Gaston Calmette, one of

145

France's most eminent journalists. On 16 March, 1914, she shot him to death in his office at *Le Figaro*, of which he was Editor, practically in the presence of his staff.

It is true that both she and her husband had had much to endure from Calmette's persistent and vicious attacks upon them, and also – as they had been legally informed – that there was no judicial action they could take to protect themselves. The attacks had become extremely personal and touched upon Henriette's honour. A woman could not challenge a man to a duel, but she could certainly have recourse to firearms, and in her view that was the only way of dealing with an outrageous situation. It is not to be supposed that she intended to kill him, but she did believe, wrongly as it turned out, that the sword, or a least the gun, was mightier than the pen.

Gaston Calmette was a journalist of repute. He believed that it was his patriotic duty to expose Joseph Caillaux who was then Minister of Finance in M. Doumergue's government and who had been guilty of some outstanding political chicanery. *Le Figaro* was Paris's most important morning paper and its campaign against Caillaux had to be taken seriously.

Joseph Caillaux was born in 1863, son of Eugène Caillaux, who in the 1870s had held the offices of Minister of Public Works and Minister of Finance. Joseph Caillaux had a brilliant academic career and lectured at the Paris School of Political Science. In 1898 he entered the Chamber of Deputies and the following year became Minister of Finance. In this capacity he showed great administrative ability. He reformed France's fiscal system. In 1906, during his second term of office, under Clemenceau, he introduced income tax. His work in this direction has been described as 'the first serious attempt at a just and democratic form of taxation in France'.

In those supposedly tranquil years before 1914 Caillaux was entrusted with delicate negotiations with Germany which later were to bring upon him accusations of treason. Already he was the subject of the splenetic pen of M. Calmette.

Joseph Caillaux also had domestic problems. When he was

in his middle forties he fell in love with a divorced lady of thirty. Henriette Rainouard. His passion for Henriette was intense and was ardently returned. The only bar to their happiness was Mme Caillaux, Joseph's first wife, who was in no mood to be cast aside for the Rainouard girl who, as everyone knew, had been born nine months before, rather than after, her parents' wedding day.

The passionate affair between Henriette and the Minister of Finance continued despite the wife's disapproval. He called her Riri and in 1909 he wrote ardent love-letters to her on official notepaper, some of which contained an injudicious mixture of politics and passion.

Realizing afterwards how dangerous these letters would be in the wrong hands, he asked his mistress to return them to him. She promptly did. Caillaux, however, intoxicated by the sweet blandishments with which he had been delighting his mistress, could not bring himself to destroy them. Instead he locked them in a drawer in his desk. It was a foolish thing for him to do, for his suspicious wife was going through his personal materials with a fine toothcomb, and locked drawers are no bar to the depredations of a betrayed wife.

As soon as Caillaux found the explosive letters missing, he accused his wife of rifling his desk. She told him flatly that she had the letters and proceeded to blackmail him with them. Finally the letters were burnt and Caillaux broke it off with his mistress. But the marriage was wrecked. Mme Caillaux tried her best to prevent a divorce. She had got photographic copies of the Riri love-letters. She also possessed a highly indiscreet letter which Caillaux had written to her in 1901 which contained the following sentence and was signed 'Ton Jo': 'I have had a very gratifying success: I have *crushed* the Income Tax Bill while appearing to defend it, thereby pleasing the Centre and the Right, without too much upsetting the Left.'

To sophisticated minds, this is just normal political practice, and Caillaux who had resumed his association with Henriette Rainouard and was determined to make her his wife refused to be intimidated. Mme Caillaux finally agreed to surrender the 'Ton Jo' letter and divorce him by mutual consent. But the lady deceived him again and had the compromising letter photographed previously.

Caillaux married Henriette in October, 1911. His first wife became known as Mme Gueydan-Caillaux. The second marriage was an undoubted success. They were much in love and their ménage was socially very successful.

Shortly after his second marriage Caillaux learnt of the way in which his first wife had deceived him. The compromising letters were being hawked around the newspaper offices of Paris. Gaston Calmette, it seemed, was the only editor with the bile to use them against him.

Calmette's campaign started in 1913 and really got underway in 1914. It was not difficult to associate Caillaux, or indeed almost any other politician, with the many rich scandals of the day. But Gaston Calmette picked upon Caillaux with especial venom and attacked him with relentless persistence.

It is not always easy to understand why journalists pick upon one particular politician and hound him without mercy. It has been said that Calmette, like many journalists, suffered from *folie de grandeur*, and that Caillaux's refusal to resign after the first exposure of his political wrongdoings caused Calmette to mount the attack with increased persistence and viciousness.

In the first three months of 1914 not a day passed without an attack on Caillaux appearing in *Le Figaro*, either in the form of an editorial or a cartoon. He was accused of using his office corruptly to make money on the Stock Exchange, of selling the French Congo to the Germans, of influencing the Director of Public Prosecutions to delay the course of justice in the Rochette case, and of making a fortune out of the Franco-Moroccan negotiations. It was also said that a tiara worth three-quarters of a million francs which was given to Henriette Caillaux as a wedding present had been paid for by the Kaiser.

One thing was held in Calmette's defence. He honestly believed that Caillaux had had traitorous dealings with Germany, and later events suggested that there was some truth in his allegations.

On 13 March *Le Figaro* published the 'Ton Jo' letter containing the embarrassing aside quoted above. Calmette's comments were the usual mixture of piety and malice.

As this was one of the letters which Mme Gueydan-Caillaux was supposed to have destroyed both Caillaux and Henriette concluded that his indiscreet love-letters of 1909 were in Calmette's hands and would soon be splashed all over *Le Figaro*. Henriette sought legal advice, but was told that there was no way of stopping Calmette by judicial means.

She was determined that something must be done. Her own honour was at stake, for the letters made it plain enough that she had been her husband's mistress before their marriage.

When their friend, Judge Monier, told them there was nothing they could do, Caillaux exclaimed to his wife: 'Very well then, if there is no solution, at least I won't let him attack you with impunity. I'll break his neck.'

Whether or not Henriette Caillaux believed in her husband's intention to stop Calmette in his tracks, it was obvious to her that the situation was so urgent that it needed a woman's determined hand. It is not likely that she thought of herself in the role of Charlotte Corday just then. There was in any case no premeditated intent to kill Calmette, if we are to believe her actions and her thoughts on the afternoon of 16 March as she told them later in court.

The fact that she was giving a dinner party the following evening and went to an employment agency to select a new cook for the occasion, would suggest that murdering Gaston Calmette would so seriously interfere with her social activities as to be quite out of the question. It was while being at the agency that it first occurred to her to go to the offices of *Le Figaro*. Her intention was to make a demonstration, a violent one certainly, but not a murderous one.

She confessed that she had always carried a small revolver. 'It was a habit inculcated in my sister and myself by our father.' A strange home life indeed, for those were not wild and violent days in France. Henriette had mislaid her lethal little toy, she told afterwards, and as the election campaign was about to begin, she intended to replace it, because she would be travelling about alone. What, if any, use she intended to make of it upon her husband's electors she did not disclose. But the excuse seemed to go down all right in 1914 France.

So Mme Caillaux decided to combine the two actions of buying a revolver and protesting at the offices of *Le Figaro*. Perhaps if this wretched scribbler Calmette saw how outraged and determined she was, he would cease his malignant campaign against her and her husband.

These were the thoughts in her mind as she went to Gastinne-Renette, the gunsmiths, and bought a Browning revolver, had it loaded with bullets and charged to her husband's account. She returned to her car and directed her chauffeur to take her to the Crédit-Lyonnais where she had some business to transact, and then she told him to drive her to 26 rue Drouot, the office of *Le Figaro*. There she demanded to see Gaston Calmette and sent up her card.

Henriette's declared intentions at this point should be read in conjunction with a note which she had left for her husband before she left the house that afternoon:

> 'My beloved husband – When I told you this morning of my interview with President Monier, from whom I learnt that in France there is no law to protect us against the libels of the Press, you told me that one of these days you would break the vile Calmette's neck. I know your decision to be irrevocable. From that instant on, my mind was made up. I will see that justice is done. France and the Republic have need of you. I will carry out the task! If you should receive this letter, it will mean that I have obtained or tried to obtain justice. Forgive me, but my patience is at an end. I love and embrace you with all my heart. – Your Henriette.'

After that letter, no one could surely have thought that her visit to the gunsmith was with the innocent intention of arming herself against the wild and licentious electorate. Could it be believed either that she had gone to see Calmette with the thought of 'merely intending to cause a fuss'?

She told that, as she sat waiting in the hall, her anger was further inflamed by a conversation between some of the employees of the paper standing nearby who were talking of a big story on Caillaux ready for the next day's issue. According to her story, her name was then called out by Calmette: 'Show in Madame Caillaux.'

'Realizing that my identity was now known, I suddenly understood how indiscreet I had been,' she explained later. 'I completely lost my head.'

Calmette had come into the office through a side entrance with Paul Bourget of the French Academy. They had been chatting for some time in Calmette's office, said Bourget later, and were on the point of leaving the building when the receptionist came up with Mme Caillaux's card, saying the lady had been waiting for some time, and wished to see M. Calmette urgently.

'But surely you won't see *her*?' exclaimed Bourget as he looked at the card.

'It is a lady. Of course I must receive her,' said Calmette, thinking perhaps that he might get a certain amount of amusement, perhaps even a story, out of the interview.

Calmette returned to his room and an office boy named Adrien Sirac showed Mme Caillaux into the presence of her great enemy.

Henriette had her hand on the Browning, thumb on the safety catch.

'No doubt my visit surprises you,' she began.

'Not at all.' Calmette went behind his desk. 'Please be seated.'

Henriette had no intention of bandying words with this fellow – this creature – this evil scribbler. She did not hesitate. She pulled out the Browning, pointed it at him and started to fire.

It happened so quickly that Sirac was still outside the door when he heard the first shot. He rushed back into the room to see Calmette reeling over behind the desk as the bullets hit him. Mme Caillaux stood there like an avenging angel pumping bullets at him. She had already fired three. She fired the fourth shot before Sirac could stop her.

As Sirac tore the gun from Mme Caillaux's hand, Calmette fell heavily to the floor.

His assassin remained calm. With splendid dignity she turned to the office boy. 'I am Madame Caillaux. Do not be afraid,' she reassured him rather unnecessarily as the young man had already disarmed her and held her smoking weapon in his hand.

The noise attracted other members of the staff who came hurrying into the room. According to them, Mme Caillaux made a number of remarks appropriate to the historic occasion. They all agreed that, like Charlotte Corday, she was the calmest person present during the pandemonium which followed the murder and was completely indifferent to the consequences of her crime.

'It was the only way to put an end to it all,' she pointed out. 'There is no justice in France, so I had to obtain it for myself.' Her most famous remark was: 'Let me go. I am a lady. I am Madame Caillaux. I have my car waiting downstairs to take me to the police station.' A superb declamation which rang around the world.

Meanwhile the stricken editor, still conscious, his clothes soaked with blood, was lifted into his chair. He is alleged to have said with rather more self-effacement than the occasion warranted: 'Forgive my causing you so much trouble, my friends.'

By then the police were upon the scene. Mme Caillaux began to explain herself by repeating: 'There is no justice in ——'

But she was interrupted by one of the members of the staff: 'Be quiet, Madame. After what you have done, the least you can do now is to remain silent.'

Mme Caillaux fixed him with a paralysing stare. How dare the fellow interrupt her?

'I was not addressing *you*, monsieur,' she snapped and then stalked magnificently out of the room and downstairs to her car, followed by the somewhat awed police. This was indeed murder with a difference.

It was a splendid performance and it created a world-wide sensation. Gaston Calmette died at midnight. Henriette Caillaux languished in jail enjoying, it was maintained, very special privileges which included the best of food brought in from a nearby restaurant.

The staff of *Le Figaro* worked hard all night producing a black-bordered edition full of emotional eulogies about their slaughtered editor. When Calmette found it necessary in justification of his high principles to attack individuals, they wrote, he suffered bitterly – though obviously he did not expect to suffer unto death. 'We weep, shuddering at the horror of the crime.'

Henriette Caillaux did neither herself nor her husband any good by her crime. The allegations against him were repeated in the Chamber of Deputies the following day by M. Fabre in terms which made Caillaux's resignation inevitable. Relieved of the burdens of the Ministry of Finance, he then directed the whole of his formidable energies and talent to the defence of his wife.

The political uproar caused by Calmette's murder resulted in a number of awful revelations. Many careers were terminated as a consequence of Madame's fusillade in Calmette's office. When the case came to trial on 20 July, 1914, it was more of a furious political wrangle and a raking over of the dead ashes of old marital disputes than a murder trial. The *partie civile*, representing the injured party, were so intent on ruining Caillaux politically and morally that the case of getting his wife condemned for Calmette's murder suffered.

The case began in the usual way with the accused being questioned by the President, M. Jean-Marie Albanel. Henriette defended herself with great skill and eloquently told of the events which led up to the shooting in Gaston Calmette's office. She spoke movingly of the great happiness of her marriage to Joseph Caillaux, then recounted in distressed tones the story of the persecution she and her husband had had to endure from the vicious pen of Gaston Calmette. After this emotional tale, she passed on to the events of 16 March. She recounted how she told her husband that Judge Monier had said there was no legal redress in France for such scurrilous newspaper attacks.

There was some dispute as to what Caillaux had actually remarked to her. According to the depositions she quoted her husband as: *'Je lui casserai la gueule'* – which is a rather vulgar French way of saying 'I'll break his neck', though it could have other meanings.

When her delicacy prevented her using such expressions in court, Maître Chenu, Counsel for the *partie civile*, objected to such fastidiousness on the part of a murderess.

'It embarrasses me to use such a phrase in public,' replied Mme Caillaux coldly.

Chenu recalled the note she had left her husband before she set out on her visit to Calmette's office. 'You wrote it then without any trouble.'

Mme Caillaux's icy gaze was unflinching. 'There are things which one writes to one's husband which one does not wish to say in public,' she informed him disdainfully, to the accompaniment of sympathetic murmurs from the crowded court. Counsel soon learned that this was no ordinary prisoner. They had to treat her with the respect befitting her station.

With deference and attention the court listened to her explanation of her action: 'Try and think how I shall be conscious all my life of having, even though I never wished it, caused a man's death. How can anyone imagine that I ever intended to commit such an action? But, moreover, apart from the problem of conscience, which is terrible enough, there is a question of logic. That a woman who had been deprived of everything through a man, who feels herself to be ruined, should have the idea of killing in order to revenge herself – that is conceivable. But I – I had everything I desired, leaving aside the outrageous slanders and the threatened publication of the letters. Why should I have wanted to kill? To kill a man – that is a frightful thing, appalling. I never said that death should be the punishment.'

As for the actual shooting itself, it was not a premeditated act on her part. In fact the killing was accidental, she claimed, and was due to a combination of events – the sinister discussion of the big story being prepared about her husband, her name being called in a loud voice, the dim light in the editorial sanctum, all this had unnerved her.

'I lost my head when I found myself in the presence of the man who had done us so much harm, who had ruined our lives for thirteen months.' The gun went off accidentally. The bullets seemed to follow each other automatically owing to the fact that she was not used to that particular gun.

Not surprisingly, the members of the staff of *Le Figaro* contradicted her on several vital points. It was denied that there was any discussion in the entrance hall on the subject of 'tomorrow's big story about Caillaux'. It was also denied that her name was called out or that Calmette's office was in semi-darkness.

On the question of the discussion in the entrance hall Mme Caillaux countered the denial with the statement that she had overheard one of the witnesses, Louis Voisin, being asked: 'Is the sheet (*feuille*) ready yet?' This was a term she had never heard before, and Voisin had replied: 'No, it's only six o'clock. Anyway, we're getting a big story on Caillaux ready for tomorrow.'

Voisin protested loudly that this was a lie. Other members of the *Figaro* staff attempted to confuse the issue by imputing political rather than personal reasons to the fear which M. and Mme Caillaux had of the paper's campaign.

Caillaux himself defended his wife with great force and eloquence, and the trial developed into a political discussion of ancient and forgotten scandals. Occasionally matters connected with the murder were mentioned for the benefit of the bemused jury. For instance, Mme Gueydan-Caillaux let it be known that it was her sister, not herself, who had had the compromising letters photographed. Naturally the former wife of the Minister of Finance was too much of a lady to sell them to the grubby scribblers of *Le Figaro* or any other newspaper, though she admitted that her sister had given them to her.

The jury were probably more interested in the scandals which went on in high places than in the shooting of the editor who exposed them. It has been charitably assumed that when they came to decide the proper issue of the trial they were so confused by the extraneous political matters brought into court for propaganda purposes by Caillaux's enemies that they scarcely knew what it was all about.

On the other hand they may possibly have thought that

Henriette Caillaux did not do such a bad thing in shooting her persecutor, and they may have been hypnotized by the magnificent manner in which she justified her action. We all know the power of the Press, and in those days it was more difficult to obtain redress than it is today.

At any event they declared her innocent of deliberate murder and also of shooting with premeditation.

The world was astonished, *Le Figaro* outraged. The self-assured Henriette Caillaux took it as the natural and inevitable result for her to walk out of the court a free woman. She had already arranged a splendid champagne party in anticipation.

It was a strange verdict. Whether it was premeditated murder or not – and her letter to her husband certainly suggested that it was – the shooting of Gaston Calmette was a crime by any standards.

*Le Figaro*, frustrated and angered at the 'shameful verdict', launched an even more virulent campaign against Caillaux and his wife. But it was 29 July, 1914, and the whole business was soon forgotten in the deep shadows of European war.

On the outbreak of war Caillaux was appointed Paymaster-General to the Forces and a few months later went on an economic mission to South America. Caillaux was against the war and accused of treason. In 1918 he was arrested and sentenced to three years' imprisonment in 1920; but he was immediately released as by then he had spent that period of time in prison. In 1925 he returned to politics and in the following year he again became Minister of Finance. He died in 1944.

Henriette Caillaux died in 1943, never doubting the rightness of what she did that afternoon in the offices of *Le Figaro*.

Caillaux himself, speaking of the incident many years later, said: 'If he had walked right up to her to disarm her, as any man of courage would have done, instead of running away, or even if he had not just crouched down, he would only have been wounded in the legs, if indeed at all.'

In other words, the man himself was to blame for getting in the way of Madame's bullets.

# Chapter 9
# The Montesi Scandal

Crimes and scandals are often said to act as catalysts in society because their very existence produces change or creates the tensions which lead to change. The Dreyfus Affair acted as a most violent catalyst by creating dissension which nearly tore France to pieces. In England the Profumo scandal acted as a catalyst of a milder kind. In Italy during the 1950s the scandal following the death of Wilma Montesi was a catalyst with results almost as violent as those of the Dreyfus Affair.

Wilma Montesi was the twenty-one-year-old daughter of a carpenter who lived in Via Tagliamento, Rome. She was attractive certainly, though she was neither gay nor sophisticated. Some even said she was dull. Her policeman-fiancé confessed that he found her heavy going.

Wilma had a sister named Wanda, also in her early twenties. On 9 April, 1953 their mother, Maria Montesi, suggested that they should all go to the pictures together. Wilma did not want to see the particular film her mother and Wanda had chosen and said that she would stay at home.

Instead she took a train to Ostia, the seaside resort near

157

the mouth of the Tiber known as the Lido of Rome. It was later suggested that Wilma went there to treat chilblains on her feet with sea water, and that while paddling in the shallows she fainted as the result of menstrual pains and was drowned. Assisted by the wind, her body drifted fifteen miles down the coast to a lonely place named Tor Vaianica where it was found on the morning of 11 April and identified by the weeping Montesi family. They accepted this explanation even though there were one or two things they could not understand. When she left home she had not taken her money, jewels, or the picture of her fiancé which she usually carried. No shoes and stockings were found. Nor was there a suspender belt.

The tragedy caused little stir at the time, but the elections were near and one of the great issues among politicians was corruption, orgies and drug-taking in high places. Someone noticed the unexplained facts about the Montesi case. There was a rather feeble joke going the rounds in Rome that Wilma's suspender belt had been brought to Roman police headquarters by a carrier pigeon. The Italian for pigeon is *piccioni*. Now the name of the Italian Foreign Minister was Attilio Piccioni whose son, Piero Piccioni, was a jazz musician and composer who had his own radio show. There was no reason at all to connect either father or son with the Montesi business, but the spreading of scandal was all part of the political game, and many of them – mostly fictitious – were exposed in that election year by both left and right. Much was also heard about trafficking in drugs and women.

It was not until January, 1954 – eight months after Wilma's death – that the Montesi scandal really broke. It started in a weekly paper called *Attualità*, edited by Silvano Muto. Muto drew attention to the fact that Wilma's body was found close to a hunting lodge, Capocotta, which once belonged to the Italian royal family. It was now owned by a syndicate of socialites. There were stories that sex orgies and drug parties went on at Capocotta. Was Wilma's death connected with this?

The rest of the Press, particularly that of the extreme left wing, took up the story with zest and in headlines inches high, using it as a means of violent attack upon the Government, big business and the princes of the Church and society. The burden of their heat and indignation was that important officials of the Government and the police had conspired to conceal a crime which had resulted in the death of the daughter of a poor and respectable working-class Roman family. Wilma's virtue was certainly in doubt, according to some who imagined her the victim of nameless orgies and unspeakable vices which went on at Capocotta.

The Government permitted the storm to run for a while, hoping it would blow itself out. But when the story was taken up in foreign newspapers and the scandal became world-wide, Silvano Muto, the editor of the paper which started it all, was put on trial for publishing falsehoods likely to disturb the public peace. The action was brought under an old Fascist law still in force. The object of bringing Muto to trial was to force out of him the source of his information.

Muto had no compunction in revealing his sources. He told the court that he got the material for his article from two signorinas – Adriana Bisaccia and Anna Maria Caglio. Adriana had intimated to him that she knew a lot about the death of Wilma Montesi and that it was not an accident. Adriana herself had been to certain parties at Capocotta patronized by people in high places. She had informed him that Wilma Montesi knew people in prominent social positions, and they were responsible for her death. When asked to name these people, Adriana had been afraid to.

Muto declared that Anna Maria Caglio had told him a similar story about drug orgies at Capocotta; she had named Ugo Montagna, one of the administrators of the shoot at Capocotta, as the man who knew all about Wilma's death. According to Adriana Bisaccia, Wilma Montesi became ill after taking drugs and died during the party. Then her body was taken to the beach by car and left there.

The Judge asked Muto where these two so-well-informed ladies were to be found, as he would like to hear their stories from their own lips. Muto did not know. The Judge declared they must be found and adjourned the hearing.

During the adjournment the scandal gathered enormous

momentum. Italy has no law which prevents discussion of such a case when it is *sub judice*. There was endless conjecture about the body of Wilma Montesi – whether she was a virgin, and if she was not, whether she had been pregnant.

Speculation rose to fever heat when Ugo Montagna was identified as a Sicilian Marquis, and when a famous film star was linked with the case. According to *Unità*, a Communist daily, the star was supposed to have said to Piero Piccioni, the son of the Foreign Minister, 'What sort of mess have you got yourself into this time? So you knew her, did you? Well, what are you going to do now? And what does Ugo think about it?'

The film actress, Alida Valli, thereupon brought herself into the heated scene by demanding of *Unità* if they were talking about her. *Unità* printed her letter but had no comment to make.

Adriana Bisaccia turned out to be a girl who was hanging around the international film colony in Rome hoping for a job. When questioned, she was vague and claimed that she really knew nothing about the Montesi affair.

But Anna Caglio who was discovered in a Florentine convent was rather more forthcoming. A dark-eyed, shapely, attractive girl of twenty-three, she admitted that Ugo Montagna had been her lover. The hunting lodge at Capocotta was the symbol of everything that was evil – according to Signorina Caglio, not only was the son of the Foreign Minister involved, but men who were pillars of State and Church as well.

All Italy reeled under a sense of shock and horror. Where was this thing going to end? Could the depths of this corruption ever be plumbed? The tales of what went on in this place of degeneration and infamous vice bordered on the fantastic when stories were told of men on horseback hunting naked girls through the woods at night.

The trial of Muto was resumed with the temperature of the nation at fever pitch. Adriana Bisaccia, just recovering from an overdose of barbiturates, wasn't much help when called to the witness stand. 'I am in no condition to remember,' she declared.

Gaston Calmette, Editor of *Le Figaro*, conducted a virulent political campaign against Joseph Caillaux (*left*) and was murdered by

Caillaux's wife, Henriette (*right*). Huge crowds attended Calmette's funeral (*below*). Caillaux's political career suffered little damage.

The Montesi case was perhaps the most amazing scandal of the century. The body of Wilma Montesi (*left*) was found on a lonely Italian beach in 1953. Even though foul play was not established, Anna Maria Moneta Caglio (*below*), the chief witness, accused two men in particular – Piero Piccioni (*bottom left*), son of the Italian Foreign Minister; and Ugo Montagna, a Sicilian Marquis (*bottom right*). All persons who were put on trial on charges of being concerned in her murder were acquitted.

Under pressure from the prosecuting attorney, she exclaimed: 'I can't invent names to keep people quiet, even if the whole nation is waiting for them. I know nothing. Why don't you bring the guilty people here? You know who they are. You are playing politics and I have been ruined in the game.'

She did admit, however, that an artist with whom she had lived had accused her of being Montagna's mistress and that one night, when she, Adriana, was having a nightmare, she had shouted out: 'Don't throw me into the sea like Wilma!'

Anna Maria Caglio was the real heroine, if that is the word, of the Montesi case. She did not have to be pressed into giving her evidence. She was in fact embarrassingly forthcoming. Throughout the two trials connected with the Montesi affair she nearly talked herself into the dock. But at first everyone believed what she said. Her story was listened to with breathless attention.

She recalled that she met Ugo Montagna in March, 1953 and became his mistress. He gave her a car, a Fiat 1400. She told the court that on one occasion she phoned Montagna at his flat and spoke to his manservant who talked in a manner which convinced her that Montagna had another girl there. She was not able to speak to him. Later she drove past his house and saw him leaving with a dark-haired girl she was sure was Wilma Montesi. Montagna drove off at full speed and she followed in her Fiat.

It was an extraordinary pursuit, she said, which led her across pavements and the wrong way down one-way streets. At one point she knocked down a pedestrian. The judge mildly asked her if the pedestrian had raised any protest.

'Poor fellow,' answered Anna Caglio. 'He was lying on the ground and he didn't look too happy. But I drove on, shouting to him to take the number of my car.'

She recounted that she had seen Montagna drop his girl passenger near the Via Condotti. If it wasn't Wilma, she said, she would like Montagna to say who it was. After this curious episode Montagna had been furious, taken her Fiat away from her and shut her up for a month in his house in the Via Gennargentu.

Despite these tempestuous interludes, however, she had resumed her love-affair with him. 'I was just amused,' she said grandly. On 12 April, the day after Wilma Montesi's body was found on the beach at Tor Vaianica, she went with Montagna to shoot quails at Capocotta. She mentioned that one of the gamekeepers told her that Wilma Montesi's fiancé had come to Tor Vaianica and had intimated to him: 'If I told all I know, there'd be some big names flying about.'

La Caglio informed the court that when she had expressed to Montagna her suspicions that Piero Piccioni was responsible for Wilma's murder and ought to pay for it, even if he was the son of the Foreign Minister, Montagna got very angry and exclaimed, 'Piero doesn't come into this business at all. He was at Amalfi when the Montesi died.' Anna Caglio did not believe this, for Piccioni had phoned Montagna in Rome when she was there. Montagna then threatened that she knew too much and it was time she had a change of air. Scared, she then went to Milan.

The court asked her about the parties and orgies which were alleged to have taken place at Capocotta. She replied that she had not taken part in such goings-on, but she had heard that things were done 'which cannot be described'. She referred to a cupboard with a special lock of which Montagna only had the key, and hinted that he made an enormous income from drugs. She asserted that when she told Montagna to his face that he was earning millions out of the drug traffic, he did not deny it. Later she broke with him completely.

The quality of Anna Caglio's evidence is well exemplified by her statement that a chauffeur called Gasparini had told her that he had often seen Montagna and Wilma Montesi together. When asked where Gasparini was, she replied that he now kept a bar in Guatemala, of all places.

Her final shot against her former lover was dramatically produced in the form of a 'testament' found by the police in the Post Office and read in court in theatrical manner. It ran: 'I know the character of Ugo Montagna and Piero Piccioni, the son of the Minister. I am afraid of disappearing and leaving no trace behind. Alas I know that the head of the gang of drug-traffickers is Ugo Montagna. He is responsible for the disappearance of many women. He is the brain of the gang, while Piero Piccioni is the murderer.'

The temperature was running high. Moral and political passions were at fever pitch. Riot squads and armed police stood guard outside the law courts during the trial.

It was time for justice to think of other things than the writings of Sylvano Muto. The hearing was adjourned indefinitely so that an investigation into the death of Wilma Montesi should take place.

Anna Maria Caglio was the heroine of the hour. Lionized, adopted by a newspaper, they called her the Black Swan, the Girl of the Century, and Joan of Arc. She was the accusing angel fearlessly exposing the social evils of Italy. Ministers, Prefects, Heads of Police, even the Pope himself got in the way of her thunderbolts.

The Montesi scandal was no joke to the ordinary Italian. It was to them the symbol of something very sick and sinister in their society. Wickedness, depravity and corruption were abroad and had permeated into high places. People believed that the whole moral structure of society was threatened, that morality itself was at stake – a similar feeling developed in England ten years later over the Profumo affair.

It is easy to smile now at a nation's gullibility. But with the mass media hard at work with their brain-washing techniques, it was easy for Italy to be convinced that some great moral spring-clean was going on during the Montesi affair. Even *Stampa* of Turin claimed that the whole of the new Italian public was on trial, not just Muto. Others were persuaded that democratic institutions themselves were in danger. As for the Communist Party, it was serenely confident that the outcome of the affair would be the downfall of Italian capitalism, after which they would carry Europe's most ancient civilization into the domain of the promised land behind the Iron Curtain.

While various unstable characters appeared on the fervid scene claiming proof of Wilma's involvement in drug trafficking, her body was exhumed from her grave in Rome's great cemetery where she lay in a wedding dress beneath a photograph of herself and an inscription which read: 'Pure creature of rare beauty; the sea of Ostia claimed you and carried you to the beach of Tor Vaianica. You seemed to be resting in the sleep of the Lord, as lovely as an angel. Your mother and your father, your sister and your brother are near you in their great love and their terrible grief.'

But such sentiments reflected the previous year. Now it was announced that the Montesi family were about to make a film, playing the parts themselves. Who was to play Wilma was undecided. What remained of the poor girl was being cut up on the pathologist's slab. Some of the Montesis' legal advisers were so shocked about the film that they abandoned the bereaved family. The film, too, was abandoned later.

Prince Maurice of Hesse, closely related to the Italian royal family, was deprived of his passport on account of a report that he had gone to Capocotta with a girl in his car on the day of Wilma's disappearance. There was much Press speculation, followed by a spate of libel actions. Even lawyers were suing each other for libel. It just showed what a state everyone had got into.

Everybody wanted to get in on the act of national purification. A girl told the examining magistrate that she had been in the sand dunes with her lover – a married man – when she saw Wilma's body being carried down to the shore by two men. The only result of this piece of fiction was that her lover's adultery – a crime in Italy – was revealed to the world, and that she went to prison for perjury, as did a number of sleazy drug addicts who trooped into the chambers of the examining magistrate in the expectation of profiting in some way from what was going on. Various men claimed to have been Wilma's lover – not aware that the post-mortem had established her as a virgin.

Adriana Bisaccia was arrested for perjury, Piero Piccioni was arrested for the culpable homicide of Wilma Montesi, and Ugo Montagna was arrested for complicity with Piccioni's alleged crime. Saverio Polito, chief of the Roman police, an old man, was also arrested on the charge of complicity.

Montagna was dining with friends when he read about his

arrest in the late evening paper. He finished his dinner and went to the Regino Coeli prison. At first he was denied entrance, but when he showed the warder the headlines in the paper, he was reluctantly admitted to prison – establishing that at least the power of the Press still meant something in Italy.

It was, of course, amazing that the three men should have been charged at all. The case against them was so slight that it would have been thrown out of a court of unqualified English country magistrates within half an hour. Yet an Italian examining magistrate had been taking statements from witnesses for months and had compiled ninety-two volumes of evidence.

The trial was long-delayed. There was much to be done, apart from the digestion of those ninety-two volumes. But the ability of the mass media to discuss the evidence fully in the meantime – one of the uncertain benefits of the Italian system of the Napoleonic Code – ensured that the public's passions on the matter were kept simmering. Also, Giuseppe Sotgiu, Muto's Communist lawyer, and his wife were involved in a grave scandal which helped to raise the political temperature.

The trial began at Venice in 1957, four years after Wilma Montesi met her death. Venice was chosen as being the town in Italy least likely to generate heat over the affair which had become such an obsession in Italy that someone had suggested nationalizing it.

The Italian form of trial is totally different to the English. They have adopted the Napoleonic Code to suit the national mood and temperament, with the result that the proceedings are more emotional and matters are pursued and investigated which would be ruled as totally irrelevant in an English courtroom. The object of the system is to search out and reach the truth, by whatever means, whereas the English system requires the court to reach a decision only upon such evidence as is permitted by the strict rules to be given in court, and the decision need not necessarily be the truth. (It has often been said that it would be better for a guilty man to escape justice than that the strict laws which govern the administration of English justice should be in the slightest way infringed.)

Hearsay evidence, which is excluded from English courts, is allowed in Italy where the courts frequently confront witnesses with each other and encourage mutual argument as a way of testing conflicting evidence.

The trial opened on 20 January before Judge Mario Tiberi. The Public Prosecutor was Cesare Palminteri. Piero Piccioni's principal counsel was Francesco Carnelutti. Montagna's main defence counsel was Girolamo Bellavista.

The trial began with the evidence of the accused. Piero Piccioni stated that on 9 April, 1953, the day of Wilma Montesi's death, he was at Amalfi with Alida Valli, the film star. He drove her to Sorrento where he waited with her until the boat sailed for Capri. After seeing her on board, he left Sorrento about ten-thirty in the morning and drove to Rome which he reached at two-thirty. He drove quickly because he had a fever and a sore throat. When he arrived home his family had just finished lunch. He did not eat much because of his difficulty in swallowing. Afterwards he lay down in great pain and his family insisted on his seeing a specialist which he did about six o'clock in the evening. The prosecution knew that he had incontrovertible evidence to prove this, and that he had a watertight alibi. Yet they proceeded with the case!

Piccioni denied that he had ever met Wilma Montesi. He had not even heard of her until he read about her death in the newspapers. The Press linked their names together about a month after her death. He considered it a political campaign to damage his father's party. As for being in complicity with Polito, he had never met him before in his life until they met in the courtroom the previous day.

Saverio Polito then gave evidence. Being thus accused at the end of his long police career had completely broken the old man.

'They have embittered the last years of my life and sought to destroy me,' he complained in a pathetic voice. 'You know, Mr President, to go from the chair of the *Questore* of Rome to the dock is a terrible thing. It is an intolerable burden, and there is nothing against me – nothing, nothing, nothing.'

When the Judge asked him what he had to say in his defence, Polito said that he had never met Piccioni until the day before. As for Montagna, he had seen him three times before in his whole life. He never took any interest in the death of Wilma Montesi until he heard the rumours going round about Piero Piccioni. He complained bitterly about the way he had been treated during the preliminary examinations. He had been questioned for eighteen hours on end, and one of the judges had a pistol on the table while he was questioning him.

He declared that the Rome police made meticulous inquiries into the death of Wilma Montesi and were absolutely certain that there was no question of foul play.

'Wilma Montesi turns out to have been a good girl, honest and discreet,' he said, 'even if certain people in pursuit of their own interests have tried to turn her into a loose woman.'

Polito considered that he was being persecuted on account of an old score from Fascist days.

Montagna then gave evidence and protested: 'I proclaim my innocence with all my strength.' He denied every one of Anna Maria Caglio's accusations. Asked about the money he gave her, he said it was fifty thousand lire a month. When the Judge pointed out that two payments of half a million had been paid into the Caglio's bank, Montagna replied with a smile that she had done pretty well out of certain big industrialists.

While Montagna was giving evidence his erstwhile mistress was holding a Press conference at Florence at which she said she had made fifteen million lire – apparently for a film she was going to make about the affair.

The evidence of 24 January established that Prince Maurice of Hesse did go to Capocotta on 10 April, 1953 with a girl in his car. But the girl was not Wilma and his visit was unconnected with her death.

An astrologer named the Wizard Orio appeared upon the scene determined to enlighten the court with his revelations. He had written a letter to the Public Prosecutor, saying that he was visited by a party of four people in either February or March 1953, who turned out to be none other than Wilma Montesi, Piero Piccioni, Anna Maria Caglio and Ugo Montagna. The Wizard's proper name was Ezio de Sanctis. He was invited to come to court and give evidence when, after repeating his tissue of fictions, he was sent to prison for eighteen months for perjury.

The Montesi family gave their evidence at the end of January. Her father, Rodolfo, a tallish man in his fifties, had suspected, at first, that Wilma had committed suicide, as she was due to get married shortly and did not want to leave home. The Judge asked him about his reaction when he was told that Wilma's body had been found without her suspender belt. Rodolfo – by this time he had presumably abandoned his suicide theory – imagined she had taken it off out of sheer high spirits. He confessed that he had been greatly distressed when he went to the police to report Wilma's disappearance and when they began to consult the register of prostitutes, telling him in effect that all fathers believed their daughters were good girls.

Wilma's mother gave similar evidence, insisting that her daughter was a good girl in every respect. Everything that happened at the trial supported the Montesis' opinion of their daughter's virtue.

Angelo Giuliana, Wilma's fiancé, said he met Wilma at a dance and two days later asked her to marry him. He had told her he was a wine merchant, not a policeman. He said their love was purely platonic, 'and not a love like others'. He had since married another girl.

Wilma's letters to Giuliana were read by the judge. They were naïve and contained none of the warmth and passion usually associated with the latin temperament. They were hardly the letters which would have been written by a girl who had led a double life – which was the only theory on which this extraordinary prosecution could be supported.

Evidence was given of the finding of the body. It was a young labourer named Fortunata Bettini who had actually found it and reported it immediately. Several persons who had passed the spot earlier had not seen it, a fact which the court found somewhat mystifying. Much contradictory evidence on the subject was given and there were some heated exchanges.

A gamekeeper named Zingarini was settling himself in the witness's chair when one of the defence counsel observed a piece of paper sticking out of his pocket, and this legal smart alec asked him if it was his criminal record.

'Don't you get at me!' exclaimed Zingarini spiritedly. 'There are some lawyers here who ought to think about their own criminal records.'

This wholly justified riposte brought about such an uproar from the legal benches that the Judge threatened to suspend the sitting.

The court then heard the medical evidence. Poor Wilma's remains had been subjected to no less than eighteen different medical examinations, but the doctors were unanimous on only two points – that she had been drowned, and that she was a virgin.

Small abrasions of the hymen and vagina had been found and had been the subject of much imaginative speculation in certain quarters. Professor Frache of the University of Sassari in Sardinia considered they were due to the action of sand in the rough sea and had been caused after her death. Professor Macaggi of the University of Genoa, on the other hand, expressed the opinion that the abrasions could have been caused before death, though he could not say with any certainty.

'Let us rest content with probabilities,' he concluded.

But no court wishes to do that. Some experts plumped for murder, some for suicide, others for accidental death. They finally fell to heated argument. Their net contribution to the court's deliberations was small.

Another clairvoyant, Del Duca, in an interlude of light relief, gave some inconsequential evidence. He believed that everyone was guilty and only a return to Fascism could save the situation and redeem Italy.

General Umberto Pompei, who had been ordered to inquire into the background of Ugo Montagna and his associates, stated that Montagna had been a member of *Oura*, Mussolini's secret police. According to Pompei there was no evidence that Montagna was engaged in drug trafficking. He had written off Anna Caglio's accusations as being due to jealousy.

As the case proceeded on its laborious and disordered way, the stories told of the police investigations strongly suggested that the whole affair had been blown up by lies and rumours out of nothing. Various members of the Press were asked where they got their information that Piccioni had killed Wilma Montesi. The answer was simply that everyone was talking about it. Where the rumours originated they could not say, though it was obvious they were politically inspired.

It was plainly time for Anna Maria Caglio – the Girl of the Century, the Italian Joan of Arc – to give a further account of herself and to explain her accusations. This La Caglio was only too happy to do. She arrived at the court smiling engagingly at a barrage of photographers' flash bulbs. All were ready to listen avidly to the words that fell from her charmed lips, and she did not disappoint her public.

She related that Ugo Montagna had had an affair with Clara Petacci – Mussolini's mistress during the war who used to hold Black Masses in her house. Mussolini, La Caglio told the court, found them together once, but was too afraid of Montagna to do anything about it. La Caglio talked about Ugo's parties at which eighteen girls were enjoyed by six men who included Bruno and Vittorio Mussolini.

These fascinating anecdotes were of course nothing to do with the matter before the court, though that seemed no reason why they should not be discussed. The Judge, however, did admonish her: 'You have already said too many things that have nothing to do with the trial.'

La Caglio informed the court that after the death of Wilma Montesi, Montagna had described Piccioni as very depraved. But *he* could talk! added Caglio, for his maid, a girl named Mina, had soon given notice, 'because they did such disgusting things in that house'.

'Shall I tell you what things?' asked Caglio after a tantalizing pause.

The Judge reminded her that she was in an open court and that the public were present. But Caglio was not to be denied her dramatic revelation. The maid had told her that they used to sit down to table stark naked. This slightly uncomfortable proceeding seemed to be more shocking to her than it was to the court which was leaning forward eagerly expecting to hear about unspeakable things.

Her evidence against Montagna and Piccioni, as before,

was little more than bald accusation. She said that when she had accused Montagna of making money out of drug trafficking and of being Piccioni's accomplice in the murder of Wilma Montesi, Montagna had not denied it, but had merely retorted that there was no proof. Pressed about her allegations that a lot of women had disappeared from Capocotta, she could only name the Montesi, and herself if they had managed to kill her. It was Sylvano Muto who told her about the other women.

Conscious of the thinness of his case, the Public Prosecutor pressed her again and again, but in vain, for proofs of her assertions. She had no evidence against the accused, only accusations. The court began to turn against her. Even the Public Prosecutor lost patience with her when she admitted that she had no proof of drug trafficking, though she insisted that 'filthy things' had gone on at Capocotta, but as she hadn't seen them, much less taken part in them, she was somewhat at a loss to describe them.

She hinted that she was working with the Jesuits in this cleansing of the Augean stables, and so the Vice-Provincial of the Roman Jesuits was called to give evidence. He recalled that Anna Caglio came to see him in November, 1953, to tell him about the immoral circle in which she had been living – about terrible orgies at Capocotta, which then she had described not only the head of a big drug organization, but also as a centre in the white-slave trade. Ship-loads of prostitutes, La Caglio had suggested to the Vice-Provincial, sailed between Sicily, North Africa and Capocotta. These fearful happenings were reported to Signor Fanfani, Minister of the Interior, and to the Pope; but no concrete evidence could be brought to support the allegations.

The credibility gap was widening. The case against Piccioni collapsed completely after witnesses had given evidence to the effect that he could not possibly have been at Capocotta at the time of Wilma Montesi's death. Chief of these was the film star Alida Valli who had since married the French writer, Felicien Marceau, and whose word was hardly to be doubted. She had not been in touch with Piccioni for the last three or four years, but although she provided Piero Piccioni with as good an alibi as he could have wished, she never once glanced at him as she gave her evidence.

With the case against her alleged murderer collapsing, the question of the dead girl's missing suspender belt and her mysterious phone calls seemed irrelevant.

More to the point was the evidence of Chief of Police Tommaso Pavone, who previously had been Chief of Public Security. He pointed out that much of the election campaign was based on the Montesi scandal; the accusations against Piccioni were merely part of a political manœuvre to discredit his father.

This had been blindingly obvious all the time, but for some reason the case proceeded and witnesses continued their procession into the box. They included Anna Caglio again who came out with further titbits which did little more than embroider her original stories. During a confrontation with her, Bruno Pescatori, a hairdresser who knew many of those involved in the scandal, exclaimed: 'The imagination of this girl is really incredible.'

A moment of comic relief was provided by Red Jenny, another fanciful character whose intervention in the case was for some reason taken seriously by the court. She wrote a letter to the investigating authorities, saying she was in danger of meeting the same fate as Wilma Montesi, as she was mixed up in drug trafficking. She would come forward if her life could be protected. She never put in an appearance.

Anna Caglio was called back to answer more questions. She began to find herself in serious trouble with the court who disbelieved the statements which she had made and which had led to the accused being in the dock. Glibly she tried to bluff her way out of the difficulties which arose when witnesses flatly contradicted certain facts in her story.

When the Judge asked for his comment, Montagna said bluntly from the dock: 'She is lying and she knows she is lying.'

This brought a certain hostile murmur from the public in the courtroom who were not yet prepared to admit that their beloved Joan of Arc had feet of clay. But it was most significant that the Public Prosecutor – whose job was to prove the guilt of the accused – turned against her.

'You go away,' the Judge told her coldly, 'and come back on 29 March.'

On 27 March Frederico Alessandrini, the assistant editor of *Osservatore Romano*, the official newspaper of the Vatican, gave evidence. He stated that in March, 1954 (eleven months after Wilma's death) a friend of Montagna had told him the story that Piccioni had been with the dead girl at the time; after certain intimacies they had supposedly gone to the edge of the sea and there she was taken ill. According to this story, Piccioni had panicked and, thinking her dead, ran away leaving her there. Montagna later tried to hush the scandal up.

Alessandrini commented that he didn't believe this story because he knew that Piero Piccioni was ill in bed at the time, and thus could have had nothing to do with Wilma Montesi's death. He was severely criticized in court for having previously concealed what he knew.

'That is the way you send people to jail!' exclaimed one of the defence counsel.

The trial had gone on for weeks, and so far no evidence had been produced which pointed to the guilt of any of the accused, surely a unique situation, and one which brought no credit on Judge Tiberi and his court. Not a single witness had been brought forward who could identify any of the three defendants as being in any way connected with the death of Wilma Montesi. Not one of the medical witnesses was prepared to say that she had been murdered. The main witness for the prosecution, Anna Maria Caglio, had no direct evidence to give about the Montesi death; and what evidence she had given, mostly hearsay, had been found to conflict over and over again with the evidence of other witnesses, so much so that the Public Prosecutor had abandoned her in despair and disgust.

Why the case was allowed to continue another day is a mystery. But it certainly didn't peter out. It took a sudden and dramatic turn when the dead girl's uncle, Giuseppe Montesi, gave evidence. Known as Zio Giuseppe (Uncle

Joseph), he had been the subject of much discussion in the Italian Press. He was a stocky, good-looking young man who had given it as his opinion that Wilma had gone to Ostia as an act of rebellion against the strictness of her father who never allowed her to go out in the evenings. Bringing up girls that way in a modern city like Rome, he commented, was only asking for trouble.

Zio Giuseppe was already under some suspicion in the public mind. When the Montesis, after dropping their initial assumption that Wilma had committed suicide, became convinced that their daughter had run away, Wilma's mother had kept repeating: 'Come back, my daughter. I'll forgive you whatever you've done, even if you come home with ten lovers and twins. I'll take them all on. But only come back.' A friend of the Montesi family in court reported Wanda's remark that whoever was guilty should be prosecuted, ominously adding – 'even if it's our own uncle'.

The court carefully went into Zio Giuseppe's movements on the afternoon of Wilma's death. He denied suggestions that he had left his place of work early that day after telephoning Wilma. Mariella Spissu, his fiancée, confirmed his story that they had been together on the night of Wilma's death.

The chief compositor of the printing works where Giuseppe was employed gave a different story. He told the court that Giuseppe on the day of Wilma's death left soon after five boasting that he was having an affair with a girl. And he had said he was going to Ostia.

Giuseppe, confronted with this witness, passionately denied it. However, he was forced to admit that he had gone out that evening, though he refused to say where. Guessing there was something which he was not prepared to say in public, the court was cleared. They need not have bothered, because the newspapers had the whole story in their next editions.

Giuseppe's guilty secret was that he was having an affair with Rossana Spissu, his fiancée's sister. On 9 April, 1953 she had telephoned him and they had gone some distance in his car along the Via Flaminia where they had parked and made love. Later on Rossana had given birth to his child.

When the public were re-admitted Wilma's mother, Maria Montesi, was again called to the witness stand. What did she think, asked the Public Prosecutor, about the newspapers' assertion that her brother-in-law, Giuseppe, had been with Wilma?

'They suspect everything, these newspapers,' Maria Montesi cried out bitterly. 'They spoke of Wilma as if she were a prostitute who sold cocaine – our lovely clean Press!' Only a few minutes previously she had affirmed her belief in Wilma whom she called 'the pearl among my children, the sweetest of the three, and I held her like a rose to my nostrils'. She thought nothing of the suspicion which had fallen on Zio Giuseppe.

'But you knew that your brother-in-law had invited Wilma and Wanda to go out with him in his car?' said the Public Prosecutor.

'That is not true.'

'But your daughter Wanda said so.'

Maria jumped to her feet and shouted at the Public Prosecutor: 'It is not true.'

'Sit down, signora, and stop acting,' commanded the Public Prosecutor.

Maria Montesi calmed down. 'In any case, Wilma did not go,' she insisted.

At the end of an eventful day Anna Caglio was recalled to the witness stand. Piccioni's counsel read out a list of twelve manifest lies which she had told in evidence, and demanded that she should be charged with perjury. She was instead sternly warned by the Judge, and the Public Prosecutor told her that she had better reconsider her evidence and advised her to draw the line between imagination and truth. The considerably deflated Caglio protested that she never had the least intention of lying. 'What I have said is true,' she declared. No one believed her any more.

The prosecution was preoccupied with Zio Giuseppe. There was in fact no other suspect in sight, and Giuseppe was only an outside chance.

Wanda Montesi was called to give evidence again. She was first asked about the suspender belt. Wilma always wore it over her pants, she said. She would never have taken it off on an open beach. Wanda added that both she and her sister sometimes did not wear their suspender belts in hot weather because they did not like the feel of them. But Wanda protested that she never entertained an 'atrocious suspicion' against her uncle Giuseppe.

Was it true that her uncle invited the two of them to go out with him in his car, and that Wilma had refused to come saying it was written all over his face that he wasn't their *uncle*? asked the Judge. Wanda replied that this was a joke, and anyway their uncle had invited both of them *and* their mother to go in his car.

Wanda admitted they had suspected that something was going on between her uncle and his fiancée's sister, though they didn't know about the baby. She called Rossana Spissu a very forward girl – she had even flirted with Wilma's father and their mother had taken great offence. There had been a most unpleasant scene.

Rossana herself gave evidence on 10 April. She was an attractive, brown-haired girl. Her sister whose fiancé she had stolen was ill suffering, according to her doctor, from a neurasthenic depressive syndrome. She was unable to appear in court.

Rossana said she spent the afternoon and evening of 9 April, 1953 with Giuseppe Montesi. She admitted she saw him every day. Counsel treated her pretty badly in the witness stand and reduced her to tears. Her story was one she could hardly be proud of, but it provided a perfect alibi for her lover – even though it contradicted, in some respects, his version of his movements on the fatal evening.

The catalogue of lies and twisted newspaper stories which made up the Montesi scandal rose to an emotional and exciting climax as the trial drew to its end.

Giuseppe had told more than one story about his activities on the afternoon of Wilma's death. Consequently, when he went into the witness stand again he was set upon not only by the Judge, but by counsel of both sides, who poured upon him a furious barrage of questions and accusations which would have daunted the most innocent of men. A transcript of this part of the trial reads like a session in a Gestapo interrogation chamber, so anxious was the court to get poor Giuseppe to admit to a murder which (perhaps they had forgotten) had manifestly not taken place.

Giuseppe came through his formidable ordeal with flying colours, though plainly shaken to the core by the fury of judge and counsel.

Leaping to his feet, he yelled at the top of his voice: 'I have told you I was with Rossana on that day. I don't have to justify anything I did. This is the last time I shall repeat it – I know nothing! I know nothing of the death of Wilma Montesi! I don't know how Wilma died!'

Nor, it might be added, did the court. But they hadn't finished with him yet. In the meantime they lowered the temperature by hearing evidence from journalists, one of whom stated that everybody in the case, including the Montesis, had made money out of the Press. They all had something to offer – even photographs of Piccioni and Wilma together for twenty million lire. A newspaper paid the expenses of Wanda's wedding, and Wilma's mother had offered to write a juicy article for *Epoca*.

Then Giuseppe's alibi that he was making love to Rossana in their usual place along the Via Flaminia on the evening of Wilma's death was challenged from a new quarter.

The wife of a tram driver, Signora Piastra, said that at six in the evening of 9 April, 1953 Rossana Spissu had been at Rome's Central Station seeing Signora Piastra's mother off to Chiusi where she lived. In support of this she produced a booklet of concessionary railway tickets to which the mother, as the wife of a railwayman, had been entitled, and on one of the counterfoils was evidence of a journey from Rome to Chiusi on 9 April, 1953.

It was a very awkward piece of evidence for both Giuseppe and Rossana. Rossana flatly denied that she had been at the railway station on that particular evening.

Naturally enough she was given another mauling by the Public Prosecutor, desperate to find someone guilty in these extraordinary proceedings, now that the three men in the dock were sitting back, arms folded and smiling, their complete innocence plain to the whole world – even though the members of this extraordinary legal tribunal were turning a blind eye to this fact.

Rossana emphasized: 'Mr President, I swear to you that I did not go to the station.'

'Signorina Rossana, tell the truth!' rapped out the Public Prosecutor.

'But I have told it. I swear on the head of my child!'

'Leave your child out of it,' cried the Public Prosecutor. 'Do not bring innocence into this room. Tell the truth and stop crying. Tears are useless.'

'I'm not crying,' Rossana countered scornfully. 'I've given up everything and everybody. Why should I lie now? It's cost me enough to tell the truth. But I've done it. I've lost my job, I can't look my mother in the face, nor my sister or my brother. What is there left for me to do? Haven't I been tortured enough?'

The Public Prosecutor had no better reply to that than that he could see she was lying by the look on her face.

They tried a confrontation between Rossana and Signorina Piastra, which turned out to be highly embarrassing for both of them. Each insisted they were telling the truth, and each begging the other not to distress her further.

They both departed in floods of tears. As she left the court Rossana took a photograph of her baby from her bag and handed it to the Judge, with the plea, 'Mr President, think of my child.'

Rossana was then brought back to confront Signor Piastra. This also ended in floods of tears and mutual recriminations. Half the court was weeping by now.

But the Public Prosecutor was not moved. You can't allow the mysteries of motherhood to stand in the way of getting at the truth, he pointed out.

After that they had another go at Zio Giuseppe, but to no avail. Giuseppe wasn't impressed by the Piastra story, or shamed into 'admitting the truth at last' by the Judge and the Public Prosecutor.

Then they confronted him with Luciano Doddoli, a journalist who had been prominent in the Montesi affair. It only

The Montesi Scandal

resulted in mutual accusation of a kind that got the court nowhere. Doddoli openly charged Giuseppe with murdering Wilma, but he had no evidence to back it up.

The Public Prosecutor, having seen the case against Piccioni and Montagna collapse, wanted an adjournment to consider whether there was a case against Giuseppe. The Judge agreed.

Slowly the farce now ground to a halt. The court ruled that there were no criminal proceedings pending against Giuseppe Montesi, and even if there were, it would not affect the outcome of the present trial. The Public Prosecutor was forced to admit that there was no case at all against the three accused men, and that most of Anna Caglio's evidence had been false.

Piero Piccioni was acquitted of having committed the crime. Ugo Montagna and Saverio Polito were acquitted because there had been no crime. Piccioni heard the decision unmoved while the other two defendants embraced everyone within reach.

No proceedings were taken against Giuseppe Montesi as the court established that his niece had not died as the result of foul play.

So ended a trial which was no credit to the Italian legal system. The case against the accused was so thin that the question arises why was the trial held at all? The Government doubtless believed that so great a head of steam had been generated by the affair that there would have been a revolution if the examining magistrate had thrown out the case against the accused as being *non prima facie*. It was perhaps necessary to have the trial in order to demonstrate the accused's innocence and deflate the dangerous uproar in Italy. It can only be assumed that the reputation of the legal system was of secondary concern compared with what the Montesi affair might have led to.

# Chapter 10
# Alma Rattenbury

Until recently women guilty of sexual immorality were at some disadvantage when up against English justice. Edith Thompson (1923), Charlotte Bryant (1936) and Ruth Ellis (1955) were all immoral women. Certainly the last two were murderesses. But all three were hanged.

The execution of Edith Thompson is generally considered a blot on English justice. Found guilty, with her lover, Frederick Bywaters, of the murder of her husband, she was hanged for adultery rather than murder. The first Lord Birkenhead – who, as F. E. Smith, had successfully defended Ethel Le Neve of being an accessory after the fact in the murder of Cora Crippen – defended Edith Thompson's execution by saying, 'Anyhow, she had the will to destroy her husband for the sake of her lover,' even though he confessed to a lingering doubt as to whether she was present at the crime for which she was hanged.

Few shared his view. Public opinion was, in fact, so shocked at the monstrous thing done to Edith Thompson that when twelve years later Alma Rattenbury was accused, with her lover, of a similar murder of passion, the Bywaters–Thompson case hung over the trial like an awful warning. Not many people believed that Mrs Rattenbury would be hanged, but her acquittal was by no means a foregone conclusion.

Alma Rattenbury was not really an attractive character. At first the evidence against her seemed overwhelming. She appeared to be a loose, immoral, drunken, callous woman who seduced a youth young enough to be her son, and after sleeping with him constantly, in the same room as her own child, she finally took part in the brutal murder of her wealthy husband.

This picture of Alma Rattenbury emerged when the case was first brought in sensational style before the public in the spring of 1935. But as usual the public image was distorted. The story was only half told. Mrs Rattenbury's sexual immorality dominated the public mind, and if she had been less fortunate in the judge who presided over her trial, it would probably have lessened her chances of justice; for one of the least admirable of Anglo-Saxon attitudes is that people found guilty of gross sexual immorality are considered capable of almost any crime.

Alma Victoria Clark was born at Victoria, British Columbia in 1897, the daughter of a printer. She grew up a talented musician and wrote many popular songs under the name 'Lozanne'. She became a quite well-known musician in Western Canada. Men found her extremely attractive. On the outbreak of war, when she was eighteen, she married a young Englishman named Caledon Dolly who joined the Canadian forces. She followed him to England where she got a job in Whitehall. When her husband was killed in action, she became a transport driver. After the war she married a man whose wife had divorced him citing her as co-respondent. A son named Christopher was born in 1922. The marriage failed. She returned to Canada and stayed with an aunt at Victoria.

Here she met Francis Mawson Rattenbury, a wealthy and successful architect of about sixty. Though married himself, he fell in love with Alma, then about thirty, and had an affair with her. His wife divorced him, citing her. Alma and Rattenbury got married in 1928, but owing to the scandal of the divorce had to leave Victoria. They came to England and rented a house, Villa Madeira, Manor Park Road, Bournemouth. In 1929 a child was born to them named John. After that they ceased marital relations.

Alma Rattenbury who a few years later was to be pilloried as the most evil woman of her day was devoted to her two sons, John and Christopher. The latter spent his holidays at Villa Madeira, and when John went to school, he came home every week-end. Alma had the domestic assistance of a companion-help, Miss Irene Riggs, who was extremely loyal to her and remembered her as the kindest and most generous person she had ever met. They were friends rather than mistress and servant and addressed each other as 'darling'. They went out together to the theatre, or to London.

Life at Villa Madeira, between the years 1928 and 1934, was very much like that in many other respectable Bournemouth homes. Rattenbury was a dull sort of man who took no great interest in his wife. He looked older than his years and had grown deaf. He grew worried about his finances which had been affected by the slump, and even talked of suicide on that account. Though he drank the better part of a bottle of whisky each day, he was not a drunkard but rather a quiet, pleasant, intelligent man who was as disappointed in his marriage as he was about his financial affairs.

Occasionally he lost his temper. Once when he was talking about suicide, Alma exclaimed impatiently to him: 'It's a pity you don't do it, instead of always talking about it.' This infuriated him and he hit her across the face, giving her a black eye. But she was not one to bear malice and they soon made it up.

He was generous and allowed her £1,000 a year, out of which she had to run the whole household, pay the food and drink bills, the servants' wages and the boys' school fees. But she was not a wise spender. She was often overdrawn and there were frequent quarrels about money.

Rattenbury ran a car, but by 1934 found driving difficult. Alma advertised in the *Bournemouth Daily Echo*: 'Daily willing lad, 14–18, for housework. Scout-trained preferred.'

This was answered by an eighteen-year-old youth named George Percy Stoner who had worked in a garage and could drive a car. He was considered eminently suitable, particularly in view of his driving ability and was given the job of chauffeur-handyman. This was in September. Two months later he had become Alma's lover and was living in the house.

Stoner was a raw youth, barely literate, not very bright, though a decent enough lad. Alma Rattenbury was a sophisticated, gay, sentimental woman, talented in her way.

She was thirty-seven. He was eighteen. It is easy to see what was the attraction so far as he was concerned. She was still good to look at, and he was full of youthful lust beneath his quiet exterior. She seduced him and completely turned his head. But why was she so attracted to this immature, rather loutish youth?

The whole tragedy turned upon Alma's physical make-up. Nature had endowed her with extremely strong sexual desires. Since the birth of John, she had developed pulmonary tuberculosis and the illness inflamed her sexual appetite. For six years she had been deprived of sexual satisfaction. By the time Stoner appeared on the scene she was on the verge of nymphomania and could endure the torment no longer. She grasped at the lad almost in despair and when the young man's virility gave her what she had so long wanted, she fell in love with him, or imagined that she had.

His virility was in fact the main attraction so far as she was concerned. 'Love' to her was the physical enjoyment of sex. But it was not as simple as that. Like many women of loose morals, she was generous-hearted and loyal. Her affair with Stoner in no way turned her against her husband, for whom she maintained a constant affection. Nor did it make her less of a devoted mother to her two sons.

No one can pretend that Alma Rattenbury was a woman of taste. That she entertained her young lover in her bedroom at Villa Madeira when her six-year-old son was asleep in the same room, was a profoundly shocking thing for which there could be little excuse. At first she admitted it and tried to excuse it in the witness-box. She said in court that she did not consider it a dreadful thing, for little John was always sound asleep. Indeed, as the family doctor confirmed, he knew of no child with a sounder sleep and John noticed nothing of what was going on around him. But the revelation did irreparable damage to her character and she later tried to deny it.

But the love affair did not make her a murderer, as Mr Justice Humphreys, one of England's great judges, was at pains to point out to the jury.

According to Stoner, Alma Rattenbury seduced him shortly after he entered her employment during a trip to Oxford which, she told her husband, was a visit to relatives in Sunderland. She said the seduction took place somewhat later, on 22 November, 1934 – in fact, just before Stoner took up residence in the house. It is of scant importance. The fact remains that throughout the winter of 1934 and the spring of 1935 the two of them regularly slept together. The adultery took place both in his bedroom and in hers.

During this time Francis Rattenbury was constantly in the house and slept downstairs. It was generally believed that he knew what was going on and did not care. Alma said at her trial: 'He must have known about it, because he told me to live my own life quite a few years ago.' The Judge called him 'not a nice character – what the French call *un mari complaisant*, a man who knew his wife was committing adultery and had no objection to it.'

No one can say for certain that Rattenbury knew what was going on. Apart from being very deaf, incurious and tired of life, he drank so much every night that not only would his marital relations have been impossible, even if he desired them any longer, but in his alcoholic haze the noises of the incautious lovers on the floor above never came to his ears. There was certainly something pathetic about him, but those who knew him – Irene Riggs and his doctor – were of the opinion that he was not the contemptible character who would consciously permit his wife to go to bed regularly with his chauffeur-handyman.

The person who was perhaps most distressed by the affair between Alma and Stoner was Irene Riggs. For her it meant the end of a pleasant and delightful intimacy with the mistress she loved with exemplary loyalty. Alma told her about the affair with Stoner. Irene considered Stoner a quite unsuitable person to enjoy the favours and love of Alma Rattenbury who at least should have chosen someone more of her own age and class. She found the liaison shocking at first, though she was forced to accept it. It meant the end of many pleasant little outings with her mistress which had given her so much pleasure. Now Mrs Rattenbury was obsessed by her teenage lover. Naturally enough, Irene Riggs resented Stoner and he didn't like her very much, though there was no open enmity between them.

In March, 1935 Alma's bank account was considerably overdrawn. She cajoled £250 out of her husband on the pretence that she had to go to London for a minor operation. She had had several such operations in the past. Rattenbury had always paid generously for them.

On 19 March Alma went to London, taking Stoner with her. They stayed at the Royal Palace Hotel, Kensington, as brother and sister, occupying rooms opposite each other. In return for the enjoyment Stoner gave her in bed, she took him to Harrods and bought him two new suits, shirts, handkerchiefs, ties, gloves, three pairs of crêpe-de-chine pyjamas, two sets of underwear and a mackintosh. He was not above taking £15 10s. from her to buy a ring which she solemnly accepted as a present.

They stayed in London four days. The experience thoroughly turned Stoner's head and was directly responsible for the tragedy which followed. Here he was no longer the servant, but the equal. He was addressed as 'sir', was waited on, ate at the same table as his mistress and was intoxicated by the presents she showered upon him. A simple labourer's son, he had never experienced anything like this before and the taste of 'high life' in London increased his vanity and his determination to make the most of the situation in which he found himself.

They returned to Villa Madeira on 22 March. It is possible that Stoner would have resigned himself once more to the easy-going life there, had not Mr and Mrs Rattenbury decided to go away together.

Rattenbury asked no questions. He did not even inquire

about the operation his wife was supposed to have gone to London for. He was utterly depressed, reading a book in which a man married to a young wife had committed suicide, and he expressed his admiration for anyone who had the courage to take his own life. In an attempt to cheer him up, Alma suggested that they should go to Bridport and see a friend of theirs, a Mr Jenks. She had no desire, it would seem, for her husband to commit suicide.

Rattenbury agreed to go. Jenks was a wealthy business-man who was associated with a block of flats for which Rattenbury was to have been the architect and which was delayed owing to the economic depression. Alma suggested that Jenks could help Rattenbury with regard to his financial worries. She telephoned Bridport, found they would be welcome at Mr Jenks's home and made arrangements to go there the following day.

The telephone was in Rattenbury's bedroom which opened off the drawing-room, and while his wife was phoning he remained in the drawing-room. During the telephone conversation Stoner, who had overheard the arrangements Alma was making, came into the bedroom in a state of fury. He held an air pistol in his hand which she took to be a revolver. He told her bluntly that if she went to Bridport with her husband he would kill her. Afraid of her husband overhearing and apparently not taking his threat seriously, Alma took Stoner into the dining-room where he accused her of having had sexual intercourse with her husband that afternoon behind closed doors in the bedroom.

Stoner was beside himself with jealousy. He knew he would have to drive Mr and Mrs Rattenbury to Bridport, and in the Jenks' big house his place would be among the servants. To be reminded of his menial status so soon after the dazzling luxury of the Royal Palace Hotel where he had stayed with Alma as her equal was intolerable. He believed that at the Jenks' house Mr and Mrs Rattenbury would have to share a bedroom, and he told Alma that if they went to Bridport he would refuse to drive them there.

Alma Rattenbury was a persuasive as well as a sympathetic woman, and she was not unaware of the way her lover felt. She assured him most convincingly, in the first place, that there had been no intercourse between herself and her husband that afternoon – indeed there hadn't been for years; and in the second place, that she and her husband would not share a room at the Jenks'. They had stayed with the Jenks before and had always had separate rooms. Her assurances only partly mollified Stoner who left brooding darkly. That evening he went to his grandparents' house and borrowed a carpenter's mallet.

It was generally assumed that Stoner was completely dominated by Alma Rattenbury. That great student of crime, the late Miss R. Tennyson Jesse, was of the opposite opinion. 'There is no woman so much under the dominance of her lover as the elderly mistress of a much younger man,' she observed and quoted Benjamin Franklin's words: 'As in the dark all cats are grey, the pleasure of corporal enjoyment with an old woman is at least equal and frequently superior; every knack being by practice capable of improvement. . . . Lastly, they are so grateful.'

Alma Rattenbury was neither elderly nor old. She was a desirable woman in her late thirties with a potent sexuality that would have appealed strongly to any man. Miss Jesse who attended her trial described her as being very attractive to men. 'In the witness box she still showed as a very elegant woman. She had a pale face, with a beautiful egg-like line of the jaw, dark grey eyes and a mouth with a very full lower lip. She was undoubtedly, and always must have been, a *femme aux hommes*, that is to say . . . first and foremost a woman to attract men and be attracted by them.'

There is nothing unusual in a youth being obsessed by such a woman. The magic of first love and the first experience of sex have a powerful effect upon the young. Every man treasures his first experience of physical passion and remembers how he confused it with love. To be initiated into the mysteries of sex by an older, experienced woman is no small advantage to a young man, though he may well suffer agonies at the time, as Stoner obviously did. Alma unfortunately did not understand how he felt about going to Bridport with her and her husband as their servant, though there is no doubt at all that she loved him dearly and was even prepared to give her life for him.

And so the inexorable events of 24 March, 1935 led them all to tragedy, death and ruin.

It was Irene Riggs's night out. Alma sat at home and played cards with her husband, kissed him good night, then went upstairs between nine-thirty and ten to pack for the trip to Bridport. Irene returned about ten-fifteen, going straight to her room. About ten minutes later she went downstairs intending to get something to eat in the kitchen, but her purpose was distracted by the sound of heavy breathing. She looked into Rattenbury's bedroom, switched on the light and saw that he was not in bed. The sound of heavy breathing seemed to come from the drawing-room. She concluded that Rattenbury had fallen asleep in his chair, as he often did after drinking nearly a bottle of whisky as a night-cap. Irene returned to her room and came out again later to go to the lavatory.

She found Stoner hanging over the banisters at the top of the stairs.

'What's the matter?' she asked.

'Nothing,' he replied. 'I was just looking to see if the lights were out.'

Irene noticed that the lights were out. She returned to her room. A little later Alma Rattenbury came in and told her about the proposed trip to Bridport. They were going by car, but she did not know whether Stoner or her husband would be driving.

Alma then returned to her own room and got into bed. About ten minutes later Stoner came into the room. She was expecting him as usual and he got into bed with her. She anticipated, and indeed wanted, the usual sexual intercourse, for she would be deprived of it while she and her husband were away at Bridport. But there was no thought of sex in Stoner's mind on that night. She immediately noticed that he was greatly agitated.

'What's the matter, darling?' she asked. He replied that he was in great trouble, but could not tell her what it was. 'But you must tell me,' she said. He told her it was so awful that she could not bear it. Alma replied she was strong enough to bear anything.

Finally he told her, 'You won't be going to Bridport tomorrow, as I have hurt Ratz.'

She did not realize quite what he meant by this remark until she heard her husband groaning downstairs. Stoner told her that he had hit Rattenbury on the head with a mallet. Alarmed, Alma jumped out of bed, saying she must go to him.

She fled down the stairs in her bare feet, into the drawing-room where she found her husband leaning back in his chair, one of his eyes swollen and discoloured. He was unconscious and there was a large pool of blood on the floor. She stumbled around the table and trod on his false teeth with her bare feet. She screamed, a wave of hysterical nausea coming over her. Yelling for Irene, she grabbed the whisky bottle thinking the neat spirit would calm her stomach which was rising in her throat. Swallowing the whisky, she picked up a towel and put it around her husband's head, then was violently sick.

After that, Alma Rattenbury swore, she remembered no more of what had happened that night. The story was taken up by Irene Riggs who came rushing downstairs to find her mistress in a state of hysteria, begging her to phone the doctor and crying, 'Oh, poor Ratz! Poor Ratz! Can't someone do something?'

To Irene Riggs Mr Rattenbury seemed to be just sitting asleep in the chair, but then she observed his black eyes and the blood on the floor near him. She phoned Dr William O'Donnell who had been both physician and friend to the Rattenburys for a number of years.

Meanwhile Alma was 'raving about the house', drinking whisky, being violently sick, and telling Irene to wipe up the blood in case her little boy should see it. Irene fetched a bowl and a cloth and bathed Rattenbury's eye, not suspecting the gravity of his injuries. She called Stoner who helped them carry the injured man to his bed.

Dr O'Donnell arrived at Villa Madeira at a quarter to midnight. He found Mrs Rattenbury drunk and hysterical, and her husband lying in bed, a bloodstained towel around his head which was itself now covered in blood.

As the doctor tried to make an examination, Alma kept getting in the way, crying, 'Look at him! Look at him! Somebody has finished him,' and trying to take his clothes off.

It was obvious to Dr O'Donnell that the insensible man was in need of urgent surgical attention. He phoned Mr Alfred Rooke, a Bournemouth surgeon, who arrived at Villa Madeira shortly after midnight.

Alma Rattenbury's behaviour again made proper examination impossible. Owing to her condition the doctors decided to remove the injured man to the Strathallan Nursing Home where they detected three deep skull wounds which looked as though caused by a blunt instrument. The skull was seriously fractured and the smashed bone driven into the brain. It was obvious that he could not live for long. Dr O'Donnell had no option but to phone the police who arrived at Villa Madeira about two o'clock.

Inspector Mills took charge of the case. They found Mrs Rattenbury very much the worse for drink – but, in their estimation, not drunk.

She already had intimated to Constable Bagwell, the first on the scene: 'At nine o'clock I was playing cards with my husband in the drawing-room and I went to bed about ten-thirty. I heard a yell. I came downstairs and saw him sitting in a chair. I sent for Dr O'Donnell and he was taken away.'

When Inspector Mills informed her that her husband was in a critical condition she exclaimed: 'Will this be against me?' He cautioned her. She confessed: 'I did it. He has lived too long. I will tell you in the morning where the mallet is. Have you told the Coroner yet? I shall make a better job of it next time. Irene does not know. I have made a proper muddle of it. I thought I was strong enough.'

It was obvious that the woman was rambling in a semi-alcoholic condition, but the Inspector could hardly ignore what she said.

Dr O'Donnell left the nursing home about 3.30 a.m. When he came out Stoner, who had driven him there in the Rattenbury's car, was peacefully asleep at the wheel, which on the surface appeared to be an indication of a clear conscience.

When the doctor arrived back at Villa Madeira he found all the lights on, the door open, and the radiogram playing. There were four police officers in the house, endeavouring to conduct an investigation amid the uproar.

Alma's hysterical conduct had caused them considerable embarrassment. When the Inspector had left the house to go to the nursing home to inquire about Rattenbury's condition P. C. Bagwell stayed alone with Alma and Irene. According to his statement Alma approached the constable with the words: 'I did it with a mallet. Ratz has lived too long. It is hidden. No, my lover did it. I would like to give you £10. No, I won't bribe you.' She then became maudlin and amorous and tried to kiss the constable. She so pestered him with her attentions that he went outside the house. She tried to follow him, but Irene prevented her, locked the door and finally had to push her into a chair and sit on her to keep her in the house.

In Dr O'Donnell's opinion, Mrs Rattenbury was in no fit condition to make a statement, for she obviously did not know what she was saying. She was in a state of uncontrollable excitement, running about saying wild things to the police officers.

When Inspector Mills asked her who she thought had done it, she named Rattenbury's son of his first marriage. Dr O'Donnell knew that the son, who was a man of thirty-two, was not in England, and he told the Inspector that Mrs Rattenbury could have no idea what she was saying, and was in no condition to be asked any questions. She was then taken to bed and the doctor gave her a large shot of morphia.

But she did not sleep for long. The police were in the house all night. Even drug-induced sleep was impossible in the state Alma was in. At six the police had her up again, and called in a police matron. They realized that she was a sick woman who had been drinking half the night and was still under the influence of the morphia. All the same, they took a statement from her at eight in the morning, an action for which they were subsequently severely criticized.

191

In the statement she alleged: 'About 9 p.m. on 24 March I was playing cards with my husband when he dared me to kill him, as he wanted to die. I picked up a mallet and he then said, "You have not the guts to do it." I then hit him with the mallet. I hid the mallet outside. I would have shot him if I had had a gun.' Detective-Inspector William G. Carter, to whom this statement was made, later recalled that she read it over aloud and then signed it.

Carter then arrested her. Before she left the house she had a moment alone with Irene Riggs and requested of her: 'You must get Stoner to give me the mallet.'

No one really knew what went on in Alma's mind during the hours after the discovery of her fatally injured husband. Afterwards she swore that everything was a total blank, and no amount of pressure would make her say otherwise. If her story of what Stoner said to her in bed was true, then she knew he had administered those terrible injuries to her husband. Judging by her actions, it seems that her very first thoughts were for her husband, her second for her young son, and her third for her lover whom she wished to save from the consequences of his deed.

She was taken to Bournemouth police station and at 8.45 a.m. was charged with causing grievous bodily harm to her husband with intent to murder.

In answer to the charge, she said: 'That is right. I did it deliberately and would do it again.'

Medical opinion considered that she was not normal when she made these statements, and many people thought that a charge should not have been made against her in view of this. When Dr O'Donnell saw her at Bournemouth police station later during the same day, she could not stand up without support. She looked dazed and her pupils were still contracted as the result of the morphia he had given her. Three days later Dr Morton, of Holloway Prison, stated his opinion that she was still suffering from confusion of mind as the result of the alcohol and the morphia. 'She kept repeating the same sentences over and over again.'

The police were in a difficult position. The victim of the assault was dying and they knew the ultimate charge

In 1935, Alma Rattenbury, aged 38, was acquitted of the murder of her wealthy husband, while her 18-year-old lover, George Percy Stoner, was sentenced to death. Broken, Mrs Rattenbury entered a nursing home (*below*). A few days later she committed suicide. After the trial the police had to clear the crowds away from the Old Bailey (*bottom*).

Ethel Le Neve (*top*). Lord Mohun
(*below left*) was acquitted of the
murder of William Mountford. The
lady involved was actress Anne
Bracegirdle, seen here (*right*) in
Dryden's play *The Indian Queen*.

would be murder. Alma Rattenbury had confessed to the crime and had in fact admitted it over and over again. They may well have underestimated the confused state of her mind, but they had no alternative but to charge her with the crime.

Later, when it seemed that after all she had not struck the fatal blow the Director of Public Prosecutions was exposed to criticism for putting her on trial; but legal authorities held that in view of her confession the D.P.P. was bound to proceed against her in the circumstances.

While Alma Rattenbury was in Holloway Prison, London, Irene Riggs and Stoner were left alone at Villa Madeira. Irene hated being in the house alone with Stoner. She was convinced of her mistress's innocence. She knew that Alma was quite incapable of hurting anyone, let alone her husband of whom she was very fond.

Dr O'Donnell had been asked by Mr Rattenbury's relatives to keep an eye on Villa Madeira. When he called there he was, however, unable to have a word alone with Irene Riggs. Stoner would not leave them and was all the time hovering suspiciously in the background.

O'Donnell called again on 28 March when Stoner had gone to Holloway to see Mrs Rattenbury. Irene told him that her mother had seen Stoner drunk the previous night. He had been going up and down the road shouting, 'Mrs Rattenbury is in jail and I have put her there."

Irene informed him also that Mrs Rattenbury had not committed the crime. Stoner had confessed to her that he had done it. He had told her there would be no fingerprints on the mallet because he had worn gloves. Dr O'Donnell took her to Bournemouth police station where she made a statement.

The following day Francis Rattenbury died and Stoner was arrested for murder on his return to Bournemouth. He asked: 'Do you know Mrs Rattenbury had nothing to do with this affair?'

After being cautioned, he told the police: 'When I did the job I believe he was asleep. I hit him and then went upstairs and told Mrs Rattenbury. She rushed down then. You see, I watched through the french window and saw her kiss him goodnight and then leave the room. I waited and crept in through the french window which was unlocked. Still, it ain't much use saying anything.' He then added, a little touchingly: 'I suppose they won't let her out yet?'

The Director of Public Prosecutions had a clear case against George Stoner, though not against Alma Rattenbury. She now denied all knowledge of what had passed at Villa Madeira during that dreadful night, and claimed to know nothing of any confessions she had made. In fact she now denied all knowledge of the crime.

All the same her confessions could not be ignored; and if the view was taken that she had made them in an attempt to protect her lover, then the assumption was irresistible that there may have been a conspiracy between them to get rid of Rattenbury. This, in the circumstances, would have been extremely difficult to prove.

On the other hand, to have released Alma Rattenbury unconditionally would have aroused a storm of criticism in view of her behaviour – the sympathy with Stoner, as the teenage victim of her lust and wanton immorality, would have been overwhelming both among the public and in the jury box.

The D.P.P. took the only course available to him. He placed them both on trial charged with the murder and left it to the jury to decide.

Mr R. P. Croom-Johnson, K.C., put it like this in court: 'It is the contention of the prosecution that one or other of the accused delivered a blow or blows at the head of Mr Rattenbury. And if that is right the prosecution suggests for your consideration that these two people, with one common object and one common design, set out to get rid of Mr Rattenbury, who, as I suggested earlier, stood in their way.'

The defence of both prisoners presented great difficulties. Alma refused to accuse Stoner, though she was prepared to go into the box and tell the truth of what had happened, but only after much pressure from her legal advisers. Her counsel, Mr Terence O'Connor, K.C., had the almost impossible task of presenting her as a sympathetic character. The prejudice against her was overwhelming, so much so that the case could not be tried at the county assizes and was transferred to the Old Bailey.

Stoner presented his counsel, Mr J. D. Casswell, with perhaps even greater difficulties. He pleaded not guilty and insisted that he was a cocaine addict. There was no evidence at all to support this, and the theory that he had attacked the murdered man in a fit of uncontrollable jealousy while the balance of his mind was upset by the drug, was quite ridiculous and made not the slightest impression on the court. Stoner didn't even know what cocaine looked like. When asked, he said it was brown with black specks in it.

When Mr Casswell went to see Stoner in Brixton Prison before the trial, he was well aware that all the young man was concerned about was ensuring that Alma was not convicted, which was considerably to his credit.

It seemed to Casswell that Stoner did not care whether he himself was convicted or not, and at the interview he was almost completely unco-operative. Though all this might be said to be very much in Stoner's favour, it put Casswell in a most difficult position. He had little hope of saving his client, except by his own art of persuasion. To put him in the box would be fatal. The only way of saving Stoner, Casswell knew, was to get the jury to believe that Mrs Rattenbury struck the fatal blows, and if he then were to put Stoner in the box he would passionately deny it and confess it was his doing.

It told heavily against Stoner that he failed to go into the witness-box while Alma did. Was he really prepared to die for her? And she for him? If so, it was certainly a great romance, whatever else might be said about the characters of this strangely-assorted Romeo and Juliet who appeared at the Old Bailey before Mr Justice Humphreys on 27 May, 1935.

Stoner's counsel has said that he did not know that Alma was going to give evidence until the morning when the trial opened and her counsel informed him that she would be giving evidence against Stoner. It was a shock to Casswell, and he took it to mean that Alma was going to give sworn evidence against her ex-lover in order to try and save her own neck.

Actually, it was not until almost the last minute that Alma had been persuaded by her counsel to give evidence. Though she was faithful to Stoner in her fashion, the first thought in her life was her children, and the terrible thing they would inherit if she was found guilty. It was this, more than anything else, that induced her to go into the box and tell the truth, and the consensus of opinion about this strange and complicated case is that Alma Rattenbury did tell the truth in the witness-box.

The prosecution's main witness was Irene Riggs, though she could be persuaded to say very little which told against the female defendant. But what she did mention about Stoner was very damaging, and it came out dramatically in court.

Mr O'Connor, Alma's counsel, cross-examined Irene. On the Monday morning, she recollected, Stoner had said to her: 'I suppose you know who did it?' She asked back: 'Well?' But he gave no reply.

O'Connor then sat down, supposing that his cross-examination was completed, when Irene added: 'There was something else on the Tuesday that I remember. I asked Stoner why he had done it.'

There was an astonished pause in court, a sudden rising of tension.

Casswell was about to rise and cross-examine her on behalf of Stoner, and naturally he would not be expected to pursue a point so damaging to his client.

Mr Justice Humphreys immediately intervened.

'Wait a minute. Do you want to put any further questions, Mr O'Connor?'

O'Connor was on his feet again in an instant. He was not going to let an opportunity like this go by.

'My lord, I think I will follow this up, if I may.'

From the witness-box Irene Riggs said: 'I should have said it when he asked me another question.'

'What was it?' asked O'Connor.

'On the Tuesday I asked Stoner why he had done it,' replied Irene.

'What did he say?'

'He said because he had seen Mr Rattenbury "living with" Mrs Rattenbury in the afternoon.'

The damage was done. It was irreparable. There was little Casswell could do to retrieve the situation as far as his client was concerned. If young Stoner had struck the blows, then he was guilty of a despicable murder.

But so far as Alma Rattenbury was concerned, it was different. The terrible Bywaters–Thompson case cast its awful shadow over the Rattenbury–Stoner trial. The consciousness of the savage fate which Edith Thompson had met at the hands of English justice in its harshest mood doubtless held back the hands of Judge, counsel and jury alike. The unease caused by the hanging of Edith Thompson not only went a long way to saving Alma Rattenbury from the hangman; it also marked the beginning of the end of capital punishment in England.

Alma's performance in the witness box caused a deep impression. She told the story of what happened on the day of her husband's death in a way which seemed both earnest and truthful. She made no attempt to evade or excuse her immoralities. Her story could not be shaken even after the most searching cross-examination.

The trial lasted four days. Observers remarked that it aged Alma by twenty years. Day by day her physical aspect changed. She seemed to grow old in the court as though time itself had in some strange way been speeded up. Stoner, on the other hand, appeared unmoved by the whole drama.

Alma Rattenbury was fortunate in her judge. Travers Humphreys's summing up was a masterly exposition of the law. But he did not spare her character. He called her 'a woman so lost to all sense of decency, so entirely without any morals that she would stop at nothing to gain her ends, particularly her sexual gratification, and if that be true, then, say the prosecution, do you think that woman would stop at the killing of her husband, particularly if she had not to do it herself?'

Speaking of the 'degradation to which this wretched woman has sunk', he went on: 'You will remember that she gave evidence herself that she was committing adultery – she is an adulteress of course – regularly in bed with her husband's servant in her bedroom and that in that bedroom in a little bed there was her own child of six, and counsel asked her: "Do you really mean that you chose that room when if you wanted to gratify your passions you could have gone into the man's room which was just along the passage and done it there? Did you really choose the room where your child was asleep?" And you will remember that the woman who was in the witness-box seemed surprised that anyone should put such a question to her, and her answer was apparently given in perfectly good faith: "Why not? The little boy was asleep. He was a sound sleeper".'

After conceding that no one could have sympathy with this woman whose morals and depravity he had so soundly berated, the Judge gave the jury a stern warning that they must not convict her of the crime of murder 'because she is an adulteress, and an adulteress, you may think, of the most unpleasant type'. The case against her, the Judge pointed out, depended neither on her character, nor on the theories of the prosecution, but solely on her statements, and these she had made only after she had drunk considerable quantities of alcohol.

The jury took forty-seven minutes to reach their verdict. They found Mrs Rattenbury not guilty and Stoner guilty, adding a recommendation to mercy with their verdict. Mr Justice Humphreys had no alternative but to sentence Stoner to death, but he added a strong recommendation of his own to the jury's plea for mercy.

Alma left the court with barely any feeling of relief. She was overwhelmed with remorse and shame, haunted with grief over the fate of Stoner, desperately miserable about her children. Hounded by the Press, execrated by society, ill physically and mentally, she did not – could not – vanish from the scene like the mysterious Adelaide Bartlett, and leave not a trace behind.

Her husband's relatives who treated her with great charity took her away with them. But wherever they went they were pursued by the Press. Even when she was finally removed to a nursing home in London, newspapermen followed her; one of them called out to the doctor who was with her: 'It doesn't matter where you take her, we will follow you.'

She was admitted to the nursing home on 3 June for 'rest and treatment'. The following afternoon, she borrowed two pounds from one of the officials at the home, saying she was going out and would be back at nine o'clock. She appeared normal and the doctor allowed her to go out.

The following day her body was found by the side of a stream near Christchurch. She had stabbed herself six times in the chest with a knife which three times she had driven into her heart. The agony, despair, self-hatred and remorse which had caused her to do this was reflected in letters which were found in her handbag. Some of these were read at the inquest.

I want to make it perfectly clear that no one is responsible for what action I may take regarding my life. I quite made up my mind at Holloway to finish things should Stoner     (*sic*)     and it would only be a matter of time and opportunity. Every night and minute is only prolonging the appalling agony of my mind.

A letter addressed to the Governor of Pentonville Prison said:

If I only thought it would help Stoner, I would stay on, but it has been pointed out to me all too vividly that I cannot help him. That is my death sentence.

Another letter read:

Eight o'clock. After so much walking I have got here. Oh, to see the swans and the spring flowers and just smell them. And how singular I should have chosen the spot Stoner said he nearly jumped out of the train once at. It was not intentional my coming here. I tossed a coin, like Stoner always did, and it came down Christchurch. It is beautiful here. What a lovely world we are in! It must be easier to be hanged than to have to do the job oneself, especially in these circumstances of being watched all the while. Pray God nothing stops me tonight. Am within five minutes of Christchurch now. God bless my children and look after them.

Yet another:

I tried this morning to throw myself under a train at Oxford Circus. Too many people about. Then a bus. Still too many people about. One must be bold to do a thing like this. It is beautiful here and I am alone. Thank God for peace at last.

Stoner lost his appeal, but he was reprieved. His mistress died in the belief that he would be hanged.

Although he had admitted in his statement to the police that he had killed Rattenbury with the mallet, Stoner later maintained that he was totally innocent of the crime.

His new story of the fatal night was that he had fetched the mallet for an innocent reason, put it in the coal shed and then went to bed. Later he went on to the landing and was looking downstairs to see if the old man had gone to bed so that he could go to Alma's bedroom as usual. This was when Irene Riggs saw him. Afterwards he went to Alma's bedroom and found her in bed terrified. He heard a sound of groaning, and Alma said, 'Hear him!' Then she got out of bed and ran downstairs. Later he found the mallet on the floor of the drawing-room and he hid it in the garden where it was subsequently found by the police.

What was the truth of the affair? Many have chosen to believe Alma Rattenbury, that sad, unbalanced, passionate creature whom society convicted and sentenced to death when judge and jury acquitted her.

# Chapter 11
# Edmund Pook

'She was poor, but she was honest' is a catch phrase which could have been applied to many Victorian crimes. Perhaps none more so than to that of Jane Clouson, a seventeen-year-old domestic servant employed by Ebeneezer Pook, a Greenwich printer, whose brutal murder was a mean and atrocious act which reflected some of the less admirable aspects of Victorian petty snobbery.

Jane's story is the familiar one of the betrayed servant girl who was foolish enough to imagine that the son of the house would marry her. She was fifteen when she went into the service of the Pooks. A respectable, good-looking girl, little is known of her parents except that her father was a night-watchman at Millwall Ironworks. She had relatives who lived near Greenwich.

Ebeneezer Pook had previously been employed by *The Times* and now owned a printing business at Greenwich. He lived with his wife and two sons at 3 London Street, Greenwich, which has since been pulled down and become Greenwich High Road. The elder son was Thomas. The younger son, Edmund, was twenty and suffered from epileptic fits, but that did not prevent him chasing after all the pretty girls in the district. Both brothers worked in their father's business in Greenwich and were interested in what was called Penny Readings, a Victorian name for amateur dramatics.

Pook, as a fairly successful businessman, had social ambitions. He considered that Thomas had married beneath him and was determined that Edmund should not make the same mistake.

Young Edmund had no thought of marriage. He was too busy pursuing his innumerable flirtations. During the time when the Pooks' affairs were occupying the attention of the nation Edmund was carrying on with a Miss Durnford, a Miss Langley, a Miss Love and a Miss Wicks. For the purpose of attracting the attentions of his ladyloves, Edmund used a whistle which he always carried with him. It played an important part in the subsequent proceedings.

Edmund of course did not enjoy the pleasures of sexual intercourse with the various girls he was pursuing. Middle-class Victorian girls, though willing for light flirtation, were not free with their favours. It was not expected of nice girls in those days.

But with Jane Clouson it was different. She was only the parlour-maid after all, and as she was living in there was ample opportunity. Moreover, the advances of the young son of the house were not unwelcome to the innocent Jane, then seventeen, who succumbed and fell in love with him.

Edmund's affair with Jane was not just an isolated seduction – a case of a youth having what he wanted and leaving it at that. Edmund enjoyed Jane's favours over a period. She had confided that much to a friend three months before her death when she considered herself pregnant by Master Edmund. She must have got over that scare, for at the time of her death she was pregnant again and the pregnancy was only two months old.

On 13 April, 1871 Mrs Pook gave Jane the sack. The Pooks explained later that it was because of her slovenliness, but Jane's friends contradicted their statement; Jane told them she was sacked because Mrs Pook discovered about her affair with Edmund. This the Pooks scornfully denied: in their view Edmund would not demean himself by being intimate with someone of the lower classes. The Pooks stuck to their story, that she was slovenly. However, Jane had been in their service for two years and it is not likely that she would suddenly have become slovenly. Jane had no reason to lie. Whether Mrs Pook knew of the girl's pregnancy is not known. Apart from possible bouts of sickness, Jane's condition can hardly have been noticeable to Mrs Pook.

Jane, sacked on the spot as was the custom of the day, went to a woman friend named Emily Wolledge, a former employee of Pook, who arranged for her to lodge with a Mrs Fanny Hamilton of 12 Ashburnham Street, Greenwich.

In the fortnight which she now had left of her young life, Jane not only became well acquainted with her landlady. She also saw something of her uncle and aunt, William and Elizabeth Trott, and her cousin Charlotte Trott, who lived at Deptford. She had also been friendly for some time with a Mrs Jane Prosser whose husband kept a general dealer's shop. It was to Mrs Prosser that Jane had confessed three months previously that she was pregnant and that Edmund Pook was responsible.

People later suggested that Mrs Prosser was an abortionist, but there was not the slightest reason to impugn the lady thus or to suppose that Jane had any such solution to her problem in mind. On the contrary, she was confident of a much happier outcome. And Mrs Prosser was an old friend in whom the girl could confide.

But it was to her cousin Charlotte that Jane told the story which ought to have put the rope around her murderer's neck and would have done in any country but England where the laws of evidence frequently prevent the jury from hearing the whole story.

There are good grounds for believing that after she had been dismissed from the Pooks' house, Jane remained in touch with Edmund. The young man had to keep her quiet in one way or another, for he must have been terrified of the truth of her condition and his responsibility for it coming to the ears of his formidable father. By now he had tired of the uneducated and clinging girl – who else indeed was there for the poor child to cling to? – and he was courting at least one much more interesting if less obliging girl.

Jane was desperate. Ruin and a bleak future stared her in the face unless Edmund stood by her. But he set her mind at rest and made her happy by promising to do so.

On Sunday, 24 April, Jane visited the Trotts, and they noticed that she was much more cheerful than she had been for weeks. In fact she was quite excited.

In the evening she made a remarkable confidence to her aunt and her cousin. Charlotte Trott later recalled what Jane had said to her:

'Charlotte, you must not be surprised if I am missing for some weeks, for Edmund says I must meet him either to-morrow night or on Tuesday to arrange to go with him into the country. He says he will have such a deal to tell me, and that we shall have to make all the arrangements. He says he is going to take me to a christening at St Ives. Then we shall go somewhere else to such a nice place where I shall be so happy. But I am not to tell anyone where I am going, or to write to anyone for some time, as he does not want anyone to know where I am. You must not be surprised if you miss me for some weeks, but you shall have the first letter I shall write to anyone. Edmund says I shall not want for money, and if it is five pounds I shall have it and I shall be happy.'

Charlotte's mother confirmed that this in substance was what Jane had told them on that last Sunday of her life.

No suspicion dawned in the mind of the innocent Jane. She could not have known that it was an immemorial trick of murderers to get their victims to tell their friends that they would be going away and would not be heard of for some time. But Edmund Pook with his experience of Penny Readings which probably included *The Murder in the Red Barn* was no doubt better informed on this particular subject.

On that last Sunday evening of her life a gay, starry-eyed Jane walked across Blackheath with Charlotte and told her the even greater secret that she and Edmund were to be married and that she was meeting him at the top of Crooms Hill either on Monday or Tuesday evening when all the arrangements were to be made. Jane went on to say she had told Edmund that she hoped his mother would be as good a friend to her as she was to the wife of Tom, the elder brother who had also married beneath him.

All the same Jane had given Edmund to understand that she was annoyed with the way Mrs Pook had dismissed her. Still, she was in no position to complain. She must get a husband or a protector at all costs.

Both Mrs Hamilton and Emily Wolledge – neither of whom had a reason to lie – stated afterwards that on the Monday Jane received a letter which she burnt as soon as she had read, and then immediately wrote a reply which she posted herself. She had told her landlady, Mrs Hamilton, that she had expected to get a job as a machinist, then later she described such a step as unnecessary, 'as Edmund was going to do something better for me'.

Jane had intimated to Charlotte the previous day that the meeting with Edmund would be either on Monday or Tuesday; she was waiting to hear. There is little doubt that the letter was from Edmund telling her to meet him on Tuesday and to burn the letter as soon as she had read it. The burning of the letter may well have sealed her fate; it certainly enabled Edmund later to make a scornful challenge to the police to produce any letter he had ever written to the murdered girl.

So we come to Tuesday, 26 April, 1871 – the last day of Jane's life. The only thing we know about her actions on that day is that in the early evening she took a walk with Mrs Hamilton into Deptford. They parted at the top of Douglas Street at about six-forty, when Jane said that she had an appointment to meet Edmund Pook at Crooms Hill at seven. Crooms Hill runs along the west side of Greenwich Park.

Jane had also told Mrs Prosser about this appointment on Tuesday evening with Edmund, when 'arrangements for her future' were to be made. Jane promised to tell Mrs Prosser later what happened.

There can be no doubt that she had this appointment with Edmund. He cannot have thought that she would talk about it, and he seems to have impressed upon her the importance of keeping it a secret. Later he denied the appointment altogether. He had in fact other arrangements of an amatory nature the same evening.

After Jane left Mrs Hamilton at the top of Douglas Street, she was not seen again by anyone until she was found dying at four o'clock the following morning.

For the last appointment of her life she wore a dark dress-and-jacket and a dark hat. Underneath her dress she had a light petticoat. On her dress was a pink rose ornament. She went to meet Edmund with a light heart, despite the difficulties of her situation.

The Kidbrooke Lane of 1871 was not the present Kidbrooke Lane, S.E.9, which turns off Westhorne Avenue. The old Kidbrooke Lane turned off Kidbrooke Park Road just opposite St James's Church, where Brooke Lane, S.E.3, now is. The whole area has been entirely rebuilt since Jane took her last evening walk there a hundred years ago.

It was then a country lane – dark, secluded, much frequented by lovers at night time. It ran towards Manor Farm which had the land all around under cultivation. A narrow stream, the Kid Brook, crossed the lane. This stretch of open country lay between Eltham on the south and Kidbrooke to the north-east which itself lies on the east side of Blackheath. Crooms Hill where Jane was to meet Edmund leads on to Blackheath. Just beyond the corner of Blackheath lies Mordern College, the grounds of which stretched to the point where Kidbrooke Lane began.

Exactly what happened in Kidbrooke Lane that Tuesday night was never discovered. Several people saw couples in the lane. Some reported hearing cries. Others recollected that a certain amount of horseplay was going on. Nothing unusual in Kidbrooke Lane apparently.

A man named Cronk declared that he heard a girl cry out 'Let me go! Let me go!' Then he saw a man and a girl struggling. The description of the girl's clothing corresponded with Jane's. Later Cronk identified Edmund Pook as the man he saw.

A certain Thomas Lazell also had seen Edmund Pook in a cornfield near Kidbrooke Lane with a girl, after seven o'clock that evening. He described Pook as wearing a billycock hat and a dark frock-coat.

William Norton, a coachman, was in the lane with a girl named Louisa Putnam. They both heard a girl screaming. Then, between eight-thirty and nine o'clock – they were vague about the time, being more interested in making love themselves – a man ran panting past them towards Mordern College. It was dark and they were unable to give a description of the man.

P.C. Donald Gunn was the constable whose beat included Kidbrooke Lane that night. He went down the lane for the first time at 10 p.m. and again at 1.45 a.m. without seeing anything unusual.

On the third time, just after 4 a.m., he saw a woman on her hands and knees, trying to crawl along. Thinking at first she was drunk, he went up to her and asked her what she was doing.

For a few moments she was unable to speak, then she groaned, 'Oh my head – my head!'

Feebly she held up her hand for help. As Gunn went closer to her with his bull's-eye torch he saw her face for the first time and was appalled at the injuries which had been inflicted upon her. There was a terrible wound on her head through which he could see part of her brain protruding. All over her face were gashed wounds, and where her right eye had been was a gaping, bloody hole.

She tried to raise herself up as she grasped his hand, then fell forward, moaning, 'Let me die – let me die!'

The shocked constable was unable to do anything for her except to try and make her comfortable while he went for help. He could get nothing out of her, not even her name. She was in a kind of delirium.

Before he left, he noticed that her gloves were beside her and her dark hat was about four feet away.

Gunn ran all the way into Eltham and returned with Sergeant George Haynes and a cab, into which they lifted the dying Jane with what tenderness they could and took her to Eltham.

Jane was still conscious, though hardly able to speak. She

moaned as the cab jolted through the April dawn to the end of Kidbrooke Lane, into Woodville Road, past the silent Manor Farm and along Kidbrooke Way (now Rochester Way) and into Eltham.

The policemen tried to make her talk and tell them what had happened to her, but the only thing she could say was, 'Oh, save me – save me!'

They took her to a Dr King in Eltham who immediately sent her to Guy's Hospital where it was seen at once that her case was hopeless.

Efforts were made to get her to speak before she died. She was conscious only for a short while. When she was asked her name, she muttered something which it was thought sounded like 'Mary Shru ——'

The questioners were expecting to hear a female name. 'Jane Clouson' could not sound like 'Mary Shru ——'. But 'Edmund Pook' muttered by a semi-conscious person might well be taken to sound like it.

When she died her body was examined. It was found that she had suffered a dozen incised wounds on her face, most of which had presumably been inflicted while she was lying on the ground. There were two large wounds on the left side of her face, one of which had depressed the temporal bone above the ear and lacerated the brain. A third wound had destroyed the right eye and fractured several bones around it. It was through this wound that the brain was protruding. Other injuries to the face left no doubt that the killer intended deliberate disfigurement. From the state of the girl's hands and knees it was deduced that she was a domestic servant, and the post-mortem showed that she was two months pregnant.

The police meanwhile were searching the scene of the crime. They found widely-spaced footprints – which were not preserved – on the soft ground, as though someone ran away from the murder spot. Not far away was the stream known as the Kid Brook, and here were found blood spots, suggesting that the killer washed the blood off himself in the water.

Other blood spots were traced which led up Kidbrooke Lane towards the grounds of Mordern College where the police found the murder weapon – a lathing hammer to which hairs and a sticky substance still adhered. This vicious weapon had a long handle and opposite the hammerhead, instead of claws, was a chopper. It was the perfect weapon for what the murderer presumably had in mind – killing and disfigurement.

The body remained unidentified until the following Sunday. The Trotts became anxious about the disappearance of their niece from Mrs Hamilton's house at 12 Ashburnham Street. They had heard about the murder in Kidbrooke Lane – the papers were full of it – and so they went to Superintendent Griffin at Blackheath Road police station.

They were reasonably certain that the clothes belonged to Jane, but when they went to Guy's to look at the body, the appalled Trotts were quite unable to recognize the battered face as that of their pretty niece. Then Mrs Trott remembered that there was a distinctive mole on Jane's left breast. The mole was there, and Jane's identity was established.

Charlotte and her aunt then told the police all that Jane had said the previous Sunday. Superintendent Griffin and Inspector Mulvany also interviewed Mrs Hamilton and Emily Wolledge. Then they went to see Edmund Pook.

Edmund created a bad impression from the outset. He was a full-faced, stockily-built young man, with long hair and side-whiskers. He was described by his contemporaries as a rather commonplace person.

He was not at the best of times a very pleasant young man, and the callous way he spoke about the dead girl whom, whether he was guilty of her murder or not, he knew quite well did much to prejudice opinion against him.

'She was a dirty young woman,' he maintained, 'and left in consequence.'

He was full of confidence, though his attitude was rather too belligerent to suggest innocence. He declared that the last time he saw Jane was when she left the house on 13 April. Mulvany who was in charge of the case fired questions at him.

'Have you written her a letter?'
'Certainly not.'

'People say you have.'

'Do they? Have you the letter? If it is in my handwriting that will prove it.'

Remembering the story of Jane burning the letter, Mulvany instinctively knew he had his man.

Mulvany invited him to account for his movements on the night of the murder. Pook said he went to Lewisham and came home about nine-fifteen.

'Who did you go to see in Lewisham?'

'A lady. But I did not see her.'

Mulvany asked to see what he was wearing at the time. It was a dark frock-coat and a billycock hat, as described by Lazell. When Mulvany found bloodstains on the clothes, he promptly arrested Edmund for the murder.

Neither the police investigations nor the trial of Edmund Pook at the Old Bailey in July 1871 reflect much credit upon the administration of justice. The police were strongly suspected of manufacturing evidence against the accused and had ignored important clues. The improper behaviour and inefficiency of Inspector Mulvany drew a rebuke from the Lord Chief Justice and questions were asked about it in Parliament.

At first it seemed that the evidence against Edmund was overwhelming. He had been seen running away from Kidbrooke Lane covered in mud after the murder. A shopkeeper identified him as the man who bought the murder weapon. There was blood on his hat and on his clothes. A woman said he had come into her shop after the murder to clean the mud off his clothes. A whistle, exactly like the one he used to attract the attention of his girl-friends, was found near the scene of the crime. There were the statements Jane had made to her aunt and cousin two days before her death. And there was of course Jane's pregnancy and the fact that she had said he was responsible for it.

Why then did Edmund get away with it?

Public opinion had been violently aroused by Jane's murder. Edmund's guilt was assumed from the start. The Pooks were hooted and reviled in the street. On 8 May an enormous crowd went to Jane's funeral, after which there was a violent demonstration in London Street outside the Pooks' house.

So anxious was everyone to see Edmund hanged that witnesses came forward who were prepared to swear to anything in their enthusiasm to incriminate him. Their stories were not tested sufficiently before they went into the witness box, with the result that much of the prosecution's case was discredited in court and the jury were greatly confused by the conflicting evidence.

Edmund's defence was clever and determined. His family stood by him with a fierce loyalty which nothing could shake. The Pooks were not interested in the truth. They were only interested in clearing the family name. In this they had the active support of the editor of *The Times* who stood by his former employee with marked partiality.

It is probable that all those who defended him so ardently believed honestly in his innocence. Indeed, the murder was such a brutal and savage one that it is difficult to imagine it could have been committed by a young man from a decent and respectable home such as Ebeneezer Pook's. It must surely have been committed by a madman.

This is an unreliable argument and one which was used at the trial of Lizzie Borden. The two cases make interesting comparison, because both Lizzie and Edmund were epileptics and capable of periods of uncontrollable passion.

The Pooks had an answer for all the evidence which seemed to incriminate Edmund so deeply. The blood on his clothes was due to his chronic nose-bleeding which was associated with his epilepsy. He went into the shop to clean the mud off his clothes after a fall on the way back from Lewisham where he had been to watch a young man whom he suspected of having designs on a girl-friend of his there.

As for his having an affair with the dead girl, it was quite out of the question. Mrs Pook declared in the witness-box that no son of hers would stoop to have an affair with a domestic servant. The evidence about Edmund buying the hammer was admittedly confusing and indecisive owing to the poor performance of the witnesses. The case against Edmund was indeed mainly circumstantial.

But what of Jane's statements on that last Sunday of her life when, radiant at the prospect of marrying Edmund, she had told her cousin and her aunt of the plans for her disappearance, and of her date with Edmund when 'her future' was to be decided? What of her statement to Mrs Hamilton on the evening of her death that she had an appointment to meet Edmund Pook at Crooms Hill at seven? Surely this was damning evidence against the accused.

So it was. But it was hearsay evidence and English law, generally speaking, sets its face like flint against hearsay evidence. Lord Chief Justice Bovill, the judge at Edmund's trial, insisted on the strict interpretation of the law and refused to allow the jury to hear the story of what Jane had told her cousin and her aunt on the Sunday before her murder.

There was also some rumour that the Lord Chief Justice was engaged in a feud with Sir John Coleridge, the Solicitor-General who led for the Crown, and was determined to obstruct the prosecution's case as much as he could.

Mrs Trott was called as a witness to identify her niece's body, but she was not permitted to repeat the conversation Jane had with her on the Sunday before her death; Charlotte was not called at all. The jury were thus kept completely in the dark about these vital conversations which put an entirely different complexion on the facts which they were permitted to hear.

The hearsay rule certainly saved Edmund's neck. He himself could not be questioned on any of these vital matters, because under the laws of evidence which were not altered until 1896 an accused person was not permitted to give evidence on his own behalf.

Edmund was saved as much by the inadmission of Jane's statements as by the fact that the Judge not only leant over backwards in his favour, but commented unfavourably on the police witnesses. The jury found him not guilty after twenty minutes' deliberation. He returned to Greenwich to the hoots and jeers of an infuriated populace who were convinced that great injustice had been done.

This was by no means the end of the affair. Edmund and

his family had to run the gauntlet of outraged public opinion. There were daily demonstrations against them.

On the Monday following the acquittal a procession of insulting effigies was towed past the house, including a truck bearing a tableau in which a woman was being repeatedly struck by a man with a lathing hammer. Afterwards a crowd numbering about four thousand demonstrated outside the Pooks' home. The police, aggrieved at the verdict, did little to stop it.

Then the pamphleteers got to work. A little booklet called *The Eltham Tragedy Reviewed* appeared in Greenwich and the neighbouring boroughs and was selling rapidly at twopence a copy.

The writer made some very critical comments about the conduct of the trial and said highly unflattering things about the Judge. He attacked the rules of evidence as practised in English courts, and raised the point that as in other countries the jury should have been told what Jane had said before she left Mrs Hamilton, since this showed the identity of the person she was intending to meet.

The most sensational part of the pamphlet was an undisguised attack on Edmund himself. One passage read:

'Now I will tell you how I shall conduct myself when I commit a murder, and I wish to let the judge, jury, police, counsel and the public know beforehand how I intend to act under the circumstances. I shall prepare myself for my diabolical task and cultivate my natural callousness and villainy by a devoted study of the most popular and sensational novels of the day. The girl I once loved and who is desperately in my way shall be my victim. An evening walk down a dark unfrequented lane and a small axe will supply me with all the conditions I shall require for accomplishing my design. Fifteen blows in fifteen seconds will be enough. When the deed is done, I shall not be miserable; I shall feel the same relief that a surgeon would feel after lopping off a mortified limb. But if my nerves should be a little agitated, a quick run home through the evening air will restore my equanimity.

'Knowing that the police can discover nothing special

against me, I shall give them every facility and treat them with the greatest apparent frankness. If they ask for any explanations why spots of blood are on my clothes, I shall promptly reply that my nose bled and this answer shall be considered conclusive and satisfactory for ever after. I shall be very unlucky if the witnesses against me are not stupid and sadly out of their reckoning of time. All hearsay evidence against me will of course be illegal, and I shall be acquitted amid the applause of an excited and bamboozled multitude.'

This was highly inflammatory stuff by any standards and it immediately provoked a libel action.

It was intended to. The Pooks didn't know who they were up against, for the author of the pamphlet was a wealthy London businessman, Newton Crossland, who felt keenly, as many did, that there had been a grave injustice. He was waging a war on behalf of this murdered servant girl whom he had never seen.

Jane's new champion was a doughty one and he briefed the foremost counsel in the land to fight her case once more in the courts.

But the libel action was different from the murder trial. At the Old Bailey Edmund was not permitted to give evidence. The principle was that it was entirely the onus of the prosecution to establish his guilt. This was not altered until the end of the century; we have the opinion of such a legal authority as Lord Birkett that the change in the law has not been to the advantage of the accused. Yet certainly it was a great advantage to Edmund that he was not subjected to cross-examination at the Old Bailey. The case would almost certainly have ended differently if he had been.

But in the civil action it was different. If he wanted to win it, he must be prepared to go into the witness-box and be cross-examined.

This was of course the last thing Edmund wanted to do. He would have preferred decent obscurity. After all, he had been very lucky at his trial and people would forget in time.

But he had no choice in the matter. He was a minor, and his father was determined to defend the family honour. Besides, the costs of the murder trial had all but ruined the Pook fortune and Pook senior saw the prospect of recouping heavy damages from the wealthy Newton Crossland.

So the wretched Edmund went into the box and endured a devastating cross-examination from Serjeant Parry, one of the great counsel of the day. It was a masterly performance on Parry's part. In effect he accused Edmund of the murder of Jane and of getting away with it at his trial.

'It is obvious,' said Parry in his final speech, 'that there are many circumstances which point to the young man being the murderer, and he cannot get over them. If the girl's lips had not been sealed by death, and if she had repeated those statements on oath, where would the plaintiff be now? Why, undergoing penal servitude for life.'

Edmund won his case, for he had undoubtedly been libelled. He had been found innocent at his trial, and it was not the province of a civil court to say that the trial verdict was wrong. But he was awarded a mere £50 damages. If the jury had been convinced that he was innocent of the murder they would have awarded him very large damages indeed in view of the deliberate nature of the libel.

Other actions followed and the whole business became finally lost in a maze of litigation which got the Pooks nothing in the way of damages. Nor did it rehabilitate Edmund in the public eye, though as the result of the libel actions no one dared say so openly during his lifetime.

The truth about this case has always been in dispute. The Pook faction told a story about Jane being affianced to a young seafaring man who returned home unexpectedly and then brutally murdered her when she confessed to her guilty intimacy with Edmund, immediately afterwards taking ship to escape justice. But if that had been the case, one would have imagined that Edmund rather than Jane would have been found done to death in Kidbrooke Lane.

Another story put out was that Jane had given Pook's name in order to conceal the real identity of the man who had put her in the family way, that she had met her mysterious seducer on the night of the murder, went with him to some place of amusement at Greenwich or New Cross, left there about eleven, took a stroll with him up Kidbrooke Lane, and there he attacked her unexpectedly, battered her into insensibility, and thinking her dead, dragged her into some dark corner. There she lay till she regained consciousness just before dawn, when she managed to crawl to the spot where P.C. Gunn found her.

Whoever was responsible for the murder, this is the most likely explanation of the mystery why the constable did not see her until 4 a.m.

But Edmund Pook's guilt has never been seriously challenged. According to Sir Edward Ridley in a letter to *The Times* in 1924, those who were in the court when Serjeant Parry defended Newton Crossland on the libel charge were fully satisfied that Parry had proved Edmund to be the murderer.

He escaped justice partly owing to the strict application of the rule against hearsay evidence and partly owing to the ineptitude of the prosecution. The police were criticized for their inefficiency and were accused of manufacturing evidence against the accused. For instance, it was suggested that the whistle found in the lane was planted there by Inspector Mulvany. Many lies were told in court and the most ardent of the perjurers were the Pooks themselves. Whether they believed in Edmund's innocence is not known. Certainly all those who have made a study of the case believe in his guilt.

Of all the precious characters in this sorry tangle of sex, murder and injustice the unfortunate victim herself had no reason to lie. What she said to her cousin and her aunt certainly had the ring of truth in it.

Poor Jane, butchered so brutally that night in Kidbrooke Lane where she had gone, in the springtime of her life, to meet the man she loved and who had promised to marry her – her story never had a hearing among the squalid din of legal battle which her death precipitated, a fact that does little credit to the way the law is sometimes practised in English courts.

# Chapter 12
# Lord Mohun

The hell-rakes of Restoration and Georgian times, like the Regency dandies and the young rowdies of today, were the delinquents of their age. Violence, uproar, cruel jokes and pranks were the delight of these young men, usually the scions of the upper classes. Young gentlemen amused themselves by torturing and mutilating innocent passers-by with their swords. Some dedicated their ample leisure to raping young girls. Others offered violence to any tradesman for the most trifling offence.

Some of these hell-rakes were men of intelligence and their behaviour is a reflection upon a society which did not know how to employ their talents.

One of the worst of these eighteenth-century rowdies was Charles, the fourth Baron Mohun, who inherited the title when a child, on the death of his father. Lord Mohun flourished under the reigns of William of Orange and Queen Anne and his behaviour caused great offence.

His boon companion was Captain Richard Hill with whom Mohun spent many a night roystering around London town, smashing windows, setting fire to houses, assaulting women and beating up the watch if they were bold enough to try and restrain them. Mohun deemed it sufficient explanation of his behaviour merely to inform the guardians of law and order that he was a peer of the realm.

Captain Hill had conceived a great passion for Anne Bracegirdle, the most popular actress of the day. Though not the most beautiful woman on the London stage, she was unquestionably the most fascinating and sought after. Lovely, black-eyed, her ravishing charms and ineffable grace of movement filled Drury Lane to capacity every night as she graced the plays of Mr Shakespeare, Mr Wycherley, Mr Congreve and Mr Vanbrugh.

Even though it was said that in the theatre she always had as many lovers as she had male spectators, no one had ever gained her favours. No man, however rich, however high in rank, had prevailed upon her to be his mistress.

Macaulay wrote rather disparagingly of her: 'Those who are acquainted with the parts which she was in the habit of playing, and with the epilogues which it was her especial business to recite, will not easily give her credit for any extraordinary measure of virtue or delicacy. She seems to have been a cold, vain and interested coquette, who perfectly understood how much the influence of her charms was increased by the fame of a severity which cost her nothing, and who could venture to flirt with a succession of admirers in the just confidence that no flame which she might kindle in them would thaw her own ice.'

Macaulay was as severe on Anne Bracegirdle as he was on Lord Mohun. Colley Cibber, an actor and dramatist who knew her, commented that she had the merit of being 'not unguarded in her private character'. During her lifetime it was said that she was secretly married to William Congreve. In any event the lady was doubtless wise to avoid involving herself in amours with the aristocracy of the period, and Macaulay, with his snobbish nineteenth-century outlook, thought she was being 'a cold, vain, interested coquette', because she refused to become the mistress of a lord. It was not until the present century that the stage was considered a respectable profession for a female. The limited comprehension of the gallants of Anne Bracegirdle's day was stretched to the point of incredulity at her refusal to permit a gentleman to honour her by enjoying her favours.

Captain Hill finally came to the conclusion that there was only one reason for her invincibility. She must have another lover, and he decided that his rival was William Mountford, one of the most notable actors of his day and a playwright as well. The possessor of a noble figure, a handsome face and a rich and splendid voice, Mountford might well have been considered a good match for the fascinating and famous Anne Bracegirdle. But Mountford was married and his affections were firmly with his wife. Captain Hill chose to believe otherwise, and he and his boon companion in debauchery and violence, Lord Mohun, plotted to kidnap the actress so that Hill could enjoy her by force – by no means an uncommon enterprise on the part of the nobility in those days.

The plot was laid on a frosty night in December, 1692, at the Three Tuns tavern in Chandos Street. They had already ordered a coach to be in readiness in Drury Lane, and outside their armed hirelings stamped up and down in the cold, awaiting their masters' pleasure.

In the Three Tuns the chosen companion of the fourth Baron and the love-lorn army captain was an unmarried lady by the name of Elizabeth Sandys, a loud-mouthed frequenter of the taverns, whose favours were available to all those who were prepared to pay her price. While his lordship fondled Elizabeth's dubious charms and pulled up her dress with increasing frequency, the three of them drank heavily and toasted the night's shabby enterprise with maudlin enthusiasm.

'Damme, she shall be yours, Dick,' cried Mohun at the cracking of each bottle. 'Not a soul shall stop you. You're my friend, and anybody who offends against my friend offends against me.'

As for Captain Hill, he expressed himself grossly offended that the object of his passion should be the mistress of a common actor like Mountford. To rescue her from the embraces of such a vulgar person would indeed be doing her a great favour. Hill had little knowledge of her circumstances or those of her supposed lover. Mountford's respectability was unquestioned among those who knew him, and Anne Bracegirdle lived in Howard Street with her mother in very reputable circumstances and was known as Mrs Bracegirdle – a courtesy title then given to unmarried women who were no longer adolescent.

The conversation of the three rowdies was loud and unrestrained, and they freely discussed their plot to seize the desired actress and take her into the country.

'This business will stand you in for fifty guineas or more, Dick,' Mohun remarked chaffingly to Hill who shrugged his shoulders saying it was worth it. He loudly repeated the slander that Mrs Bracegirdle was Mountford's mistress, a fact which, if anything, inflamed his own desire for the lady.

All this was heard by witnesses in the Three Tuns, but the two men cared little for that. Their plans had been laid with elaboration and they were certain of their success. The coach stood by ready to take Hill and his unwilling victim to a house in the country where the scene of her proposed rape had been prepared with some care. He had even placed a parcel containing night attire for her in the waiting coach.

Young Lord Mohun, then only eighteen, took a vicarious delight in the whole affair. The pursuit, capture and violation of a virtuous and beautiful woman was the very spice of life. Again and again he raised his glass and swore that Anne Bracegirdle would be taken by Captain Hill and whoever tried to prevent it would have to answer to him.

Supposing Mountford should leave the theatre with Mrs Bracegirdle and attempt to stop the enterprise? This suggestion came from Elizabeth Sandys.

'If the villain does, I'll stab him,' declared Hill.

'And I will stand by my friend,' exclaimed Mohun melodramatically. 'After all, one low actor more or less won't be missed. And the fellow's nothing but a damned seducer of women.' An observation which came well from a young man doing his best to become the most debauched and vice-loving member of the peerage.

Eventually they judged the time had come when Anne Bracegirdle would be leaving the theatre. They settled the score with the landlord and after bidding their female companion a rumbustious farewell, they directed their uncertain steps to Drury Lane Theatre with their posse of ruffians in their wake.

When they got to the theatre a surprise was in store for them. The lady they sought was not billed to appear that night. If Hill was disappointed, his lordship was not going to allow such a small thing to spoil the evening's entertainment.

'We'll soon find out where she is,' he blustered alcoholically, dragging his bemused companion to the pit door where he bought two tickets. Not wishing to be recognized by the fashionable theatre-goers among whom they were well known, they exchanged coats which hardly accomplished much in the way of disguise. It was a fruitless search in the pit and they went on the stage where the attendant asked them for more money.

Mohun told the man they would not pay any more, and in case he fetched his superiors they would all get their noses slit.

They gathered from talk behind the scenes that Mrs Bracegirdle was taking supper with her friends, the Pages, in Drury Lane. Still hot on the scent, Mohun and Hill left the theatre and replanned the operation, giving fresh instructions to their ruffianly retainers. All they had to do was to wait.

But it looked like being a long, cold wait. There was no sign of anyone coming out of the Pages' house. They dispatched the coach to Howard Street, off the Strand, where Mrs Bracegirdle lived, to ensure that the lady had not already returned home. The coach returned with the news that she had not. They waited with what patience they possessed. Mohun in the coach with several cases of pistols, Hill and his paid thugs lurking in a dark turning.

About ten o'clock Anne Bracegirdle emerged from a house in Drury Lane with her mother and to the accompaniment of cheery good-byes. Then, escorted by their host, Mr Page, the two ladies began to walk home.

They approached the coach in which Lord Mohun sat. Mrs Bracegirdle remarked on the fact that the door was open. At that moment Captain Hill leaped upon her from out of the darkness and tried to force her into the coach.

Anne screamed for help at the top of her voice, and she certainly had splendid, theatrically-trained lungs. Both her mother and Page sprang to her rescue. Page tackled Hill, but the captain, maddened with both alcohol and passion, knocked him down, turned once more upon the intended victim and tried to drag her to the coach. However, Anne's mother got her arms around her daughter's waist and hung on like grim death. She was a stout and formidable woman and the captain could not dislodge her.

The screams and uproar were heard by the watch in a neighbouring street and they came to investigate at the double. The whole neighbourhood was now aroused and the watch arrived upon a scene of great confusion. The courageous determination with which Anne's mother clung to her daughter doubtless frustrated the kidnapping. The watch soon outnumbered the ruffians. The paid hands vanished into the night, only the miscreants' personal attendants remained.

Lord Mohun who had taken no part in the vulgar brawl then descended gallantly from his coach. Gesturing Captain Hill to silence he swept off his headgear, bowed low to the ladies, and using language of elegance and chivalry tried to convince them that what had happened was nothing more than gross bad manners. No offence or injury had been intended. His lordship said that he and the captain humbly begged their pardon. He apologized to the watch for disturbing the peace. He then coolly proposed that he and the gallant captain should escort the ladies to their home.

His offer was scornfully refused and the two ladies, accompanied by Page, walked towards Howard Street. In the whole neighbourhood everyone was at their window. The casements were open despite the frosty air. The wild aristocrats were abroad creating drunken uproar, assault and possibly rape; and the entertainment was free. Between Drury Lane and the Strand keen ears heard everything that went on.

They saw the famous actress walking between her mother and Mr Page, followed by the two hell-rakes who, though no one believed that their intention could be anything but the worst, now seemed to be trying to make amends. It was Mohun who did most of the talking. Captain Hill was choked by his frustration and inability to get his hands on the delectable Anne whose progress down towards the Strand he watched with lustful eyes.

Mohun endeavoured to explain in honeyed tones that the whole incident had been misunderstood. He tried to make their peace with the outraged ladies and their escort. He even suggested that they should all get together in the parlour of Mrs Bracegirdle's house and have an amicable end to the affair.

Against the background of Mohun's persuasive apologies, Captain Hill could be heard muttering ominously in angry frustration, uttering dark threats and swearing he would be avenged, though he didn't say upon whom.

When they reached Anne Bracegirdle's house Mohun tried to enter, but the door was shut firmly in his face. Both men were furious at the presumption of this common chit of an actress in refusing their apology. For two hours they stormed up and down outside the house with drawn swords, shouting that they would not go until the lady had seen them.

Again, all the neighbours were aroused. Many sat at their windows watching the antics of the foiled villains. Hill loudly declared that Mountford was already within the house enjoying the lady's favours or, if not, he would soon arrive there to spend the night with her.

Lord Mohun did not exactly agree with his friend and would have preferred, it seemed, to have made the peace. But Hill refused to be mollified and they sent for more wine to keep out the cold and maintain their spirits.

In Mrs Bracegirdle's house there was, not unnaturally, considerable alarm. The windows were stoutly shuttered and the heavy front door firmly locked and bolted, as was necessary in those boisterous times. The gentleman-ruffians could not get in, but what Anne and her mother were concerned about was the safety of William Mountford. They knew that he was the innocent cause of Hill's insane jealousy. He lived nearby in Norfolk Street and was usually on his way home from his nightly haunts at about this time. Mrs Bracegirdle sent servants from the back entrance of her house to warn Mrs Mountford of the danger. But Mountford was not at home. Servants were sent in search of him to warn him.

Meanwhile Lord Mohun and the gallant captain had thoroughly revived their flagging belligerency with copious swillings of potent wine and were roaring with alcoholic pugnacity. The watch came by and asked them what they were doing with their swords drawn in the street.

Lord Mohun told them he was a peer of the land and dared them to touch him at their peril. As for Captain Hill, he had accidentally lost his scabbard. Mohun bade the watch go about their business and the guardians of the law retreated to a nearby alehouse. This was a matter for superior officers to deal with, so strong was privilege in those days and so weak the law.

While this was going on, William Mountford was returning to his house alone. He walked along Howard Street while the watch was in the alehouse awaiting help and advice from their superiors. One of Mrs Bracegirdle's maids had slipped out of the house and hurried along Howard Street to intercept Mountford and warn him. Mountford, however, mistaking her for a street-woman with a new kind of approach, brushed her aside and strode on, heedless of the girl's pleas.

He thus walked straight into the path of Mohun and Hill. It was Mohun who accosted him first, according to the onlookers.

'Damme, sir,' he exclaimed, standing astride on the pavement in the actor's path, 'what are you doing here at this hour?'

Mountford who knew them both glanced apprehensively at the glowering Hill and replied that he was passing by chance.

'I suggest you have heard about the lady,' Mohun continued threateningly.

'I hope my wife has given your lordship no offence,' said the actor.

Lord Mohun was furious, thinking the impertinent fellow was deliberately and insolently trying to misunderstand. 'Damn you, sir. It's Mrs Bracegirdle I mean,' he exclaimed.

Mountford shrugged. 'Mrs Bracegirdle is no concern of mine. But I hope your lordship does not countenance any ill action of Mr Hill.'

As Mountford said these words Hill came forward and hit the actor a tremendous blow on the ear. Mountford staggered, growling, 'Damme, what's that for?' Hill thrust at him savagely with his sword, running him through several times. Mountford fell beside the pavement crying out, 'He has killed me!'

The spectators at the windows, and there were plenty of them, immediately raised a shout of 'Murder! Murder!' The watch came rushing out of the alehouse to meet a scene of tumult in the street. A number of men had come out of their houses when they saw Mountford run through and fall mortally wounded. In the confusion Hill escaped and was not seen again.

Mohun, however, stood on the pavement gazing at the distorted face of the dying actor lying in the gutter. Officers of the law, previously summoned by the watch, were already on the scene. Mr Page called upon the constable to arrest Lord Mohun, and according to the constable the gallant peer was shaking and quaking with horror and fright at what had happened. His hand shook so violently that when the officer seized his loose sleeve he thought 'the lace would be torn'.

Mohun was taken to the Round House. By the time he got there he had recovered his nerve. He asked if Hill had been taken. When he was informed that the brave captain had fled leaving him to face the music alone, and was not to be found, he exclaimed, 'God damme, I'm glad he is not taken. But I am sorry he had no more money with him. I wish he had some of mine. I do not care a farthing if I am hanged for him.'

Mountford's wound was mortal, but he lingered until one o'clock the next afternoon. Before he died he confided to Bancroft, the surgeon: 'My lord Mohun offered me no violence, but whilst I was talking with my lord Mohun Hill struck me with his left hand, and with his right hand ran me through before I could put my hand to my sword.'

The Grand Jury of Middlesex found a true bill of murder

against Mohun and Hill, but only Mohun remained to face the charge as Hill was not to be found.

Lady Mohun, the accused peer's mother, threw herself at the feet of King William of Orange, then in his third year on the English throne, and begged in vain for royal intervention. 'It was a cruel act,' said the King. 'I shall leave it to the law.'

Lord Mohun chose to be tried by his peers, and so on 31 January, 1693 the Lord High Steward led a solemn procession of his retinue and peers from the House of Lords to Westminster Hall. All were splendidly robed – Garter King-at-Arms, Black Rod, serjeants-at-arms, yeoman ushers, eight judges, the peers themselves, all in strict order of precedence. When all were settled in the famous hall which is still in use today the Deputy-Governor of the Tower was commanded to produce his prisoner. Lord Mohun came to the bar of the court escorted by the Gentleman Gaoler who bore the axe with its edge turned away from the prisoner. If he were convicted, then the edge would be turned towards him.

The law of the time permitted Mohun no counsel to argue his case, although the Crown arraigned against him its full panoply of legal might – Sir John Somers, the Attorney-General; Sir Thomas Trevor, Solicitor-General, and Serjeant Thompson. The prisoner was permitted counsel only if a point of law arose to be argued – a harsh state of affairs which even Judge Jeffreys had pronounced unfair.

But Mohun who was not yet twenty at the time conducted his defence with remarkable skill which drew the admiration of his peers, many of whom expressed the hope that he would put his talents to a more worthy use once he had sown his wild oats.

Lord Mohun knelt at the bar and heard the charge against him that he did 'with malice aforethought, aid, abet, comfort, assist and maintain Richard Hill to kill and murder one, William Mountford', the penalty for which was death. He pleaded not guilty.

The Lord High Steward in his opening addressed him thus: 'My lord, you are a very young man and therefore it is to be hoped you cannot so easily have had your hands in blood.

And the same reason, because you are so young, may perhaps make you conceive that you are under some disadvantage in making your defence than you would be if your experience had been longer. But to remove any apprehension you may have of that kind, it is very proper to put your lordship in mind that you have the good fortune now to be tried for this face in full Parliament where no evidence will be received but such as may be manifest and plain beyond all contradiction, so that you have nothing to fear here but your own guilt.'

Lord Mohun was permitted to cross-examine the witnesses which the Crown brought against him, and the manner in which he did it displayed a remarkable skill and judiciousness.

One of the most dangerous witnesses was Elizabeth Sandys who told of the wild talk in the Three Tuns on the night of Mountford's death. She told her story volubly and repeated his own words: 'I'll stand by you, Dick.'

Mohun had no intention of contesting her story. He merely wanted to discredit her. He dealt with the point brilliantly by turning to the Lord High Steward and asking with some disdain: 'My Lord, is it permissible to inquire whether this witness is a *married* woman?' When the reply was found to be in the negative, he said no more but shrugged his shoulders expressively. No respectable woman would go to a tavern except with her husband. Would their lordships condemn him upon the word of a town harlot?

His defence was that he had taken no part in the scuffle. He put this point to several of the Crown witnesses, all of whom agreed. The suggestion was put forward, however, that he had detained Mountford in friendly conversation in order that Hill might more easily run him through.

Richard Rowe who had witnessed the affray in Howard Street swore on oath that he had heard Mohun's footboy exclaim: 'Pray, my lord, good, my lord, don't do it. Alter your resolution.' This seemed to confirm the evidence of other witnesses who had observed Mohun attack Mountford with his sword drawn, though there were plenty who maintained that Mohun's sword was in his scabbard at the time. But Mohun's footboy could not be found and his missing evidence was somewhat in his master's favour.

After the Crown had completed its case, Mohun called his own witnesses.

Thomas Lake, Hill's footboy who had been present, stated that the fight was between Hill and Mountford only, and that they both had drawn swords.

Mohun then called Anne Bracegirdle's maid, Elizabeth Walker, to give evidence on his behalf – a rather interesting switch of allegiance upon which a number of interpretations could be placed. After the crime she had vanished and the prosecution had searched for her in vain. It was she who had taken possession of Mountford's sword which according to a number of defence witnesses had been broken in the fight, but this vital piece of evidence was not produced.

Asked by the prosecution why she had vanished, Elizabeth Walker explained that she had been threatened by Mountford's theatrical friends. Defence witnesses had sworn that both men had fought with naked swords – Elizabeth's way of putting it – 'I have never seen men naked fighting so before' – drew a great shout of laughter from the court.

The evidence having been completed the Solicitor-General summed up. The evidence proved that the prisoner and Hill had a common design against the dead man. Hill committed murder while Lord Mohun stood by his friend without offering to part the murderer and victim. It had been established, the Solicitor-General submitted, that Mohun was privy to Hill's design.

The Solicitor-General's eloquence was interrupted by a lady having a fit in the gallery. The proceedings were suspended while she was removed.

Mohun admitted that he had been involved in a scandalous and criminal conspiracy to abduct Anne Bracegirdle – as he was not charged with that offence, however, he risked nothing in admitting it. He made an eloquent final speech.

'My lords, I hope it will be no disadvantage to me in my summing up that I have made it clear by various questions to the witnesses that there was no quarrel or malice between Mountford and myself. I hope too that I have made it abundantly clear that the reason why I stayed so long in the street with Captain Hill was because he was my friend and I wished to persuade him to approach Mrs Bracegirdle in all humility and beg her pardon for an offence against good taste. My conscience is clear of all other motive and I commit myself to the honourable House.'

Following that, there was much debate among their lordships. For hours the lawyers argued over a point of law which has haunted English justice for centuries; it causes dispute even nowadays.

Could the accused be found guilty of murder merely because he had been present when Hill killed Mountford with his sword, even though he knew beforehand of his friend's intention? The judges finally gave their opinion that merely being in the company of the murderer did not of itself render his companion equally guilty of murder.

On 4 February the Lords reassembled to vote on the indictment. The Lord High Steward called upon each one of them, and as each heard his name he rose and placing his right hand on his breast, answered either 'Guilty upon my honour' or 'Not guilty upon my honour'. It was quickly seen that the majority were for acquittal. After the vote the Lord High Steward called Lord Mohun and told him that he had been acquitted by 69 votes to 14, and was discharged.

Silence was then proclaimed and the Commission was solemnly dissolved. The Lord High Steward then held the White Staff above his head in both hands and broke it in two. Then all went in solemn procession to the House of Lords.

Although modern students of this case believe that Lord Mohun was rightly acquitted, his contemporaries took a different view. So did Macaulay who said that no one who studied the report in the *State Trials* 'can doubt that the crime of murder was fully brought home to the prisoner. Such was the opinion of the King, who was present during the trial; and such was the almost unanimous opinion of the public. Had the issue been tried by Holt and twelve plain men at the Old Bailey there can be no doubt that a verdict of guilty would have been returned.'

Macaulay maintained that Mohun's trial was conducted

unfairly on the basis of class favouritism and privilege. He wrote: 'One great nobleman was so brutal and stupid as to say "After all, the fellow was but a player; and players are rogues." All the newsletters, all the coffee-house orators complained that the blood of the poor was shed with impunity by the great. Wits remarked that the only fair thing about the trial was the show of ladies in the galleries. Letters and journals are still extant in which men of all shades of opinion, Whigs, Tories, Nonjurors, condemn the partiality of the tribunal.'

Recent opinion disagrees, though perhaps a certain suspicion remains. There seemed to be no design to murder Mountford. The meeting was by chance and Hill acted without premeditation. The affair was over in seconds. Lord Mohun did not seem to know what was afoot; he did not appear to aid and abet the murderer. He was therefore guiltless of murder.

His conduct that night was of course reprehensible in the extreme, but he was not charged with outrageous conduct or with the attempted abduction of Anne Bracegirdle. His peers acquitted him of the charge of murder on the advice of the judges, and not on account of class prejudice. The public, even the King, generally ignorant of legal matters, condemned him because he was a ruffian, a boor and a profligate.

Lord Mohun learnt no lesson from the Mountford murder. Hill was never found and the charge of attempting to abduct Mrs Bracegirdle was not brought. Mohun did not live down the scandal, and he continued his wild life until 1699 when he was involved in another murder scandal. Once more he appeared before the House of Lords on a capital charge.

On 29 October Mohun was one of a drinking party at the Greyhound in the Strand. His fellow carousers were the Earl of Warwick, now his boon companion, three army captains – Coote, French and James – and a man named Dockwra. It was a loud-mouthed, rather quarrelsome party at which talk of slander, treachery and murder was bandied about without regard to listeners.

When they left the Greyhound in a quarrelling mood at 1 a.m. they had themselves conveyed in sedan chairs to the end of St Martin's Lane where they stopped. Here Captain Coote continued the bitter quarrel and insisted on settling it with the sword. They proceeded to a spot where Green Street (now Irving Street) runs into Leicester Square, and a mixed duel seems to have taken place in the pitch dark of Leicester Fields in which Coote was killed and French badly injured. Mohun had a slight wound in his hand.

Mohun was once more tried for murder, and Warwick for manslaughter. Mohun in his defence claimed that he had not wanted to fight and had only done so after exhausting all efforts of the others to abandon the affair. Certainly, if he had drawn back he would according to the code of honour of his day have shown himself a coward. He was tried in the same solemn manner as before and unanimously found not guilty of murder.

The Earl of Warwick was convicted of manslaughter, but he pleaded benefit of clergy – a curious survival of medieval law which enabled a person with the ability to read to claim exemption from the jurisdiction of the courts. Warwick was indeed allowed to go free on the strength of the medieval reverence for the ability to read.

When Lord Mohun was acquitted by his peers for the second time, they made a solemn plea to him to change his ways. He promised to reform and kept his word. He served in the army and made a number of not unimportant speeches in the House of Lords.

But his propensity for duelling was finally the end of him. In 1712 he was involved in a bitter dispute with the fourth Duke of Hamilton over a long-standing debt. On 15 November he forced the Duke to a duel in Hyde Park. It was a long and desperate fight. Mohun drew the first blood and called on Hamilton to give. But the Duke, though mortally wounded, refused and made a last dying thrust at Mohun who received the blade in his stomach and was killed.

# Chapter 13
# Ethel Le Neve

It was Alexander Woollcott who said that the Crippen case has entered into the legends of crime incalculably the stronger, because his fellow-fugitive had the romantic name of Ethel Le Neve.

Actually her real name was Neave. It was given thus on the 'Wanted' bill issued by the Metropolitan Police in July, 1910.

She was born about 1883 to a commercial traveller who lived in Camden Town. When she was sixteen she went out to work and earned her living as a typist in the City of London, a young pleasant-faced girl, and perhaps better able to look after herself amid the temptations of the city than legend and her defender in court suggested.

She went to work at Munyons, an American firm which sold patent medicines of doubtful value through advertisements and whose London office was in Shaftesbury Avenue.

In 1900 an unremarkable little American doctor was appointed from the head office in New York to manage the English branch. His name was Dr Hawley Harvey Crippen. He was to leave his mark upon the scene of murder in an almost unwarranted way, for he committed the very ordinary crime of killing his wife and burying her remains in the cellar, for the very ordinary reason that he wanted another woman. It was the only decisive act in his inconsequential life and Ethel Le Neve was his inspiration to commit this commonplace murder which has given him immortality in the archives of crime.

It is perhaps the personalities in the case which has made the murder of the florid Mrs Crippen 'the one indisputable murder classic of the twentieth century'. Crippen was a little man, insignificant, rather amiable, dominated completely by his flamboyant wife. He was slight, undersized, with bulbous eyes that looked at you through gold-rimmed spectacles, and had a sandy rather straggling moustache. With his choker-collar and unassuming manners, he was typical of his age.

Ethel Le Neve was a quiet, not unattractive girl, gentle, affectionate. She was anaemic and suffered from neuralgia. About both of them was an air of indestructible respectability. Mrs Cora Crippen – Belle Elmore – was their exact opposite. Vivacious, loud-voiced, gay, uninhibited, unconventional and dominant, she was good-looking, with large dark eyes and black hair. She always wore elaborate clothes in the brightest of colours. She was also a somewhat pathetic character with invincible delusions about her non-existent stage talents. Belle Elmore was the stage name under which she made only one dismal appearance and under which she posed as a star.

This strange and rather sad trio had all the elements of classic tragedy. Mrs Crippen nagged her husband and treated him as though he was a piece of furniture. She was over-fond of other men, to whom she was sexually attractive, and it is assumed, though without any certainty, that she had extra-marital love affairs. In 1902 Munyons recalled Crippen to Philadelphia for six months and during his absence Cora Crippen saw a great deal of an American music-hall performer named Bruce Miller.

'It is distasteful to speak of Mrs Crippen's relations with other men,' Filson Young quaintly remarks in his introduction to the *Notable British Trials* volume on Crippen, 'but it is obvious that the avenue to her affections was not very narrow or difficult of access.' Why it should be tasteless to talk of Cora's alleged infidelities when the whole case revolves around her husband's adulteries with Le Neve, is not clear.

It seems that Ethel Le Neve first met Peter Crippen (he had adopted this Christian name in England where the Hawley Harvey was thought rather stridently American) when she was working for the Drouet Institute, a patent-medicine firm in which Crippen had an interest. She knew him for six or seven years before they began their memorable affair. It was not likely that the insignificant little doctor would have aroused feelings of romance and passion in her or indeed in any girl, but the fact that he was the boss would naturally make things easier for him to have affairs with his girl typists.

But during the first years of the century Crippen was contented enough with Cora, basking in her reflected glory among their theatrical friends. In 1905 they moved to 39 Hilldrop Crescent, and then things began to deteriorate. Cora's stage ambitions came to naught, though she still pretended that Belle Elmore had been a theatrical star. She no longer concealed from her husband that she preferred other men, and she told him that Bruce Miller was in love with her – a thing Miller strongly denied at the trial.

It was no surprise, therefore, that Crippen began to look elsewhere for feminine sympathy and understanding. He did not have to look far. He found it quickly enough in the person of his young typist. What really appealed to him were those refined, ladylike qualities so desirable in a girl in those days, and which Ethel Le Neve had acquired almost to perfection despite her ill education and somewhat monotonous life. Ethel was the direct opposite of the flamboyant and somewhat vulgar Cora Crippen, and doubtless this was part of the attraction so far as he was concerned.

What she saw in him remains something of a mystery. The general opinion of Crippen as a rather nice little man who killed in sheer desperation, or even by accident, is not shared by all who met him. A doctor who examined him in Quebec described him as the most 'horrifying little man I have ever

234

met'. His reaction of course might have been coloured by the knowledge of what he had done to his wife. Certainly Crippen had no such effect upon Ethel Le Neve. But while she was plainly not repulsed by her unromantic little admirer she can hardly have regarded him as a Don Juan or a great lover, and there is no evidence at all that her feelings for him went very deep. When she fell for his blandishments she must have been thinking what she would get out of it. He was the boss. He was well-heeled or appeared to be, and better educated than she was. He moved in higher circles, would take her to places she would never have gone otherwise.

Ethel Le Neve was a martyr to respectability as well as to neuralgia, and doubtless Crippen had to do a lot of persuading before she finally consented to become his mistress. Whatever tales he told her, whatever reservations and fears she had of taking the step into adultery from which there could be no drawing back and which was an awful thing in those days after her years of ladylike strivings, it is impossible to accept F. E. Smith's picture of these two as he presented in court at her trial.

Smith described Crippen as 'unscrupulous, dominating, fearing neither God nor man, insinuating, attractive, immoral, one of the most dangerous and remarkable men who have lived in this century'; and Le Neve he depicted as gentle, retiring, and coming under the demoralizing influence of this monster when she was a bare schoolgirl. Smith's description of Crippen would have made Cora laugh her silly head off and wonder what she had been missing. She of course knew him much better than the great F. E. who was in full forensic flood and fighting a just battle for his frail little client in the dock. Ethel Le Neve was twenty-five when she became Crippen's mistress. She was a calculating young woman rather than a frightened schoolgirl. In those days girls of twenty-five were on the shelf and virginity was not so important as opportunism, though it was of much more importance than it is today.

It was about 1908 when she yielded to the desires of the boss and flung respectability out of the hotel window as she got into bed with him.

In September of that year she left home and took a bed-sitting room at an apartment house at 30 Constantine Road, Hampstead, owned by a Mrs Emily Jackson. The two soon became close friends. Mrs Jackson frequently went up to Ethel's room for long cosy chats and during the two or three years that Ethel was Crippen's mistress, a real affection grew between them, rather as mother and daughter; according to Mrs Jackson the girl actually called her 'Mother'. Mrs Jackson knew all about the affair between Ethel and Crippen and tried to discourage it.

At Hilldrop Crescent life became increasingly irksome to Crippen. His wife started to take lodgers – men of course – and kept what they paid her for pin money. Crippen was earning a comfortable living now, paying all the household expenses. He didn't take very kindly to having to clean the lodgers' boots, bring in the coal and help generally in the extra housework involved.

But he did it all with a certain good nature, for after all he had the docile Ethel to console himself with. He had what so many middle-aged men desire, a young mistress, and he had without a doubt fallen very much in love with her. As for Ethel, her anxieties about her irregular situation sometimes made her ill.

But she certainly enjoyed the fruits of being the mistress, and naturally enough desired to be the wife of a reasonably well-off doctor, whether she loved him or not. It would be a great step up in the world for her. As it was, she was already dressing much more smartly, for Crippen was buying her nice clothes and presents. One of the doctors at Munyons told her stuffily to dress in a manner more in keeping with her station in life. This must have hurt her deeply. Was it not on the tip of her tongue to say who had given her the offending clothes? And in the bitter humiliation of her position she must have longed for the day – would it ever come? – when Cora Crippen would be no more, and she could at last attain respectability by marrying Peter and becoming a doctor's wife.

Crippen by now was considerably at odds with his wife. She had said more than once that she was going to leave him, that she preferred other men, in particular Bruce Miller.

Crippen's preference for Ethel Le Neve seems to have been an ill-kept secret. Le Neve said that she had visited the Crippens' home at Hilldrop Crescent socially, and Cora Crippen had received her well. Cora had found out about her husband's liaison with his typist and she didn't like it at all. She had more than once told her friends that if her husband did not give the girl up she would leave him and take all the money with her.

The money she referred to was £600 on deposit in the Charing Cross Bank under the joint names of Belle Elmore and H. H. Crippen. On 15 December, 1909 Belle Elmore notified the bank that she wanted to draw out the £600, and the bank said that they would have eventually paid without Crippen's signature.

This is believed to be the true motive behind the murder. Crippen had been generous to his wife, but it is thought that the £600 included money presents she had received from various men. Such a sum of course would be worth perhaps three times more then than it would today.

On 31 January, 1910 the Crippens gave a dinner party at Hilldrop Crescent. Among those present were Paul Martinetti and his wife Clara, who was a member of the Music Hall Ladies Guild of which Belle Elmore was now the honorary treasurer. It was a comparatively amicable evening, spoilt only by an angry outburst by Mrs Crippen against her husband over some inconsequential matter. The Martinettis left at 1.30 a.m.

Cora Crippen was never seen alive again. Three days later Crippen wrote a letter containing her resignation to the Ladies Guild. He said she had to leave suddenly for America owing to the illness of a relative. On the same day he started pawning her jewellery.

At this time Mrs Emily Jackson, Ethel Le Neve's affectionate landlady, observed that there was something strange about Ethel's manner. She became miserable and depressed, and one night at about the end of January – Cora was murdered about that time – she came in looking tired and strange, greatly agitated and went to bed without her supper.

'I went into the bedroom after her,' said Mrs Jackson. 'I

could see that her whole body was trembling and that she was in a terrible state. I asked her what was the matter, and she did not seem to have the strength to speak. I asked her again, and she said she would be all right in the morning.'

The next morning, according to Mrs Jackson, Ethel still looked ill and was unable even to drink a cup of tea. Mrs Jackson phoned up Miss Le Neve's place of business and told them that the girl was unwell and would not be at work, and then went to her room.

'You must tell me what is the matter, dear,' she pressed. 'There must be something dreadful on your mind. You'll go mad if you keep it to yourself.'

After a while Ethel said: 'Would you be surprised if I told you it is the doctor?'

'But what about the doctor? I thought that was all past and gone.'

Ethel burst into tears again. 'It is Miss Elmore.'

Mrs Jackson looked puzzled. 'Miss Elmore? Who is she?'

'She is his wife, you know. Mrs Crippen. When I see them go away together, it makes me realize what my position is.'

'My dear girl,' said the down-to-earth Mrs Jackson, 'what is the use of worrying about another woman's husband?'

To that Ethel Le Neve replied: 'She has been threatening to go away with another man, and that is all we are waiting for, and when she does the doctor is going to divorce her and marry me.'

Mrs Jackson was sceptical. 'Are you sure he will marry you? It seems to me that what he is asking is most unfair. Why don't you tell him that he has placed you in a most difficult position?'

Ethel Le Neve promised Mrs Jackson to tell Crippen precisely that – which she did. As she later told Mrs Jackson, Crippen was very glad that she had done so.

This was Mrs Jackson's story and there is no reason to disbelieve it. The state tried to use it to prove that Ethel Le Neve knew about Mrs Crippen's murder and was therefore an accessory after the fact. The state may very well have been right, but the trouble was that Mrs Jackson was never very clear about her dates.

Mrs Crippen was murdered either on 31 January, after the dinner party, or on the following day. Suspicions were not aroused for some months. Meanwhile – and the story is still Mrs Jackson's – perhaps a week or so after the murder, Ethel Le Neve began to stay away from her lodgings and not come home at night. The question naturally arises: how long does it take a doctor, working in his spare time, to dismember, eviscerate, and bury the remains of his wife in his cellar?

A week after the illness, Mrs Jackson recounted, Ethel came to see her, looking happy, even radiant. She said 'somebody' had gone away at last. After that she began staying out at nights regularly. She told Mrs Jackson that she had been at Hilldrop Crescent searching for a bank-book, and during the search some jewellery had come to light which Dr Crippen sold, to put the money into his business. She then began to bring presents of clothing to Mrs Jackson – a fur coat, a black feather boa, long coats of green, black and brown, blouses, skirts, nightgowns, hats and stockings. Once Crippen came with Ethel and brought some things for Mrs Jackson in a dress basket.

Why this generosity to Mrs Jackson? Was it to sweeten her – to keep her quiet in case anything came out?

One can imagine those two going through the loot at 39 Hilldrop Crescent in that first week in February, when the grisly work of dismemberment and evisceration had been done by the gentle doctor and the cement was still fresh on the cellar floor.

To Ethel Le Neve it must have been like going through a treasure-trove, Pandora's box. All of Cora Crippen's gorgeous and glittering belongings were there, including her furs and jewellery. Crippen said he had told Ethel that his wife had gone abroad with another man. Le Neve had met Mrs Crippen and knew what sort of woman she was. Did she honestly believe that the gorgeous Belle Elmore, self-appointed star of the music halls, had gone off with her paramour without taking a single belonging with her? Did she imagine that the peacock was parading naked, without a single feather, along the sidewalks of New York?

It was true that this very circumstance did not arouse suspicion in the dense mind of Inspector Dew who later investigated the crime. But Dew was not at Hilldrop Crescent until July. Ethel Le Neve was there in February, sorting everything out, when the murder was fresh, the victim's clothes almost warm. She was a woman of twenty-seven, neither unworldly nor a thoughtless young girl. Could she really have imagined that Cora Crippen had gone away leaving every single thing to the smallest and most personal piece of jewellery behind her? Was Ethel Le Neve such a fool as that? Could she really have believed that Cora Crippen had gone away at all?

On 20 February there was the dinner and ball of the Ladies Guild Benevolent Fund, of which Mrs Crippen was the treasurer. It was perhaps expected that Crippen would go, but no one suspected he would have the bad taste to take his young mistress with him. She herself had the even worse taste to deck herself out in Mrs Crippen's jewellery. Was this bravado, sheer madness, or incredible naïvety? What could have been in her mind when she was putting them on? And how must she have felt under the cold suspicious eyes of Mrs Crippen's friends as she cringed there next to the little doctor, swallowing down her dinner?

'Miss Le Neve, I thought, was very quiet,' remarked Mrs Martinetti, speaking later of the occasion. 'At the ball I did not speak to her. Afterwards we sat at the same table with Dr Crippen between us. Other friends at the gathering knew her quite well. She wore the jewellery without any attempt at concealment.'

Naturally enough the incident started the tongues wagging, and when in March Ethel Le Neve took up residence at 39 Hilldrop Crescent, ostensibly as Dr Crippen's housekeeper, scandal loomed large. But this the 'respectable' Miss Le Neve had to endure. It was neck or nothing now if she wanted to become the third wife of Dr Crippen.

She lived with him there until July in terms, one presumes, of relative bliss. At Easter they went to Dieppe together for a short holiday, and some people think that Crippen took his wife's head among his luggage and dropped it overboard in mid-Channel in a weighted bag.

Back in London questions were still being asked. Crippen, if he was to enjoy the fruits of his deed without having to pay the price, knew that he had to satisfy the niggling curiosity of the members of the Ladies Guild. They kept asking about the return of their esteemed treasurer and favourite extrovert from her mysterious and extended journey to America. And why had she not written to anybody?

Crippen was prepared for this. On 24 March he announced with great sorrow that he had just heard that Belle Elmore had died in faraway California and he put the melancholy news on record in the *Era*.

But the ladies were not satisfied. There was that Le Neve girl dressed in finery, living openly with the sorrowing widower and just as openly preening herself in poor Belle's furs. They wanted to send a wreath to Belle's grave in California; they were told that she had been cremated. But she was a Catholic! they protested in horror. Crippen explained that he had had her cremated so that he could have her ashes at Hilldrop Crescent. Obviously he could not go six thousand miles to her funeral.

Suspicions exploded when one of Mrs Crippen's friends, a man named Nash, returned from a short visit to the United States where he had tried unsuccessfully to discover any news of her death. Nash asked Crippen a lot of awkward questions and thoroughly put him on his guard. On 30 June Nash went to Scotland Yard.

On 8 July Inspector Dew called at 39 Hilldrop Crescent and was admitted by a French maid who had been engaged by Crippen perhaps to impress on his mistress that she had gone up in the world. The Inspector told Ethel Le Neve that he wanted to see Dr Crippen about his wife's disappearance. Ethel conducted him personally to Albion House where Crippen had an office and surgery. The eagle eye of the Inspector noted that she was wearing a brooch which was later identified as belonging to the late Mrs Crippen.

At the office Crippen received Dew with candour and frankness and openly admitted that he realized the time had come to tell the truth. His wife was not dead, but had run away with another man. He had told the lie to cover up the scandal. Dew spent most of the day at Crippen's office-surgery. Crippen dictated an extensive account of his whole career, every now and then going into another room to pull a tooth, for the little doctor numbered dentistry among his numerous accomplishments. He had told the lie, he declared, out of regard for his wife's reputation, deliberately deceiving her friends.

Dew had an amicable lunch with Crippen and completed the busy day's work by returning with him to Hilldrop Crescent to search the house. The inspection revealed nothing suspicious, and apparently Dew did not wonder why the bird had flown leaving all her bright plumage behind.

Throughout this somewhat terrifying day Ethel Le Neve had been hovering on the fringe of the scene. It took nearly six hours to make the statement at Albion House, and during all this time she was waiting in another room, full of fear and apprehension.

They asked her to make a statement, and this is what she said:

'I am a single woman, twenty-seven years of age, and am a shorthand typist. My father and mother reside at 17b Goldington Buildings, Great College Street, Camden Town. My father is a commercial traveller. Since the latter end of February I have been living at 39 Hilldrop Crescent with Dr Crippen as his wife. Before that I lived at 30 Constantine Road, Hampstead. I have been on intimate terms with Mr Crippen for two or three years, but I have known him for ten years. I made his acquaintance by being in the same employ as he was. I know Mrs Crippen and have visited Hilldrop Crescent. She treated me as a friend.

'In the early part of February I received a note from Mr Crippen saying Mrs Crippen had gone to America, and asking me to hand over a packet he enclosed to Miss May [secretary of the Music Hall Ladies Guild]. About four p.m. the same day he came to our business place, Albion House, and told me his wife had gone to America. He said she had packed up and gone. I had been in the habit for the past two or three years of going about with him, and continued doing so.

'About a week after he had told me she had gone to America, I went to Hilldrop Crescent to put the place straight, as there were no servants kept, but at night I went to my lodgings. I did this daily for about a fortnight. The place appeared to be all right and quite as usual. He took me to the Benevolent Fund dinner, and lent me a diamond brooch to wear. Later on he told me I could keep it.

'After this he told me she had caught a chill on board the ship and had got pneumonia. Afterwards he told me she was dead. He told me he could not go to the funeral as it was too far, and she would have been buried before he got there. Before he ever told me this I had been away with him for five or six days at Dieppe and stayed at an hotel with him in the names of Mr and Mrs Crippen. When we came back he took me to Hilldrop Crescent and I remained there with him. The same night, or the night after, he told me that Belle was dead. I was very much astonished, but I do not think I said anything to him about it. Have not had any conversation with him about it since. He gave me some furs of his wife to wear and I have been living with him ever since as his wife. My father and mother do not know what I am doing, and think I am a housekeeper at Hilldrop Crescent. When Mr Crippen told me his wife had gone to America, I don't remember if he told me she was coming back or not. I can't remember if he went into mourning.'

After she had made this statement which is the only one Ethel Le Neve ever made she returned to Hilldrop Crescent with Crippen, Dew and a police-sergeant and was there while the house was searched.

Dew explained to Crippen: 'Of course I shall have to find Mrs Crippen to clear things up.' It was imperative in fact that she should be found; otherwise Crippen would be in serious trouble. Crippen promised he would advertise in the American papers.

At this point Dew was satisfied that there had been no foul play, though he had no intention of admitting this to Crippen. (Dew later told this to Filson Young, although Sir Travers Humphreys, who was one of the Counsel for the Crown in the case against Crippen, has said this was not so, and the police attitude was one of 'not sufficient evidence at present to justify any action'. A fine distinction perhaps.)

Telling Crippen that he had better locate his wife or he would be in trouble was a mere policeman's bluff. If a man's wife is missing there is no onus on him to find her just to satisfy her friends' suspicions. Even police suspicions have to be very well founded for pressure to be exerted on the suspect. Dew considered he did not have sufficient grounds for such suspicion, though he was later severely criticized for not assessing the true importance of the fact that the missing woman had not taken her belongings with her. Richard Muir who led for the Crown described Dew as suffering from sleepy sickness.

Crippen was not to know what was in Dew's mind. But he was a pretty cool customer. He had played his cards right, though he had made enough mistakes to put the rope round his neck finally.

But on the night of 8 July something cracked. It has been suggested that Crippen was so overwhelmed with guilt that he was afraid to face another police inquisition. It is most likely Ethel Le Neve's nerve cracked first, and that she spent half the night persuading him that their only solution lay in flight and a new life in America. The plan for her to dress as a boy and pose as his son was laid. The very thought of disguising herself thus must have been distasteful to her Edwardian susceptibilities. For a girl those days to wear trousers was a vulgar thing, and grossly 'unladylike'. To what a pass must Ethel have been driven to discard in this way everything she understood by the word 'ladylike'. But it was essential, Crippen convinced her. The police would be after them, and would be looking for a man and a girl, not a father and son as they proposed to travel.

It was obvious to Ethel Le Neve by now that her lover was not in a position to answer certain questions by the police about what had happened to his wife – even if she had not known this all along, from the night when she arrived at Mrs Jackson's, trembling, terrified, after having had a terrible shock. Unless one takes the unikely view that she was naïve enough to be utterly innocent of what had happened, or was so desperately in love with him that she was prepared to stick by him no matter what he had done, then the flight of Crippen and Le Neve was a flight of two guilty persons.

The irony of the whole thing is that if they had stayed there and brazened it out, the police after a few more questions would almost certainly have dropped their inquiries, with the result that the body of Cora Crippen would not have been found until the house was pulled down, and perhaps not even then.

But one or the other of them decided otherwise. Crippen spent half the night writing letters to put his affairs in order. Early in the morning he went to his offices at Albion House and sent his dental mechanic out to buy some boy's clothes – a singularly foolish thing to do as it revealed to the police the manner in which they intended to camouflage their flight.

That day he and Le Neve left for Rotterdam and then went on to Antwerp where, in the names of Mr and Master Robinson, Crippen booked passages to Quebec on the steamship *Montrose* which was due to sail on 20 July.

Meanwhile Dew pursued his inquiries, and on 11 July he went to call on Crippen at Albion House and found him gone. When neither he nor Miss Le Neve were to be found his worst suspicions were aroused.

A search at 39 Hilldrop Crescent resulted in the discovery of human remains, subsequently proved to be those of Cora Crippen, buried under the brick floor of the cellar. On 16 July a warrant was issued for the arrest of Crippen and Le Neve.

The story was big news in all the papers during the time Crippen and Le Neve stayed at Antwerp.

Did Ethel see the English papers while she was at Antwerp? If so, she knew the worst and should have realized that to continue the flight with Crippen made her guilty of being his accessory. It was denied on her behalf that she ever saw the English papers in Antwerp. It was an important point at the trial, but not so important in retrospect.

On 20 July they embarked on the *Montrose* and travelled

in a double cabin as Mr John Robinson and Master Robinson. The commander of the *Montrose* was a certain Captain Kendall who claimed credit for his supposed astuteness in spotting the couple. It was not, however, a very difficult task to spot Crippen – though without his distinctive moustache now – and his inadequately disguised fellow fugitive. Before he sailed from Antwerp, Kendall, in common with all other transatlantic captains, had been alerted to look out for Crippen and Le Neve. As he had been tipped off that Le Neve would probably be posing as a boy, Captain Kendall's famous detecting act did not amount to much. It was easy to divine from Master Robinson's back view that he was no youth, and as Crippen could hardly keep his hands off his companion, it was plain that here was no father-and-son relationship. Crippen was not difficult to recognize even without his moustache. His small, slight build was distinctive and he also had an unusual way of walking.

With all this information to hand Kendall had, or should have had, no difficulty in spotting the fugitives. After he had been at sea for two days he sent a wireless message announcing that Crippen and Le Neve were on board. Inspector Dew and Sergeant Mitchell promptly embarked on the *Laurentic* which was a faster ship and would enable them to be in Canada ahead of the *Montrose*.

In the meantime the lovers, thinking blissfully of a golden future, were totally unaware that man's latest scientific marvel would bring about their utter ruin and downfall. During each enchanted night they made secret love in the cabin, while during the daytime they carefully maintained the fiction of their supposed identities. Ethel did not speak very much, posing as a very shy youth in case her female voice gave her away.

But whatever were Ethel's secret thoughts on this memorable crossing, it is clear that Crippen was tormented in his mind. Even if he escaped justice, he could not escape from his conscience. All the same, he was determined to go through with it.

He became friendly with the quartermaster, and when the *Montrose* was a day or two from the St Lawrence this

man informed him of what had been going on over the
wireless waves and that he was going to be arrested at
Quebec.

The quartermaster apparently believed in Crippen's innocence and helped him plan an escape. Crippen was going to
leave suicide notes in his cabin stating his decision to make
an end of things and jump overboard one night. The quartermaster would drop something in the sea to make a splash and
then tell the captain that someone had gone overboard.
Crippen in the meantime would hide in the cargo, and the
quartermaster – who would be in charge of the unloading at
Quebec – would be able to smuggle him ashore quite easily.
Crippen would make a rendezvous in the United States with
his mistress and join her there when the trouble had blown
over.

It was not a very good idea. Crippen didn't know that a
warrant had been issued for Le Neve, and even if he had got
away she would have been taken back to England for trial –
and things might have ended very differently for her than
they did.

Fortunately for Ethel Le Neve, if not for Crippen, the
plan was foiled by the sudden arrival of Inspector Dew at
Father Point which is the place in the entrance of the St
Lawrence where the *Montrose* was due to take on her
pilot.

Dew arrived on board disguised as a pilot. With him was
Chief Inspector M'Carthy of the Canadian Provincial Police.
Crippen was taken into the captain's cabin and formally
arrested by Dew for the murder and mutilation of his wife.
When he was searched some of his wife's jewellery was found
on him.

His reply to the charge was: 'I am not sorry. The anxiety
has been too much.'

Ethel Le Neve was found in the cabin in her boy's clothes.
She was brought into the captain's cabin and told she would
be arrested and charged with Crippen for the murder. She
fainted.

Crippen was handcuffed, he was informed, because of the
suicide notes he had written.

Captain Kendall promised Ethel Le Neve that he would do all he could for her – whatever that meant. She must have thought that he had done enough.

Had she seen the letter from her father in the papers? he asked.

She shook her head. 'No, I have not seen any papers since I left London. I know nothing about it. If I had, I should have communicated at once.'

She added to Dew: 'I assure you, Mr Dew, I know nothing about it. I intended to write to my sister when I got to Quebec.'

The arrested couple were of course in the charge of the Canadian police until they could be extradited to England.

Inspector M'Carthy warned Crippen and almost certainly also Le Neve during this time: 'We deal very differently with people in Canada when we arrest them to what they do in England. We tell them they must not say anything. Don't you say a word on anything. Cut out your tongue. Have nothing to say.'

Dew did not thank M'Carthy for mentioning this point to the arrested persons. Dew had hoped for a confession from the pair of them, which would have completed the splendour of his triumphant return with his prisoners at Liverpool.

But both of his prisoners heeded the advice of M'Carthy, and neither said a word to Dew, much to his chagrin. He got them extradited in Quebec and brought them back to England on a White Star liner.

'On the voyage from Canada,' reported Dew, 'Crippen was perfectly cool and collected. He conversed with me on various subjects other than this case.'

But Crippen was most concerned about Le Neve. They had of course been completely separated since the arrest.

'When you took me off the ship,' he remarked to Dew, 'I did not see her. I don't know how things may go. They may go all right, or they may go all wrong with me, and I may never see her again. I want to ask you if you will just let me see her. I won't speak to her. She has been my only comfort for the last three years.'

This pathetic request was not granted him and he did

not set eyes on her again until they appeared together in the dock at Bow Street when they were both committed. Crippen was tried first at the Old Bailey. His case lasted a week. He was found guilty on 22 October and sentenced to death.*

On 25 October Ethel Le Neve appeared at the Old Bailey charged with being an accessory to the murder after the fact. In order to prove her guilty all the Crown had to do was to establish that she assisted Crippen to escape, knowing that he was a murderer. Lord Alverstone, the Lord Chief Justice, was the presiding Judge. He had been the Judge at Crippen's trial and had been most fair and impartial. Richard Muir who had led the prosecution and subjected Crippen to one of the most devastating cross-examinations in the history of murder trials also led for the Crown against Le Neve. Her defence was brilliantly conducted by F. E. Smith, later Lord Birkenhead, one of the most famous lawyer-politicians of his day.

The case against Crippen had been strong. Apart from the other evidence against him and the guilty impression created by his flight, Muir had only to prove that he buried Cora in the cellar. If you bury someone in your cellar, you are automatically found guilty of having murdered them.

The case against Ethel Le Neve was much more difficult to prove, and it relied mainly on Mrs Jackson's story of her lodger's arrival home at about the time of the murder in a state of shock, and such guilt as could be assumed from the fact that she fled with Crippen.

Muir in his opening address said that it was up to the defence to make an explanation of her admittedly suspicious conduct. He had some interesting arguments against Le Neve which are worth considering. She had explained her illness to Mrs Jackson by saying that she was feeling her equivocal position and could not bear to think of her lover living with his wife. Muir considered this explanation unacceptable, as this situation had lasted for years. And then suddenly she had

* Crippen's case and trial is dealt with more fully in *The World's Worst Murderers*, by Charles Franklin, published by Odhams.

recovered her spirits and had begun to wear the dead woman's finery and to give her clothes to Mrs Jackson. When Dew had come to investigate Mrs Crippen's disappearance, Le Neve had obviously been disturbed enough to take instant flight abroad with her guilty lover. She had had ample opportunity to make an explanation of her conduct, but she had made none. The time had come, Muir emphasized, for her to make an explanation.

Smith took refuge in the rules of English legal procedure which enables an accused person to maintain complete silence. It protects him from being asked any inconvenient questions at all. If Le Neve had been tried, say, in France, the President of the court would have turned to her and asked her to explain herself. She could have refused, 'No, I stand by my rights and refuse to say anything. It is for the prosecution to prove my guilt.' But such an attitude would not have created a very good impression on the jury, for in France it would not have been an unreasonable request on the part of justice to ask her for an explanation of her conduct. English justice, however, does not work like that. The rules are strict and cannot be departed from one iota, even if the truth is at stake. Truth is not the most important thing in English courts which are concerned only at arriving at a conclusion upon the facts which the jury are permitted by the rules to hear. The prisoner's privilege of complete silence in court has saved many a guilty person from conviction, and of course the reverse can be said too.

So weak was the Crown's case on matters of fact, that Ethel Le Neve could rest content in the dock and listen to her brilliant counsel putting her case. He called no evidence, but rebutted the charge in a single skilful speech to the jury.

Smith ridiculed the Crown's demand for explanations. 'It is not for my learned friend to invite explanations from me,' Smith stressed. 'Nor to indicate that there is a point obscure here, or a detail in which I can assist him by offering an explanation. It is for him to discharge the onus, and to discharge it fully. The law places it on him and says "You shall prove that this woman knew that Crippen murdered his wife".'

Mrs Jackson's story was easily discredited because she perhaps understandably could not be definite about the dates of Le Neve's mysterious ailment. To make such evidence stick the witness had to be unshakeable.

Smith dealt at length with the suggestion that Le Neve had full knowledge about the murder and had even been told about it by Crippen himself. Smith ridiculed the suggestion. 'My learned friend's case really is this,' he exaggerated, 'that Crippen said in effect to Le Neve: "This is how I treated the woman who last shared my home, and I invite you to come and share it with me now." ' The comment was hardly fair, because many murders have taken place under precisely these circumstances with the knowledge, even urging of the third party.

Smith put forward the following suggestion, and it must be recalled that Dew had, foolishly, warned Crippen that it would be the worse for him if he could not produce his wife. 'Suppose Crippen had said something like this to Le Neve: "Inspector Dew, as you know, has asked me some nasty questions about my wife. She has gone away and I do not know where she is, and if she does not turn up it may be very awkward for me and I may be liable to arrest." Would that not be a circumstance in which one can well understand an inexperienced girl would have gone away? You cannot consider this as being a case of two adults of equal age dealing with one another. They were two very different persons. Crippen had acquired this enormous power over her and she was utterly ignorant of the laws of England. She was confronted with the problem as to whether she would stay in England or go with him.'

This was clever, typical F. E. Smith stuff. He had just been talking about her as being a schoolgirl when she first came under the malevolent influence of the monstrous little doctor. It was in 1900, when she was seventeen that she first saw him. At the time of the murder she was twenty-seven, had been his mistress for three years. Hardly a child, and why should she be utterly ignorant of the law, any more so than any other English person approaching thirty?

Muir of course was dying to get her into the box. He was

the most devastating cross-examiner of his day. His questioning would have gone on for hours, for he was laborious, persistent, but subtly effective in destroying a witness's story. He had practically made Crippen say that black was white. Crippen had been clever, had given an impression of honesty, but Muir utterly annihilated him.

We don't know how Ethel Le Neve would have fared at his hands, but Smith was determined that she should be spared an ordeal which might have proved fatal for her case. He was right of course. The case against her was not really strong, and he was not going to take the chance of Muir dragging some disastrous admission out of her. He told the jury:

'I am not prepared after what that woman has gone through, in the state of health in which she is, to submit her, on facts like these and on evidence such as that which has been presented, to the deadly cross-examination of my learned friend. It would be different in a case in which the prosecution had brought forward massive and weighty evidence . . . Knowing that she is a young and inexperienced woman, without any knowledge of the world, that she is dazed and shattered, I have taken the responsibility upon myself and I am content to support it.

'When she leaves this dock acquitted by your verdict the prospect which opens out to her is not one of happiness. She will be known all over London and all over England as one who has been the mistress of this murderer. When she leaves the dock, in any event there must be a most unhappy future for her. Let her at least have the satisfaction of knowing that she leaves it with the assent of twelve jurymen who have heard this case and who, though not blind to her faults, acquitted her. I do not ask you for mercy. I ask you only for justice, and I am content you will judge her in her hour of agony with that consideration that you would wish shown to a daughter of your own if she were placed in the same position.'

It was an effective finish to a splendid speech. The Judge summed up rather in her favour and the jury not unexpectedly found her not guilty.

There is in fact more than one mystery in the Crippen case. His own guilt has been disputed. The fact that he maintained his innocence right to the end and created such an excellent impression of sincerity and truthfulness among the hardened prison officials whose job it was to look after him while he awaited the hangman, has made people wonder whether after all he was innocent.

What was proved at his trial without any doubt was that the remains found in the cellar were Mrs Crippen's and that he buried them there. That was sufficient and that was fatal to him.

Although attempts to prove that Crippen was psychologically incapable of murder can hardly be taken seriously, the possibility that he killed his wife accidentally cannot be discounted with certainty. It was suggested that he had administered the hyocine of which she died in order to put her into a deep sleep while he was entertaining his young mistress at Hilldrop Crescent, but that he accidentally gave her too much. According to this theory Ethel Le Neve's state of shock as reported by Mrs Jackson was due to her guilty knowledge of what had happened.

A more fanciful variation of this theory was that Crippen used the hyocine to damp down his wife's nymphomaniac demands upon him which Crippen, frail and no longer young, was unable to satisfy, in addition to the more welcome demands of his young mistress. Crippen categorically stated that he and his wife had shared separate rooms for years. And if Cora Crippen was a nymphomaniac she had a decided taste for other men and would not have had to rely upon her husband to satisfy her appetite.

The sympathy for Crippen was aroused by his intense loyalty to Ethel Le Neve and his touching love-letters to her on the last day of his life. Whether she deserved such faithfulness-unto-death we don't really know.

She flitted through the scene of the century's most famous murder like a ghost, and after it was over she vanished like a ghost. Occasionally out of the shadows of a well-chosen oblivion the ghost emerged. Someone wrote about her. Her address was said to be known to every news editor in

Fleet Street. She kept a hat shop at Eastbourne. Now she is finally reported to have died. Whatever may be the truth of this strangely interesting murder story, she had been punished enough, and he, we would now say, was punished too much.

# Chapter 14
# Lizzie Borden

The most famous and controversial acquittal of all was that of Lizzie Borden. She was accused of one of the great crimes in the history of murder. She was acquitted by a court which was biased very much in her favour.

Her innocence has never been convincingly established despite many ingenious attempts to do so. The public's belief in her guilt has been confirmed by new facts which have been recently revealed.

Governor Robinson, her defence counsel, crystallized the thoughts of those who maintain her innocence in these words: 'To find her guilty, you must believe she is a fiend. Gentlemen, does she look like it?' It seemed an impossible thing to believe. Of course such a nice lady could not have done such a terrible thing to her ma and pa!

More than one murderer has got away with it under this sort of argument. Lizzie Borden certainly did. The nineteenth-century mind did not like to associate women with ferocious murder, although the age produced some female murderers of unexampled savagery.

All the same, one of the reasons for the Lizzie Borden

255

legend was the fact that it was so hard to imagine that such a person could have committed this nightmare of a murder, ferocious, barbarous, the work of a madman. Yet all the evidence points overwhelmingly to the guilt of this thirty-two-year-old Massachusetts spinster, daughter of respectable and respected parents who had lived a gentle, sheltered life in an exclusive New England community. She was a Sunday school teacher, the secretary of the Christian Endeavour Society, a temperance worker and an ardent churchgoer.

Lizzie was born in 1860. Her father Andrew Jackson Borden was of vintage New England stock. He was a crusty, tight-fisted puritanical businessman who made a lot of money in Fall River out of real estate and banking. Her mother died when she was two, and her father married again.

Her stepmother, Abby Borden, was a pasty-faced, squat, plump, dull woman with an unhealthily large appetite, quite incapable of a motherly affinity with her two stepdaughters. Lizzie turned to her sister Emma who was nine years her senior. A close relationship developed between them. As they grew up both Lizzie and Emma disliked their stepmother more and more.

About twenty years before the murder, the Bordens moved to 92 Second Street, Fall River, and as the murders took place there this oddly constructed house is worth a brief description.

It was a two-storeyed building with a staircase at the front and at the back. There were no corridors on either floor, with the result that each room had doors opening into it from all sides. The only lavatory was in the cellar, and the only running water was in a sink room off the kitchen. It had originally been planned for use by two families, but it is difficult to imagine a more badly designed house or one so lacking in the normal conveniences expected even in the nineteenth century.

Here the Bordens, wealthy by any standards, lived in unhealthy discomfort and increasing enmity.

Lizzie and Emma venerated their dead mother and detested their stepmother in a way which was perfectly plain to Abby Borden. Abby had done nothing to deserve this treatment. She lived an innocuous existence and was an uninteresting person. But all the Bordens including Lizzie were dull and uninteresting: tedious, stodgy people who led lives of dedicated banality. Lizzie herself only flamed across the skies of history because her greed combined with her peculiar medical condition to enable her to commit and brazen her way out of the world's most daring double murder.

Of the Bordens only Andrew himself had any qualities, though these were not all admirable ones. He was at least an astute businessman, and though mean he was scrupulously honest. He had a sense of fairness and a genuine affection for his family. Between him and Lizzie there was an especial bond. When Lizzie was expected, he had wanted a son, not another daughter. Nevertheless he did not reject her, but merely signified his disappointment by having her christened Lizzie Andrew Borden. After her graduation, she gave him a ring to wear as a sign of the bond between them. She killed him while he was wearing this ring, and it remains today on his finger as he lies in his coffin.

Why Lizzie killed at all has always been a mystery and is the main reason why the idea of her guilt has been rejected by so many. Why she killed her father is the greatest mystery of all. Those who knew her best, the exclusive little community of Fall River, among whom she lived and who rejected her completely after her acquittal, have no doubts about her guilt.

According to a recent book written by one of the members of the Fall River community* it was a Borden family secret that Lizzie had 'peculiar spells', a mild form of epilepsy. This is called the Jacksonian, or *partial epilepsy*. Most epileptics lose consciousness during an attack, but Jacksonian epileptics retain a kind of dimmed consciousness and are only partly able to control their actions. Attacks associated with this milder form of epilepsy are accompanied (according to the *Encylopædia Britannica*) by dangerous and violent acts which

---

* Victoria Lincoln in *A Private Disgrace: Lizzie Borden by Daylight* (Victor Gollancz, 1968)

replace or immediately follow the short period of unconsciousness. 'The subject is one of the greatest medico-legal interest and importance in regard to criminal responsibility.' Lizzie's epilepsy occurred only three or four times a year, during her menstrual periods.

Edmund Pook was another Jacksonian epileptic, and he undoubtedly killed Jane Clouson during one of these attacks. He also used an axe and smashed in the girl's face and skull in exactly the same way as Lizzie Borden did. Atrocious deeds committed by apparently normal people can be fully accounted for in this way.

There must of course be a motive. In the case of Pook, the unfortunate Jane whom he had made pregnant was desperately in his way. Lizzie Borden also had a good motive – greed and self-interest. People have murdered for far less.

About five years before the murders Andrew Borden put up the money to buy the house in which his wife's half-sister was living, as she was in danger of being turned out. He gave the title deeds of the house to his wife as a present. Emma and Lizzie were furious. They were not even placated when Andrew gave them the title deeds of a house he owned in Ferry Street. In order to soothe Lizzie's clamour, he paid for her to have a three months' tour of Europe, and she visited Britain, France and Italy. Emma preferred to stay at home. During the return voyage across the Atlantic Lizzie talked bitterly to her cabin companion about the hated stepmother and the awful home she was returning to.

Although her enmity was especially directed towards Abby, Andrew also got his share of it. Both the girls considered not only that they should be living in a better house, but that the entire family fortune should go to them. Andrew not unnaturally was determined to provide for Abby as well.

Tension mounted. Lizzie took to calling Abby 'Mrs Borden'. They locked their doors against each other. Conversation was non-existent. As Emma put it, they spoke; they did not talk.

Lizzie had grown up tallish, thick-set, unattractive, with

large, protruding eyes and a bad complexion. There was no romance in her life. She was sex-repressed, bitterly discontented and tormented by her 'peculiar spells' which were kept a dead secret by the family. Her father was wealthy yet refused to live up to his station in life. Like so many men of his type who have made money the hard way, Andrew Borden preferred to keep it in the bank.

It was a not unusual situation in those days. In many a nineteenth-century household the desires, loves, hatreds and natural instincts of its women were trampled upon and repressed for years. The explosion in the Borden house that hot August morning in 1892 was perhaps not so extraordinary as people have thought, especially when Lizzie's 'peculiar spells', until recently a closely guarded secret, are taken into consideration.

Lizzie and Emma's dull and pointless lives had been punctuated by an annual summer holiday on their father's farm at Swansea, a few miles up country. The grand European tour was not repeated, and there were not even trips to other parts of the United States. But Andrew Borden who knew something of Lizzie's peculiarities may well have been worried about her and may have tried to keep her happy by little acts of generosity which were somewhat out of character. Abby, on the other hand, had a healthy fear of Lizzie who did not conceal her hatred. When it was suggested that the deeds of the Swansea farm should be made over to her, Abby was terrified of the effect this would have on Lizzie.

The girls no longer vacationed at Swansea and John Vinnicum Morse, the brother of the first Mrs Borden, offered to live there and farm the place. Andrew agreed and proposed to transfer the deeds to his wife. It was perhaps not the wisest thing to do in view of the row there had been over the previous transfer of property to Abby, but Andrew was a hard and obstinate man and was not going to be dictated to by his daughters. He knew well enough that there would be plenty for the three of them when he died. In fact he left over half a million.

Abby, though a glutton for her food, was not an avaricious

woman. She was not interested in acquiring property, especially as it caused so much trouble with the girls. But she was accustomed to obeying her husband, and she may well have got him to promise that the transfer should be made in secret without the girls' knowledge.

In that first week of August an unprecedented heat wave struck Fall River. Emma went to Fairhaven, less than twenty miles away, to visit friends. Lizzie stayed at home.

She had some idea that something was afoot between her father and Abby which had to do with money. A new will perhaps? The transfer of the Swansea property? She was waiting, ready to pounce. Her menstrual period began – always a dangerous time for her as it might bring on one of her strange spells. It did.

There was no need for her to have stayed in Fall River during that blistering heat wave. Some of her friends had rented a seaside cottage at Marion, not far away, and had invited her to join them. But she preferred to stay at home.

She went to a local drug store and tried to buy prussic acid, but the druggist refused to sell it to her without a prescription.

On the Sunday Bridget Sullivan, the Bordens' Irish maid, cooked a huge joint of mutton which was to be their staple food for most of the meals during the week. There was mutton for breakfast, mutton for dinner, mutton for supper, and there was hot mutton soup always on the go. The temperature climbed up into the nineties, but the mutton, frequently warmed up, still dominated the menu.

By midweek all the family not surprisingly had upset stomachs. Andrew and Abby spent most of Tuesday night vomiting and retching. On Wednesday morning Abby called in the doctor. She thought someone was trying to poison them, though she didn't say who she thought that someone was. Dr Bowen who lived across the street and generally attended them dismissed her ideas of poison and said that some food must have gone off during the heat. Mild food poisoning was common enough in the days before refrigerators.

Andrew was angry when he heard that Dr Bowen had been called in. He told the doctor to his face that no money of his would be used to pay his bill.

On Wednesday Lizzie went to see her friend Alice Russell and had a strange conversation with her.

After telling her about the poisoning, and the rude and discourteous way her father had of treating people, Lizzie mentioned she was afraid one of his enemies would take revenge on him.

'I feel depressed,' she said. 'I feel as though something was hanging over me that I can't shake off.' This was doubtless a reference to her 'peculiar spells' and her fear of them.

After priming her friend with predictions of disaster, Lizzie returned home. Did she know that she was going to murder Abby and that it would happen during one of her 'peculiar spells', and was she trying to ask Alice Russell to do something about it and try to stop her?

Alice was quite unable to grasp what was in Lizzie's mind, and like a practical and sensible person did her best to soothe her troubled premonitions.

The temperature was in the eighties by seven o'clock the following morning – Thursday, 4 August, 1892 – when Andrew and Abby Borden were tucking into the last breakfast of their lives which consisted of coffee, bread, cookies, johnnycakes, mutton and hot mutton soup, followed by fresh fruit. John Vinnicum Morse breakfasted with them. Lizzie had not yet got up. Abby told the Irish maid, Bridget, that she wanted her to wash the windows. Bridget was feeling the effects of the food poisoning now, but that did not excuse her the window-washing.

Morse left the house just after half past eight, and a little later Lizzie came down and made a more sensible breakfast off coffee and cookies.

It is believed that she knew very well from what she had overheard that the property transfer was to take place that morning, and that Abby was to go secretly to the bank to meet Andrew and sign the transfer deeds.

Bridget, still racked with stomach pains, began her

window-washing, but couldn't continue and spent some time vomiting in the garden. Bridget is a favourite suspect among those who persist in Lizzie's innocence, though how on earth she could have brought herself to butcher her master and mistress with an axe in the most bloody fashion, with her stomach in that state, has not been explained. The case against her isn't very convincing. Bridget's discrepancies in the statements she later made could well be accounted for by the fact that she was confused in mind as well as in body by having to wash windows while she was feeling ill. She was finally forced to retire to her bed. She was hardly the person to perpetrate what has been called the greatest murder of the century.

After breakfast Abby began her usual rounds of the house with her feather-duster. Lizzie stayed downstairs and did some ironing. Presumably about this time her attack of mild epilepsy started and she was in one of her 'peculiar spells' which put her into a semi-hypnotic state, almost like a sleep walker.

According to her later story a note was delivered to Abby from an unnamed sick person and Abby said she was going to visit this invalid. This note was never found and no one came forward to claim authorship of it. But it may have been that a note was delivered, possibly from Andrew telling his wife to meet him to sign the property transfer while pretending all the time to go somewhere else.

Lizzie intercepted the note. It was the final straw, the proof that her father was intending to make his property over to Abby secretly, keeping his daughters in the dark. She had always hated Abby. Now her hatred, inflamed by her attack of epilepsy, turned her into a fiend.

She went upstairs to where Abby was dusting in the guest room, the axe concealed perhaps under some clothes she had just been ironing. Taken totally by surprise, Abby did not even cry out. The first blow killed her. The other blows were rained down on her skull, as she lay on the floor, in exactly the same way as the blows of that other epileptic, Edmund Pook, in Kidbrooke Lane, London S.E., twenty years previously.

Just how long Lizzie's spell lasted we do not know, but there was little doubt that she was aware of what she had done. Many people think that Bridget knew also.

At ten-forty-five Andrew Borden arrived home and found the door at the foot of the front staircase locked in such a manner that he could not open it with his key. Bridget came to his assistance and gave a shout of surprise when she found the door double-locked from the inside.

She said she heard Lizzie, who was just coming down the stairs, laugh, although Lizzie said later that she was in the kitchen when her father came home. In any event, she apparently greeted him in daughterly fashion, asking him if he felt better after the sickness. She told him that Abby had gone out to see a sick friend and that she herself was also going out.

Borden naturally enough said nothing about the secret appointment he was supposed to have made with Abby. As she had not turned up he had returned home. He wasn't feeling too well. The heat was overpowering. The transfer of the property could be signed another time, perhaps when Lizzie was not at home. He may well have had vague apprehensions about Lizzie's bouts of strangeness, though obviously he did not fear for his own life.

He went up to his bedroom, using the back stairs, which was the only way as the bedrooms of Lizzie and Emma were permanently locked and sealed off from the bedroom and dressing-room used by Mr and Mrs Borden. The girls had to use the front staircase to get to their rooms.

Abby lay butchered on the flowered carpet in the guest room which was accessible only from the girls' bedrooms and the front staircase. There was no chance of Andrew seeing her body when he went to his room. When he came downstairs again he lay down on the sofa in the sitting-room, exhausted, and began to doze.

According to Bridget, whose story must always be suspect owing to her sudden acquisition of wealth after the trial, she was cleaning the dining-room windows when Andrew Borden went into the sitting-room for a snooze. Lizzie brought an ironing-board from the kitchen, started to iron on the dining-room table, and kept Bridget in conversation with some small talk.

It should be remembered that Lizzie and Bridget had always got on well together, and that Lizzie was the only member of the Borden household whom Bridget liked.

Lizzie mentioned to her that there was a dress sale in town that afternoon. Bridget answered that she would go and get herself a dress. She finished the window-washing, and about eleven o'clock, she said, she went upstairs to lie down on her bed in her attic room as she still felt unwell.

About a quarter of an hour later she heard Lizzie calling urgently up to her: 'Come down quick! Father's dead. Someone came in and killed him.'

No one can really understand what went on in the mind of a person like Lizzie Borden. If, as has been credibly supposed, she killed her stepmother during a fit of partial epilepsy, it is likely that the fit would have passed by the time she killed her father. Whether the mood of hatred which the epilepsy inflamed had passed we do not know. The original prompting in Lizzie's mind was greed, sheer naked greed.

It has been suggested that Lizzie loved her father so much that she could not bear to let him suffer the horror of discovering what she had done to Abby – so she completed the job with her axe while the mood was still on her. A curious way of sparing her beloved father's feelings. Anyway, it was mercifully quick. The first blow killed him apparently.

No one denies that she was or used to be fond of him. But she was fonder of money now. And the way she had spoken about him to Alice Russell was not in the manner of a fond and dutiful daughter. Taking all the circumstances into consideration she spoke rather as though she had the thought of murdering him on her mind.

She would gain everything she wanted by his death. And now, with Abby cut neatly out of the will by her axe, why not inherit the lot with a few more blows? Lizzie had nothing at all to lose by the second murder and everything to gain, even though the first murder might have been committed under a compulsive force which she could not control. Diminished responsibility was an unknown term in those days. Lizzie banked on the fact that no one would believe that she, of all people, could have done such a thing. And she was right.

After the murders Lizzie appeared neat and clean, her clothes unstained with blood – it was considered that such butchery would have drenched her with gore. According to scientific opinion, however, the murderer would not have been spattered with blood, because the blood-spurts in both cases had been in the opposite direction from that in which the blows came.

Lizzie's wardrobe was not thoroughly examined by the police, and afterwards she burnt one of her dresses as she said it was stained with paint. She had ample time to change and wash between the murders.

Friends crowded into the house – Alice Russell, the doctor from across the road, the Churchills from next door. The second body was found. Extravagant horror was expressed. Lizzie was the coolest of all, cooler even than the police who suspected her from the start. Her story contained a number of inconsistencies which were never satisfactorily explained. But what told against her more than anything else was the fact that she had admittedly been up and down those stairs past the open doorway where Mrs Borden's body lay.

At the inquest which was held in secret she shifted her ground and changed her story more than once. By some dispensation of the court in her favour none of this self-condemnatory evidence was read over at the trial, at which she did not give evidence.

The prosecution, though convinced of her guilt, had little confidence in getting a 'guilty' verdict at the trial where she was acquitted by a hand-picked jury of her fellow citizens. The Judge, Justice Mason, was accused of being unduly prejudiced in her favour, so much so that the prosecution considered walking out of the court. The Judge ruled her vital inquest evidence inadmissible. He also refused to allow the chemist – who was prepared to swear that Lizzie tried to buy prussic acid – to give evidence, on the grounds that it was irrelevant.

Lizzie was thus at a great advantage. Both Emma and

Bridget gave evidence impressively in her favour and much belittled the intense animosity in the Borden family preceding the murders. Lizzie was skilfully defended by ex-Governor George Robinson who knew the way to handle a New England jury.

With a gesture towards the modest, refined young lady who was accused of this appalling act of bloody butchery, he invited them to ask themselves whether she looked the kind of fiend who would do such a thing. The naïve gentlemen of Fall River who composed the jury did not know about the general experience that women murderers never look capable of the appalling acts they sometimes commit. They had no hesitation in pronouncing her innocence.

Emma knew that Lizzie was guilty. A police matron at the prison, after Lizzie's arrest, had overheard a quarrel between the two sisters from which only that inference could be drawn. Emma may well have tried to shut her eyes to the fact of Lizzie's guilt or even blamed it on one of her 'peculiar spells'. Later the two sisters irreparably quarrelled.

Lizzie's fellow-citizens at Fall River tumultuously applauded the verdict. For them it was the society of Fall River which had been found innocent as much as Lizzie Borden. But they quickly turned against her afterwards. A conspiracy of silence descended. It was not a thing to be discussed. As many records referring to it as possible were destroyed or hidden away. The official transcript of the inquest containing Lizzie's damaging admissions completely vanished, though a full newspaper report of the inquest survives. Legal papers referring to the case remain buried in archives.

After the acquittal Lizzie and Emma, now rich, were able to live up to the style which they had always considered their right. They bought a splendid house in Fall River, though it would certainly have been wiser for Lizzie to have gone elsewhere. Fall River society shunned her, particularly when she developed a strong friendship with an actress named Nance O'Neil which was suspected of having a lesbian flavour. About this time she and Emma parted. As for Lizzie's 'peculiar spells', they ceased with her menopause.

Lizzie lived on in defiance of a society which had rejected

her and never ceased to believe in her guilt. She died in 1927, and Emma died a few days later.

They buried them in the family grave next to Abby and Andrew and the first Mrs Borden who was their mother.

Lizzie's acquittal was the most famous of all, and it sparked off the greatest controversy in the immemorial history of murder.

# Bibliography

Marie Besnard, *The Trial of Marie Besnard*, translated by Denise Folliot (William Heinemann 1963)

1st Earl of Birkenhead, *Famous Trials* (Hutchinson)

Lord Birkett (ed.), *The New Newgate Calendar* (Folio Society 1960)

Yseult Bridges, *Poison and Adelaide Bartlett* (Hutchinson 1962)

J. D. Casswell, *A Lance for Liberty* (Harrap 1961)

Elbur Ford, *Poison in Pimlico* (Werner Laurie 1950)

Roger Fulford, *The Trial of Queen Caroline* (Batsford 1967)

Roger Garnett, *The Remarkable Mr Bartlett* (Edgar Wallace Mystery Magazine, June 1965)

Alister Kershaw, *Murder in France* (Constable 1955)

Isabel Leighton (ed.), *The Aspirin Age* (The Bodley Head 1950, Penguin 1964)

Victoria Lincoln, *A Private Disgrace: Lizzie Borden by Daylight* (Gollancz 1968)

Alfred Lyall, *Warren Hastings* (Macmillan 1889)

Lord Macaulay, *History of England*, vol. 2 (Longmans Green 1886)

Edward Radin, *Lizzie Borden: The Untold Story* (Gollancz 1961)

Lord Russell of Liverpool, *Caroline, the Unhappy Queen* (Robert Hale 1967)

Jack Smith-Hughes, *Unfair Comment upon some Victorian Murder Trials* (Cassell 1951)

James Stephen, *History of Criminal Law*

Lately Thomas, *The Vanishing Evangelist* (Heinemann 1960)

George Woodcock, *The Paradox of Oscar Wilde* (T. V. Boardman 1949)

Wayland Young, *The Montesi Scandal* (Faber & Faber 1957)

*Notable British Trials Series* (published by William Hodge):

*The Trial of Adelaide Bartlett*, edited by John Hall

*The Trials of Oscar Wilde*, edited by H. Montgomery Hyde

*The Trial of Alma Victoria Rattenbury and George Percy Stoner*, edited by F. Tennyson Jesse

*The Trial of H. H. Crippen,* edited by Filson Young

Howell, *State Trials*

The Annual Register, 1806, 1820

# Index

# Index

# Index

271

# Index